THE MAKING OF THE NATION

THE
MAKING OF THE NATION

1783-1817

BY

FRANCIS A. WALKER, Ph.D., LL.D.

PRESIDENT MASSACHUSETTS INSTITUTE OF TECHNOLOGY

WITH MAPS AND APPENDICES

NEW YORK
CHARLES SCRIBNER'S SONS
1897

TROW DIRECTORY
PRINTING AND BOOKBINDING COMPANY
NEW YORK

PREFACE

I DESIRE most cordially to acknowledge my obligations to Professor Charles H. Levermore and to Professor Charles F. A. Currier for their assistance in reading the manuscripts or the proofs of this volume, and for suggestions at many points by which I have been saved from errors such as beset every one who undertakes to write of the life of any people through any considerable period of time, or by which I have been helped to make this narrative more comprehensive and life-like. Neither of these gentlemen, however, can be held responsible for any mistakes which may be found to exist in spite of their friendly revision. All of these are wholly my own. Professor Currier has made up the bibliography, which is appended, with far more knowledge of the historical literature of the period than I could claim to possess.

BOSTON, March 22, 1895.

CONTENTS

CHAPTER I.

CHAPTER II.

stitution—The Massachusetts Convention Ratifies, 187 to
168—Maryland and South Carolina Join the Union—New
Hampshire, the Ninth State, Accedes—The Constitution
Formally Accepted—Great Importance of Securing, also,
New York and Virginia—The Conventions in those
States—The Constitution Fiercely Opposed—General Con-
sent to the Subsequent Adoption of Amendments in the
Nature of a Bill of Rights—Virginia and New York Fi-
nally Ratify, the Latter, 30 to 27—North Carolina and
Rhode Island Stay Out—The Government Organized—
George Washington Chosen President—John Adams, Vice-
President—Congress Assembles, March 4, 1789 : No Quo-
rum until April 6th—Inauguration of Washington, April
30th — The Beneficent Influence of Washington in the
Establishment of the New Government — Extent of the
United States : Population—The Western Colonies—The
State of the Arts—Agriculture the Predominant Occupa-
tion of the People — Reasons for the High Productive
Power of the United States : A Vast Breadth of Virgin
Lands ; Popular Tenure of the Soil ; the Cultivating Class
not a Peasantry—The Remarkable Mechanical and In-
ventive Genius of the People : The Genesis of this Trait
Explained.

CHAPTER V.

CHAPTER VI.

CHAPTER VII.

CHAPTER VIII.

CHAPTER IX.

CHAPTER X.

APPENDIX III.

APPENDIX IV.

MAPS

DISTRIBUTION OF POPULAITON 1790

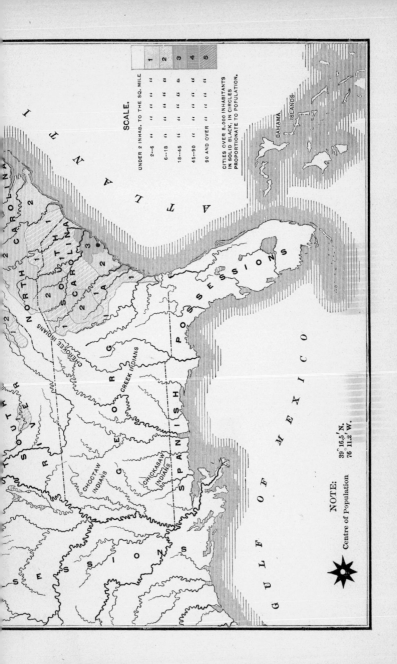

SCALE.

UNDER 2 INHAB. TO THE SQ. MILE.

2—6 " " " " "

6—18 " " " " "

18—45 " " " " "

45—90 " " " " "

90 AND OVER " " " " "

CITIES OVER 8,000 INHABITANTS
IN SOLID BLACK. IN CIRCLES
PROPORTIONATE TO POPULATION.

ATLANTIC

NORTH CAROLINA

SOUTH CAROLINA

CHEROKEE INDIANS

GEORGIA

CREEK INDIANS

CHOCTAW INDIANS

CHICKASAW INDIANS

SPANISH POSSESSIONS

POSSESSIONS

BAHAMA ISLANDS

GULF OF MEXICO

NOTE:

Centre of Population

39° 16.5′ N.
76° 11.2′ W.

THE MAKING OF THE NATION

CHAPTER I

THE CONFEDERATION, 1783–87

THE close of the Revolutionary War found the States which had, by their common efforts and sacrifices, achieved independence of Great Britain very loosely bound together. The ties between them were such as were not unlikely to snap in the first serious strain, even if they did not wear out and drop away under the mere commonplace, vulgar irritation and dissatisfaction inseparable from the restraints and obligations of ordinary, peaceful political life. One great object had brought the insurgent colonies together, though it had not sufficed to make them hearty and harmonious in council, in camp, and in battle. That object attained, the force which had produced a

Weakness of the Confederation.

very incomplete and unsatisfactory confederation was found to be largely exhausted.

It is hard for Americans, in this day, to feel there could have been any question whether there should be an American nation, or not. To us it seems a matter of course. Yet, in fact, the gravest doubts existed, in 1783, whether the union, formed at first for the purposes of resisting the aggressions of the mother country, and afterward for the achievement of independence, would long be continued. The most probable result, to the mind of an enlightened thinker, at the time our story begins, was that there would be two or three nations, or leagues of States, established along the Atlantic coast. Prior to the outbreak of the Revolution, in 1775, hardly a trace of a sentiment of American nationality had manifested itself among the colonies. Carolinians were content to be Carolinians ; Virginians to be Virginians ; New Yorkers to be New Yorkers. Even the exigencies of war against a common enemy, the French and the Indians, had not developed the sense of common interest and a common destiny.

Lack of American nationality.

In large part, the indifference to union, prior to the Revolution, had been due to the geographical relations of the colonies. The early settlements had been made along the seaboard, with the result, speaking generally, that each colony had its own coast-line, its own harbors, its own interior waterways. In consequence, the colonies had little dependence upon each other, and few causes of dispute among themselves. Massachusetts and Connecticut did, indeed, for a little while (1647–50) quarrel, in a small way, over the dues levied at the mouth of the Connecticut River (Saybrook) upon goods destined for Springfield ; New York, Connecticut, and New Jersey might quarrel, as, in fact, they did, after a fashion, even subsequently to

Geographical relations of the colonies.

the adoption of the Constitution, over the navigation of
the waters of New York Bay ; * Virginia and Maryland
had cause of dispute, traditions of which survive to this
day in the petty war of oyster-men in the Chesapeake
and the Potomac ; and several of the colonies had reason
to complain that their neighbors took advantage of a better geographical position to tax their products.† Perhaps
the greatest apparent danger to the peace of the early
colonies arose from the geographical relations of Pennsylvania and Delaware, the former being inland from the
latter.   But the danger in this case was practically removed by the fact that, even after Delaware secured a
separate legislature, the two colonies had a common governor.   If, on the contrary, we suppose the thirteen colonies to have been planted up and down the Mississippi
and its tributaries, we shall see how strong would have
been the reason, almost the necessity, for an early union,
arising from their geographical relations.   Some colonies
would have been at the mercy of those who controlled
the navigation of the streams below.   In such a situation even the Crown could hardly have kept the peace,
unless there had been some form of government com-

---

* The question was as to the exclusive right of certain patentees of
New York State to navigate the waters of New York with steam-vessels.
Mr. Webster, in his argument in Gibbons and Ogden, describes the sit-
uation as follows : "The North River shut up by a monopoly from New
York ; the Sound interdicted by a penal law of Connecticut ; reprisals
authorized by New Jersey against citizens of New York."

† Virginia had taxed the tobacco of North Carolina ; Pennsylvania had
taxed the products of Maryland, of New Jersey, and Delaware (Curtis,
History of the Constitution, vol i., p. 290). Newport took advantage
of certain Massachusetts towns in its vicinity ; and was enabled to levy
duties on imported goods which those towns paid, rather than go to the
expense of carting goods overland. It was, later, one of the arguments
of the opponents of the Constitution in New York, that that State would,
by the adoption of such a form of government, lose the large income it
derived from taxing products entering the port of New York but destined for consumption by the people of Connecticut and New Jersey.

mon to all the colonies, which the most grasping and
aggressive would have been compelled to respect. This
view is corroborated when we consider how quickly the
free navigation of the Mississippi became a vital issue
with the pioneers who passed the Alleghanies after the
peace of 1783 ; and how constantly, ever after, until the
question was finally settled by the acquisition of Louisiana, that region was embroiled by disputes arising from
this source.

Other causes which had from the beginning tended to
keep the colonies apart from each other were found in
differences of race, of religion, and, though to a smaller
degree, of language,* giving rise to prejudices, to jealousies, and even to practical difficulties in arranging for
any form of common government. While the settlers
of the Atlantic coast were predominantly English,
there were important exceptions ; and those exceptions
existed at just that point, geographically, where they
would naturally exert the greatest force in opposing a
movement for confederation.† The two almost purely
English groups of colonies, those of New England and
those of the South, were separated from each other by
the middle group, consisting of New York, New Jersey,
Pennsylvania, and Delaware, three of which,
the first and the last two, had been extensively settled by people of other races, chiefly
Dutch, Germans, and Swedes, with an admixture of
French and even of Finns. It does not need to be said
that differences of race and speech, with the differences
as to usage, habits, and institutions which are sure to

Differences
of race and
language.

* There was a time when the laws of New York were regularly printed
in three languages.

† One will obtain a lively sense of the prejudices which existed, for example, between the Dutch of New York and their New England neighbors, and which remained in full force far into the present century, by
reading some of the local novels of Fenimore Cooper.

accompany these, constitute a powerful obstacle to political union, even as against a strong and earnest movement toward union.   In the absence of any such impulse, they might suffice to keep neighboring communities apart and distinct for centuries.

Perhaps differences of religious belief and practice exerted even more influence than did differences of race and speech, in producing among the colonies that distrust and dislike, those prejudices and animosities, which would have withstood even a strong motive to confederation.   When one mentions religious differences, the instances first rising to the mind are apt to be those of the Catholics of Maryland, the Quakers of Pennsylvania, and the Baptists of Rhode Island, the last two confessions being almost as fully outlawed, in the view of the Englishmen of *Religious differences.* the eighteenth century, as the first.   But it is doubtful whether these three communions exerted an influence hostile to a common government equal to that exerted by divisions of belief, of practice, and of organization among the other colonists.   The bitterness of religious controversy is often not according to the largeness of the differences existing, but according to the smallness of them.   With reference to the subject we are considering, the distinction between Lutheran and Calvinist, between the Independent and the disciple of the Church of England, was even more important than that between Protestant and Catholic.

Finally, since we are asking why there was not earlier a movement toward American nationality, it is to be remembered that population was still sparse *Sparseness of population.* upon the Atlantic shore ; that many communities were separated from their nearest neighbors by bays, swamps, and streams, by mountains or barren lands ; that the industries of the people were as yet primitive and simple, involving little intercourse with distant points, while the means of transport and travel were not much more advanced than they had been two thousand years before. Not only does the close contact of population tend to remove the prejudices which are founded upon report and tradition, but from it arise many positive reasons for political association.

Such are the considerations which may serve to explain the absence of any strong sentiment of American nationality prior to the beginning of the quarrel with the mother country. Increasing resistance on the part of the colonists to what they regarded as unconstitutional and oppressive taxation, and finally the actual outbreak of the Revolution, led to the meeting of a Continental Congress. As the war progressed, the exigencies of the struggle induced the people to give the Congress some part of the powers of government ; but The Confeder- the most that was thus conceded was paination formed. fully inadequate to the gigantic task of combating Great Britain in arms. Late in 1777, Congress had been educated by bitter experience up to the point of proposing to the several States the formation of a permanent Confederation. Yet, notwithstanding the urgent, the overwhelming, reasons for at once creating some form of real government, it required nearly three years and a half to secure the ratification of the Articles by all the insurgent States. It should be said, however, that this almost suicidal delay was in Cession of Western lands. part due to the fact that some of the States had a vast extent of public lands in the West beyond the mountains, while others had none.* At last, the

* The objections of the States which, like Delaware, Maryland, New Jersey, and others, had no Western lands, to the adoption of the Articles of Confederation without the cession of the lands belonging to the more favored States, were two: First, that the latter States could pay their share of the requisitions of the common government by sales of

cession of the Western lands by individual States had gone so far as to make it reasonably certain that the whole would ultimately be accomplished ; and in March, 1781, the Articles of Confederation were ratified.

It would not be reasonable to attribute much of the final result of independence to this cause ; the war was nearly over ; Cornwallis surrendered at Yorktown to the united armies of Washington and Rochambeau in the October following ; the courage and the endurance of the Americans, aided greatly by the alliance with France, had already substantially achieved the victory. It is by its workings as the fundamental law of the United States, not in war, but in peace, after the treaty of 1783, that the Confederation is to be judged. It is here our story properly begins. Not only did the close of the war remove the principal force which had been making for nationality ; there was even, in some quarters and in a multitude of minds, a reaction toward sep- Reaction to-arate Statehood. The State governments ward separate had a real and vital existence. They were Statehood. well organized, with compulsory powers. The town governments at the North, the county governments at the South, while efficiently securing local interests, were held in due subordination. The States dealt with the really larger interests of society, the care of the peace, the protection of person and property, the domestic relations, the ordinary course of private, social, and industrial life. They had control of the resources of their people as a whole ; and they exercised complete command over the acts and lives of their individual citizens, subject only to the established principles of English lib-

land, instead of by taxes ; secondly, that the communities to be founded west of the mountains, upon the soil belonging to, say, Virginia, would become Virginian in political thought and feeling, and would make themselves the allies, on all public questions, of the parent State.

erty. On the other hand, the Confederation, which had been made up into the feeble resemblance of a nation, had no real and vital control. It had no compulsory powers ; it could not even protect itself. It stood for nothing which the people cared much about. Its functions were only in the lowest degree beneficent. It had to do mainly with debts and financial obligations, matters which were wholly in the nature of a burden upon the people, and which were associated with much that was unpleasant in the past. Even so, however, the Confederation might have maintained itself, at least for a while, and have done its work tolerably well, but for certain specific defects of organization which were soon made manifest.

The Articles of Confederation presented several points of weakness. Among these, three were almost inevitably fatal. First, the government had no power of taxation ; but was obliged to depend for its revenues wholly upon contributions by the States, in response to the requisitions of Congress. Secondly, the Confederation had no adequate control of foreign commerce. Thirdly, the Confederation had no power of enforcing its authority by the arrest and trial of offending and delinquent individuals ; but was obliged to look to the States, as bodies, to assert and maintain its rights. A government lacking these powers can scarcely be said to be a government at all. The Confederation, as instituted, was not, even in form, a nation, but only a league of sovereign states.

The sources of weakness.

Of the three points of weakness indicated, the first was that which during the few years following came to manifest itself most conspicuously, though the others could not have failed, on further trial, to prove the source of disaster. It was the lack of any power of taxation which brought the Con-

Lack of revenue powers.

federation to ruin almost at the start. The war had left a debt which was very formidable, according to the standards of those days ; and the recurring inter-est-charges required a large ånd constant income, in ad-dition to all that was needed for the support of the offices and services of peace. That income, as the result proved, and as might have been anticipated, was not to be obtained by the system of requisitions upon the States. Instead of responding cheerfully and promptly to the calls upon them, the States vied with each other in delinquency, each making the delay of its neighbors to pay their quotas an excuse for its own tardiness. Thus delinquency grew to be a habit, and was almost es-teemed a virtue. As each State was afraid it should pay more than others, the most backward set the pace for all. Under a thoroughly false system, such as this was, it is amazing how much meanness and selfishness will come out. Our fathers at the close of the Revolu-tionary War were not an impoverished people. They were able to give all that was demanded of them. It chiefly was a bad political mechanism which set every man and every State to evading obligations or procras-tinating payments. During this period, 1783–87, after independence had been won, there was little for an American to be proud of, much to make him ashamed.*

Two things, however, should be said in explanation of, and partial excuse for, the conduct of our fathers. One was that the Confederation was not the every-day government of the peo-ple. The States provided for the common interests of

Explana-tion of the States' delin-quency.

---

* From the 1st of November, 1781, to the 1st of January, 1786, less than two and a half millions of dollars had been received from the re-quisitions, made during that period, amounting to more than ten millions. For the last fourteen months the receipts from requisitions amounted to no more than four hundred thousand dollars, which was less than the interest due on the foreign debt alone.

life, for the care of the peace, the preservation of property, the protection of the home and of the domestic relations, the building of highways and bridges, the support of schools. To the States, then, the Americans of this period felt that they owed their first obligations. Those obligations, especially as the States had the power of direct individual taxation, to be enforced if necessary by bringing the delinquents into court, were on the whole cheerfully met. On the other hand, the people encountered the Federal Government at few points; they knew it mainly as the authority having control of relations with foreign nations.

The other thing which requires to be said, in explanation of the backwardness to honor the requisitions of the new Congress, is that these demands were mainly made for the purpose of paying the war debts of the Revolution. In communities which are still in a primitive financial and industrial state, nothing tries men's honesty so much as the payment of debt. Where one man will steal, many will, unless brought up by the law, do what is little better than stealing, in order to avoid or procrastinate the payment of indisputable obligations. When money has been had and spent, when the object for which it was borrowed has already been enjoyed, there are few who do not instinctively grudge to pay it back. It almost seems as though a wrong was being done to require them to forego present enjoyment, perhaps the comforts of life, to make good a transaction of the past. It is, however, not private but public debts which bring the hardest strain upon the virtue of a people. Long after a community has been educated up to Indisposition the point of paying individual debts promptto pay debts. ly, its members will shrink from the burden of providing for the payment of obligations contracted for general uses, of which they have individually had no enjoyment; no part of the consideration for which has passed through their own hands. We have seen abundant instances of this in our own day; yet the Americans of the last century were far behind those of the present age in the matter of political and financial education. They had, indeed, been brought up in a very bad school, so far as this matter was concerned. Almost all the colonies had indulged in paper-money issues of the worst character. The people had been accustomed to see public credit depreciated and the notes of their commonwealths at a discount, if not, indeed, treated as worthless rags. Some of the colonies had " run a rig " of paper money inflation which had bordered on madness. During the Revolution the exigencies of the general treasury had seemed to require issues of " continental currency," which rose by millions until the officers who put it out ceased to keep a record of the amount; and its value sank to a point where it almost took " a wagon-load of money to buy a wagon-load of provisions." It is not altogether strange that a people with such an experience should be reluctant to contribute toward the payment of the foreign and domestic creditors who had furnished the means of carrying on a war which was ended and over.

But however we may explain or excuse the delays of the States in answering the requisitions of the Congress of the Confederation, the fact of such delay made the maintenance of the new government impossible. That government began its career without resources or credit; and every day sank lower and lower into the abyss of bankruptcy. The volume of the public debt   Embarrass-
was continually swelling, under accretions of ments of the
  Confedera-
unpaid interest; and at last even the means tion.
of carrying on the public service were wanting. In 1781, and again in 1783, Congress proposed to the

States the adoption * of a revenue system, under which it should have power to levy customs duties for its own support. This system was not adopted ; but the discussion of the proposition paved the way for the reform of the government.

The embarrassments of the Confederation were not wholly financial. Though the Congress was, by the Articles of 1781, empowered to settle disputes between the States as to boundary, and to make treaties of commerce with foreign countries, its authority might be denied and defied with impunity by any State which felt itself aggrieved. In 1784 the residents of Eastern Tennessee, which then belonged to North Carolina, angered by the action of that State in regard to the cession of its Western lands, undertook, in conjunction with a section of Virginia, to set up a State under the name of Franklin or Frankland. In 1786 a convention met at Portland to effect the separation of the district of Maine from the State of Massachusetts. Other instances amounting to little less than flat rebellion occurred. The decisions of Congress were treated as of no account. Even the provisions of the treaty of peace with Great Britain could not be carried out because individual States refused to allow the payment of English creditors and the restoration of the confiscated estates of American " loyalists ; " and England kept possession of some of the Western posts as a means of compelling the United States to comply with its promises : a condition, surely, of great humiliation !

States defy the Confederate authority.

Meanwhile the country had been suffering continual loss in its trade and industry through the lack of adequate powers to regulate commerce. The Articles of Confederation reserved to the States the right of laying

* Unanimous consent to a measure of this character was necessary under the articles of Confederation.

duties on imports, excepting such as would interfere with any treaties that might be made pursuant to the treaties proposed to France and Spain. As a result of this, any State could, for itself, practically nullify any treaty which Congress might en- ter into with foreign countries. A striking example of the evil effect of this appears in the almost total fail- ure of the efforts made by the Confederation, in 1784 and the following year, to frame advantageous treaties of commerce with the nations of Europe. A spe- cial commission, consisting of three most distinguished citizens — John Adams, Benjamin Franklin, and Thom- as Jefferson — was appointed for this purpose ; but of the fifteen governments approached, only one, and that a country of little commercial importance, Prussia, thought it worth while to go to the trouble of making a treaty with a country which could not enforce it.

Lack of power to reg- ulate com- merce.

In such a situation as has thus been described, it was inevitable that Congress should fall off rapidly, both in the character of its members and in its repu- tation and authority among the people ; and this in turn reacted to increase the weakness of the Government. The Continental Congress had at the be- ginning been a most illustrious body ; but, as the war went on, its membership steadily declined. Some went into the military service ; some returned to their States and became governors or legislators ; some, and those among the ablest, were sent abroad as ministers to foreign countries ; some States withdrew the whole or a greater part of their delegations from motives of economy or from lack of interest, until, in the later part of the war, Con- gress became a very inferior body, at times almost de- serving the designation of a Rump. The Articles of Confederation required the assent of nine States in Con- gress to all matters of principal importance, and of seven

Decline of Congress.

States to all other matters except adjournment. Although a full Congress would have consisted of ninety-one members, only twenty or even fifteen members were at times present, perhaps from seven, perhaps from only five, States. Washington's resignation was received by a body of twenty members, representing seven States. The States voted as bodies, and as equal bodies, in the single house which was provided for by the Articles of 1781 ; and much of the dignity and authority belonging to a representative who speaks and votes in his own right and name was thereby lost. Men of character and influence found little to attract them ; and preferred public service at home. The delegates were poorly and irregularly paid by the States which sent them. At times Congress was obliged for weeks to await the arrival of a sufficient number of delegates to transact business. Even the ratification of the Treaty of Peace was delayed by lack of a quorum. Poor as it was in its membership, the government of the Confederation had not even a fixed seat ; and Congress went from city to city, a vagrant body, commanding less and less respect with each migration.

Finally domestic violence began to threaten the new nation. In addition to the selfish and malignant forces which are in all countries always ready to break the bounds of law, if not held in check by a strong and resolute government, there were special causes of disorder in the situation of the United States at this time. The war, especially through the pernicious agency of an irredeemable and rapidly depreciating paper money, had effected an enormous disturbance in the distribution of wealth. Every time the value of money changed, a certain amount of wealth was thrown, unearned, into the hands of the trading and speculative, at the cost of

Social disturbance due to Revolutionary paper money.

the productive, classes ; into the hands of those already rich, at the expense of those less favored by fortune. Any man of nerve can pick up a live coal and throw it into the fire without pain. This is because he holds it only a fraction of a second. Let him retain it a little longer and he will be burned to the bone. So it always is with depreciating paper money. Those who are in a position of advantage, who have means to pay with, who are close to the market, who are dealing largely, who have abundant and often secret opportunities of securing information, all these gain. On the other hand, the poor, the ignorant, those who have not capital and cannot readily command credit, those who deal only on a small scale and at irregular intervals, those who are at a distance from the market, those who buy raw materials for the manufacture of goods which will not be ready to be sold for weeks or months to come—all these classes lose and lose every time. The fluctuations of the "Continental currency" during the first few years of the war had been extreme ; its discredit at the end became total. There were those whose farms were deeply mortgaged and who yet had in their attics boxes full of paper money ; while those who had bought cattle, grain, and provisions, to sell them to the army, and had quickly turned the funds into houses and lands, or into mortgages on houses and lands, had become rich. A vulgar aristocracy, such as is always created by a paper-money era, flourished under the public eye, while names which had been honored throughout colonial history disappeared through a poverty which had come without blame, perhaps only through trusting the government too readily in its hour of need. In addition to all that was involved in this state of things, the close of the war itself brought distress, in the immediate instance, to many. The farmers missed the market for their produce which the

army had afforded.   The soldiers thrown out of service
could not readily find employment and remained too
often discontented and dangerous men.   One class pros-
pered ; but its good fortune was at the expense of the
general welfare ; and in time excited envy and animosity.   These were the lawyers, who flourished on the
multiplicity of suits growing out of the extensive transfer of values and the general unsettlement of society.

Such a condition was most unfortunate and deeply to
be regretted.   It would not have been dangerous but for
a vicious political organization.   As things were in
1783–87, it was possible that the elements of disorder
and violence in a group of States might at any time con-
front the military and political forces of one State * of
that group.   For example, if resistance to the law were
to break out in Massachusetts, the discontented classes
of all New England might pour into that State, confident that they would have to deal with its power alone.
This was, in fact, what occurred in the latter part of
1786.   Under the leadership of Daniel Shays, formerly

Shays's Re-   a captain in the Continental Army, those in
bellion in   Worcester County and in Western Massachu-
Massachu-
setts.   setts who felt themselves wronged by suits
at law, and by the foreclosure of mortgages of which the
depreciated paper-money of the Revolutionary government had been the real cause, gathered together, with the
purpose of closing the courts which had especial jurisdiction in their cases.   With the ordinary operation of
the courts, in the preservation of the peace and the protection of life and person, they did not wish to interfere ;
but they mistakenly believed that by unlawful violence

* " In the convention which framed the Constitution it was very early
declared that the Confederation had neither constitutional power nor
means to interfere in the case of a rebellion in any State."—Curtis, History of the Constitution.

they could undo some part of the injustice which had been wrought by unsound and pernicious financial conditions. The insurgents were largely, at least in the first instance, sober, decent, and industrious men, wrought to madness by what they deemed their wrongs; but they were, of course, joined by the idle, the dissipated, the discontented, the destructive classes, as the insurrection grew. The insurgents complained, not merely of the enforcement of payment in case of debts contracted in continental currency, and of the foreclosure of mortgages due to the same cause, but of the excessive cost of the collection of debts, fattening the legal profession at the expense of the debtor class, and of the scarcity of money in which to make the payments required, even where sufficient property for the purpose existed. These last complaints the General Court had sought to remove, at a previous session, by reducing the legal fees and by allowing payments of tax-arrears and of private debts in certain articles of produce at specified prices. But the discontent had become too deep to be appeased.

In December, Shays, at the head of an armed force, prevented the sitting of the Supreme Court at Worcester; and, a few days later, repeated the same acts of violence in Springfield. At the latter point the gathering of the insurgents menaced society with a new danger, since the United States arsenal was then, as now, situated in Springfield, and though Shays's followers had manifested no intention of destroying the State government or of proceeding further than to arrest the action of the courts in issuing executions for debts and in foreclosing mortgages, it was impossible to foresee to what extremities they might not proceed, should they secure an abundant supply of arms. In view of the threatening state of things, Congress had already, under pretence of making war upon the Northwestern

2

Indians, voted to enlist a considerable force and had
made a special requisition for funds; but the intervention of the Federal government was certain to be
too tardy for the emergency. The threatened commonwealth was saved by the promptness and energy of its
chief executive, and the public spirit of a few citizens
who contributed the necessary funds out of their own
means and at their own risk. Governor Bowdoin at
once called out the militia of Eastern Massachusetts,
under the command of General Benjamin Lincoln, a
distinguished veteran of the Revolution. These troops
promptly marched, in the depth of a severe winter, to
the relief of the beleaguered garrison. Before they
The Rebellion arrived the insurgents had been repulsed
put down. with some loss of life; and the approach of
the relieving force caused them to withdraw to a more
difficult country. By the rapid movements of General Lincoln the rebels were finally broken up and dis-
persed.

While Massachusetts was thus struggling for its life
with armed insurgents, other communities were being
rapidly drawn toward the fatal vortex of inconvertible
paper-money. A fresh craze for this delusive resort,
New paper- "this alcohol of commerce," broke out in
money craze. 1785–86, and soon infected a majority of the
States. All the teachings of the past seemed to have
been forgotten; and one commonwealth after another
took the plunge into the abyss of discredit and dishonor.
In some States the new paper-money was not made a
legal tender; in some, its acceptance was compulsory;
in others, still, it was sought to give the notes currency
by means of physical violence or of "boycotts" (to use
a modern phrase) directed against those who should decline to receive them. But, whatever form the issues
took, there could possibly be but one end for them all,

unless some superior authority should be established which could curb this delusive and destructive passion.

Shays's rebellion and the paper-money craze of 1785–86 completed the demonstration of the entire insufficiency of the Confederation under the Articles of 1781. The leaders of political opinion, the statesmen of that period, had not waited so long to be of the opinion that something must be done if the States which together had won independence were to remain in concord and union. In 1785 Governor Bowdoin suggested the appointment of delegates from the several States, to settle and define the powers with which Congress should be invested; but, the representatives from Massachusetts not concurring in this proposal, it was not submitted to Congress. Virginia was more active in the work of reform. That State, having been in controversy with Maryland over the navigation of the Chesapeake and the Potomac, appointed commissioners to confer with representatives of the latter State regarding their conflicting rights. This negotiation failed; but it led to an invitation given by Virginia, in January, 1786, to all the States to meet in convention, to decide upon the commercial relations of the country. Twelve States had already agreed to the proposed revenue system of 1783; but the hostile action of New York killed the measure. That State, however, while refusing to assent to this scheme, sent delegates, foremost among them Alexander Hamilton, to the convention, which was held at Annapolis, in September, 1786. The convention itself was a failure, since only New York, New Jersey, Delaware, Pennsylvania, and Virginia were represented; but it opened the way to a larger success than had even been in contemplation. That very failure showed the uselessness of any effort short of a general constitutional convention. The dele-

The Annapolis Convention.

gates to Annapolis departed after addressing Congress in terms, drawn by Hamilton, which induced that body to call a convention of the States, to meet at Philadelphia in May, 1787, "for the sole and express purpose of revising the Articles of Confederation." So desperate had the situation become, that the call of Congress was not unheeded, although one of the States was not represented, and the delegates came with very different minds as to what could and should be done. It is the proceedings of the body thus assembled, the Constitutional Convention of 1787, which is to form the subject of our next chapter. Only one word more remains to be said. While the career of the Confederation had been a most unhappy one, its existence had not been wholly without results of good. It had bridged over the interval till the people should be ready to establish a real and effective government; it had kept the idea of American nationality before the minds of all; and its very misfortunes and calamities had served to convince the country that something more must be done to secure the union of the States which had together won their independence.

CHAPTER II

THE CONSTITUTIONAL CONVENTION OF 1787

The Convention meets May 14th—Absence of Rhode Island—Delegates Appointed, 62—Number Attending at any Time, 55—Number Signing the Constitution, 39—Eminent Character of the State Delegations—Respective Contributions of Different Classes of Delegates—The Party of Obstruction—The Leading Spirits of the Convention—Doubts as to a Successful Result—Views Held as to the Relations between the Confederation and the States—The Three dominating Issues of the Convention—A Federal or a National Government—Equal or Proportional Representation of the States—Representation on Account of Slaves—Results on these Issues—The Work of the Committee on Detail Introduces Three New Issues—Taxation of Exports—The Slave trade—Two-thirds Vote on Navigation Acts—Extensive Disaffection of Delegates—Withdrawal of Some—Adoption of the Constitution—Nine States Sufficient for Ratification—This Measure Revolutionary—The Whole Work of the Convention Revolutionary—Called to Amend the Articles of Confederation, it Throws them Over at the Beginning—Impossibility of Deriving the Constitution Legitimately from Either the Confederation or the Revolutionary Congress—The Ordinance of 1787 among the Closing Acts of the Congress of the Confederation—Importance of this Measure.

THE Convention met on May 14th ; but there were not, on that day, delegates present from a majority of the States. Rhode Island was not represent- Absence of ed then or at any stage of the Convention ; Rhode Island from the Convention. but its Governor sent an address urging the vention. Convention to consider the interests and rights of that State in their deliberations, and holding out hopes that it would join the movement at a later period. The ab-

sence of Rhode Island has generally been explained by
the domination of the paper-money party in the Legislature.   Of all the offenders in the matter of paper-issues
before the Revolution, Rhode Island had easily been the
worst ; and the passion for bad money thus created had
not lost its hold upon the public mind.   Now, if anything was certain in regard to a new Constitution, it was
that it would prohibit paper-money issues by the States.
Other and perhaps equally valid explanations of Rhode
Island's absence from the Constitutional Convention
have, however, been given.*   From New Hampshire
delegates did not arrive till July 23d ; but by May 25th,
a quorum, that is, at least two delegates from each of a
majority of the thirteen States, had been obtained ; and
the Convention proceeded to its immensely important
business.   That business was in form, that is, according
to the call, a revision of the Articles of Confederation of
1781 ; but only the briefest time elapsed before it was
clearly seen that, if the Convention was to accomplish
anything at all, it would be not through revision, but
through the adoption of a substantially new form of
government.   The Articles of Confederation had been
too conclusively found wanting, to make any change in
them, however extensive, satisfactory.

The total number of delegates, by all the States appointed, was 62.   Of these, however, only 55 were at

Member-   any time, earlier or later, in attendance.   In
ship of the   the final result only 39 members signed the
Convention.
Constitution.   In its membership the Convention was a noble body, recalling the early days of the
Revolutionary Congress.   After the unhappy experiences of the Congress of the Confederation, through so
many years, this change was indeed refreshing, and gave

* See a very able paper read before the Rhode Island Historical Society, in 1890, by Hon. Horatio Rogers.

at least the hope of doing something. No commonplace gathering of second-rate men would have had the slightest chance of carrying the country with them in anything which they might propose.

The contributions which the several members of the Convention were destined to make to the successful result of its deliberations and decisions were *Contributions of different* very different. Some stood, first, foremost, *classes of* and always, for union—for union in spite of *delegates.* obstacles; for union in defiance of State rights and local interests; for union under almost any form, provided only a strong and self-supporting government should be created. This was their contribution: zeal for union, devotion to the prime object of the Convention. Some of these delegates enjoyed the advantage of skill in debate, persuasive discourse, and fiery eloquence. Others made their influence felt mainly in personal conference and in the spirit with which, simply as voting members, they met and rose over the successive obstacles which for the time stopped the work of the Convention or threatened its dissolution. Others there were whose qualities of mind and temper fitted them especially to contribute to a fortunate result through the analysis of methods and details. A few were jurists and publicists, widely read in constitutional history and of a learning and intellectual power to lift discussion, at critical points, out of the common and the vulgar, up to high planes of statesmanship. Some contributed through prestige, derived from services in peace and in war, lending dignity and authority to the cause of union, both within and without the Convention, whether or not they were adroit in debate, or learned in political history, or powerful in appeal. Some contributed by parliamentary skill and tact, knowing how to avoid difficulties; how to pass around obstacles; how to conciliate opposition;

when to yield and when to press vigorously for an advantage. All were needed ; without the help of any one we cannot confidently say that the Convention would, in the final result, have proposed the Constitution.

A few there were whose part was a less gracious one, that, namely, of making objections; of insisting upon concessions to State prejudices and to local interests ; of seeming to be ready, perhaps of being ready, to abandon the entire object of the Convention rather than that certain results should not be secured. We will not liken them to the false mother in the story of Solomon's judgment. Perhaps, had they not made these issues in the Convention, the work of the Convention would have been defeated before the people by the very prejudices and interests which they represented. But it is at least allowable to say that the spirit of the true mother in that beautiful tale animated not a few noble souls : rather than that the life they loved should be sacrificed, they were ready to make any concession, to mortify their own pride, to surrender their cherished views and purposes, and to yield the guardianship of the nation to other hands.

The party of obstruction.

First among the delegates must be named George Washington. Unskilled in debate, destitute of juridical and historical learning, he yet stood all the time for union, for union somehow, for union anyhow ; and the splendor of his fame shone through the Convention and over the whole land, giving hope amid the deepest despondency. Benjamin Franklin, too, was there, infirm in body and nearly past the time of public usefulness, but still holding authority by virtue of his great services. The measures he proposed were of comparatively little value ; listened to rather from respect to the man than from concurrence with his views ; but his presence, his prudence, and his devotion

Washington and Franklin.

to the larger interests of the country were a constant force in the Convention. Not only did Dr. Franklin exert a strong influence through his zeal for union ; but his thoroughly democratic sentiments were of excellent effect, as opposed to the decidedly aristocratic tendencies of many members.* The American of to-day is amazed to read in Madison's " Journal " the frank expression of opinions hostile to popular suffrage, distrust of the people, and even imputations against the honesty and patriotism of the country. The history of the nation has shown that the aged philosopher was more nearly right in his estimate of the virtue and public spirit of the American people than were his more conservative colleagues. With Washington and Franklin was another of the noble group of five, who, in 1776, laid upon the table of the President of Congress the Declaration of Independence, viz., Roger Sherman, of Connecticut, devoted to the cause of union, though perhaps too persistent at times in presenting objections to the wishes of the majority of the Convention. Among those who contributed most through juridical and historical knowledge, or through long experience in public affairs, were George Mason and James Madison, of Virginia ; Rufus King, of Massachusetts ; James Wilson, of Pennsylvania ; Oliver Ellsworth, of Connecticut.

But amid that brilliant assemblage one spirit burned with a fire surpassing all in its zeal for union. Alexander Hamilton, of New York, had been for Alexander many years the most conspicuous advocate Hamilton. of a strong and efficient government for the insurgent,

* The proposition was even made, and was strenuously supported, that wealth should be the basis of representation in the Senate. Let the reader try to imagine anyone daring to make such a proposal in this day. For a time, the principle that there should be property qualifications for the executive, the members of the legislature, and the judiciary triumphed in the Convention, though ultimately defeated.

and finally for the independent, States. Possessed of a singular eloquence, he had, since 1780, labored by speech and pen to bring the American people to appreciate the necessity of conceding ample powers to the common Congress. Upon his own State he had not ceased to urge the grant of liberal rights of revenue ; and he had been foremost in the measures which led to the Annapolis Convention, and subsequently to the Constitutional Convention at Philadelphia. In the latter body his usefulness, so far as constructive details were concerned, was greatly impaired by his desire for a more consolidated organization of the country and a more aristocratic form of government than would have met the sympathy of perhaps a single one of his colleagues, so that few of his practical propositions were adopted ; but his burning zeal for a real and vital union of some kind, his eloquence, and his readiness to concede anything and everything to reach that end, made him an immense power for good. Thus, while Hamilton contributed little to the text of the Constitution, he did perhaps as much as any man to give it being.

Among delegates from States south of Virginia were several men, notably Rutledge and the two Pinckneys, who were of the highest character and abilities, and of unquestioned patriotism ; but the rôle they felt themselves obliged to act, namely, that of objecting to the progress of the work, unless certain concessions should be made to the views and interests peculiar to their constituents, must always give them a lower place and make them less romantic figures in the history of the Convention of 1787. Perhaps the part they played was as necessary as that of others who were unconditionally for union ; certainly we have no right to impute selfish or sinister motives to them. Still, if that part was necessary, it was not

The extreme Southern delegates.

heroic ; and has not aroused in the American people the same gratitude as has been accorded to their colleagues.

Among the members of the Convention who took a very prominent part in its proceedings were three we have not mentioned — Edmund Randolph, of Virginia ; John Dickinson, of Delaware ; and Luther Martin, of Maryland. Ran- Randolph, Dickinson, and Martin. dolph, as we shall see, prepared the general plan of government which was in substance adopted ; but his subsequent course produced an impression of vacillation and inconsistency which seriously impaired the prestige he might have expected to derive from this source. Dickinson's part was marked by such a degree of conservatism, and by so much of what was considered, whether rightly or wrongly, a disposition to cavil and find fault, that his influence was deemed rather a burden than a help to constructive work. Martin, strong, impatient, and aggressive in disposition, was at several stages foremost in opposition to what then seemed to be, and is now seen to have been, essential to any real progress toward the union of the States. In such a body as we have described, there could be but one first choice for president ; and George Washington, with the immortal laurels of a patriot war carried to a successful conclusion by his matchless resolution, patriotism, and fidelity, was chosen to preside over its deliberations.

But while the Convention was thus nobly constituted, and while its members had generally, perhaps without exception, come together desirous of framing a form of government which should secure the continuance of an American union ; and while all probably were in a frame of mind to make some concessions from what they would individually have desired ; Doubts as to a fortunate result. yet the prospect of any considerable positive result was not favorable. The questions at issue were of the grav-

est nature; and the feelings and sentiments which drew
the delegates to one side or the other of these questions
were deeply founded and often passionately held.
There were not a few who were known to regard their
positions on certain points as of a higher value than the
formation of a new constitution, if not, indeed, of more
consequence than the continuance of union under any
form. There were some who, while willing fairly to
consider the schemes suggested, had from the start so
little expectation of any successful result, that their influence was almost the same as if they had desired a
failure. Possibly some even felt that it would not be a
wholly unfortunate outcome if the country were compelled to drag itself along for a few years more under
the Articles of 1781, bad as these were and certain to be
in time changed, rather than force an issue at present
and rush on to decisions which would be irrevocable.
Altogether the mood of at least a majority of the Convention was unfavorable. Yet there were among the
delegates some who believed that it was a case of "now
or never;" who burned with zeal to consummate a definitive union; and to this end were ready to make almost any concession and accept almost any plan. The
energy and devotion of these men could not fail profoundly to move their more sceptical colleagues. A
few there were, and these among the greatest intellects
of the Convention, who were fairly on fire with their
enthusiasm and determination. These men seem, in
their passion for union, to have risen to the heights of
prophecy, and fully to have appreciated the momentous
consequences of what should there be done in that
summer of 1787, as if they could look down the ages and
see the puissant nation which was to rise out of the
gloom and the confusion of the present; but there were
more who, whether because they were commonplace by

nature, or because they had been so deeply infected by the distrust, doubts, and jealousies of the miserable period then closing, looked at everything with the narrowest vision, and found it impossible to lift themselves above sectional interests and personal prejudices.

On the subject of the relations of the several States to the United States, there was in the Convention a great diversity of opinion; but, in a general way, three distinct views may be said to have been held. First, that the States still remained, in spite of all that had been granted to the Revolutionary Congress for the sake of carrying on the war, and in spite of all that had been conceded in the Articles of 1781, sovereign and independent States, of undiminished authority and competent at any time to resume the entire control of their own interests, by simply "denouncing" the Articles of Confederation. The second view was that which held that the course of events during the Revolution and the grants of power made to the Continental Congress and the Confederacy of 1781 had established a nation which existed of its own right, which had the full constitutional authority, even though the power might be lacking, to assert itself against individual States, were that necessary. Some who held this view went even so far as to claim, not that the States themselves had by an irrevocable act created a nation; but that the United States did, in fact, by and through the Declaration of Independence, pre-exist; and that the States came into existence only as integral parts of the Union. The advocates of this view pointed to the record that the Continental Congress recommended to the States to form constitutions and organize governments which should meet the fact of separation from the mother country. This view of the relations of the several States to the United States we

Two views of the relation of the States to the Confederation.

may call the High Federalist view. It is the view set
forth by Chief - Justice Jay in 1792, in the case of
Chisholm *vs.* the State of Georgia. It is the view subsequently defended by Mr. Webster in the Senate ; the
view adopted by Judge Story, in his " Commentaries on
the Constitution ; " the view elaborately expounded by
Mr. George Ticknor Curtis in his " History of the Constitution." So strongly was the opinion of the supremacy
of the United States maintained by some members of the
Convention, that they proposed that the existing States
should be broken up and the territory redivided into
States more nearly equal in extent and population. Even
those high Federalists who would not have approved of
breaking up the States, agreed with their brethren in
looking upon them as existing for the purposes of local,
as distinguished from national, government, and in denying to them the attributes of sovereignty. It is a curious
fact that those who held advanced views on this question were able to quote in their own support the words
of so ardent a defender of State rights as Patrick Henry,
who had once, in the passion of his eloquence, spoken
of the country as " thrown into one mass."

Between the two extreme views which have been described was the opinion held, probably with better reason, which may be expressed in the language of Elbridge
Gerry : " We were neither the same nation nor different nations." These members held both that the States
had, by their own repeated acts, deeply compromised
their independent existence ; and that powerful considerations of public policy, and even of public necessity,
urged them, here and now, to create an indestructible
T h e middle union of a truly national character. But, on
     view.   the other hand, they maintained that the
States were still, in spite of all, free political agents ;
nor did they admit that the States, in entering such a

union as was to be desired, would become mere territorial subdivisions, for purposes of local government, like the counties which in turn made up the State. The two extreme views of the relations of the several States to the United States were characteristic of the lawyer. The middle view was more worthy of the statesman.

While there were a hundred matters, no one of them unimportant, which were necessarily to be subjects of debate and division in the Convention, there were certain dominating issues with which the members had at once to deal, if the first step of progress was to be made. One of these was the issue between a strong and a weak government ; between a Constitution which should recognize the existence of a nation, or of what might in time become a nation, and a Constitution which should establish a league of States, brought together only for a few purposes, with little or no surrender of political power on the part of the constituent members. This issue was made in the very earliest days of the Convention when Edmund Randolph, on behalf of the delegates from Virginia, as the State at whose invitation the Convention had been called, presented a series of resolutions outlining a National Constitution for the United States of America. The resolutions were at once considered in Committee of the Whole, where the general idea of a strong and self-sufficient government was adopted by a narrow majority, made up mostly of the larger States. Had New Hampshire and Rhode Island, two small States, been represented, the decision would probably have been the other way. But, while the principle of a close union, instead of a loose confederation, prevailed thus in the first encounter, that victory was a dear one, in that it cost the influence and the interest of some delegates in the Convention and of a large number of

A national or a federal government ?

citizens outside. These persons were not prepared to establish a national government : they did not believe in it : they dreaded it : and, as they saw things inclining that way, they became disaffected, if not inimical.

An issue which arose at the same time with the foregoing, and which was intimately, though not logically, connected with it, in debate and in vote, was that between equal and proportional representation in the legislature of the proposed new government. Equal or proportional representation? The larger, that is, the more populous, States were generally disposed to insist upon having power in Congress in proportion to their inhabitants. The small States declared that they would not enter a government in which three or four of them might be weighed down by a single large State. This contest was a fierce one ; and without a compromise it would have been impossible to frame a constitution and then secure its adoption. Yet no compromise was hit upon in Committee of the Whole ; and the principle of proportional representation was accepted by a majority of six States to five. Here, again, was a victory which was costly, so costly, indeed, that, had it been pressed, the whole scheme of union would have gone to pieces.

The third great issue in the Convention was how the slaves, who were very numerous in the four southernmost States — Virginia, North and South Carolina, and Georgia—should be considered and treated in dealing with the basis of representation. Should they be counted as a part of the population, or not ? The States named were earnest in holding that the slaves should be included. The other States, most of which had few slaves, were indisposed to yield this point. Slaves were property : why should they be treated as persons for the purposes of representation ? Why should certain States have vastly increased power in Congress because they had many slaves? The contest here was a severe one, and not a little embittered. There was great danger of wrecking the whole scheme upon this obstacle. A compromise, suggested by James Wilson, of Pennsylvania, was adopted, to the effect that slaves should be counted in the basis of representation to the extent of three - fifths their actual number. That is, if a State had two hundred thousand, each, of free persons and of slaves, it should be taken, for this purpose, to have a population of 320,000. Such were the three main issues of the Convention in the first stage of its deliberations. Other matters were debated and decided which were important, which were, indeed, certain to be of the highest consequence in the history of the new government, if it should be founded; but none of these were vital in the sense that upon them turned the question whether there should be a union, or, rather, whether a constitution should even be framed for the States to consider. The continued existence of slavery was not among matters dealt with, for it was assumed from the start that the Convention could not interfere with this relation as existing within individual States.

The Committee of the Whole having reported the results which have been stated, the contest at once began all over again upon the presentation by Mr. Patterson, a delegate from New Jersey, of a series of resolutions providing for the establishment of a federal, instead of a national, government. In this stage of the proceedings, a compromise as to the basis of representation was reached, upon the suggestion of the delegates from Connecticut. It was agreed that the States should have equal power in the Senate, while in the House they should have representation in proportion to population. The rule as to the count-

The compromise as to representation.

ing of slaves, which has already been mentioned, was also, after a passionate debate, reaffirmed. The compromise thus effected was of the highest importance. Without this, it is not reasonable to suppose that a constitution would have been recommended to the States for consideration. Even this did not secure the ultimate adoption of the work of the Convention, but it did make it tolerably certain that that body would itself come to an agreement of some sort.

The contest over the basis of representation had been severe, and much sectional feeling had been developed. New York, not then counted among the large States, though now largest of all, and consequently deriving most benefit from proportional representation, had opposed the adoption of that principle in regard to the House of Representatives ; and, upon the success of that plan, Yates and Lansing returned home in disgust, leaving Hamilton alone to speak for New York in the Convention, though without any authority to bind his State. The struggle had left other wounds which would endanger ratification ; but from this time forward the work of framing a constitution on the Virginia plan, with the compromises already agreed to, went rapidly on. A Committee of Detail was appointed, consisting of Rutledge, Randolph, Gorham, and Wilson. After what seemed an impossibly brief delay, this committee brought in a rough draft of the Constitution as it was finally adopted. The committee gave to the chief Executive of

Committee of Detail introduces new issues.

the proposed government the title of President ; to its legislature, the name of Congress, while the upper chamber was to be known as the Senate, and the lower as the House of Representatives. The most important features introduced by the committee upon their own judgment were the provisions that no duties should be levied upon exports ; that the slave-trade should not be prohibited ; and that no "navigation act" should be passed except by a two-thirds vote. All these provisions had been inserted upon the demands of delegates from the southernmost States. The provision as to the taxation of exports was for the protection of the rice and indigo of Georgia and South Carolina. The provision of the two-thirds vote on navigation acts was proposed because the ship-building of the country was mainly in the northern States. The provision regarding the slave-trade requires no explanation. Each of these new provisions added by the Committee on Detail led to earnest and even acrimonious debate. The third was finally given up by the southern representatives, but the first and second were adopted, except that the prohibition of interference with the slave-trade was limited to the term of twenty years. Thus the last of the "Compromises of the Constitution" was effected. Much as anyone may dislike the principle on which these were based, it is hardly possible for a candid man to deny that, without them, or something very like them, that instrument could not have been framed by the Convention and adopted by the States. Who, in this age, can doubt that it was far better for the States to come together, as they then did, than that the effort at union should have been abandoned, and the American people have remained apart in separate States, or have founded two or three confederations along the Atlantic slope, with the vast western country to fight over in the near future? * The last clause brings to view a consideration which, though not the work of the Convention, had been a constant force mak-

* The idea that, upon the failure of the Convention to agree upon a form of government, there would arise two confederacies on the Atlantic coast, was a very common one. Mr. Wilson remarked during one of the debates, that "he knew there were some respectable men who preferred three confederacies, united by offensive and defensive alliances."

ing steadily for agreement and co-operation. The existence beyond the Alleghanies of nearly half a million
square miles of territory, much of which had been formally ceded to the United States, constituted an argument for union, the force of which it would be impossible to over-estimate. As Webster, in his famous speech
on the Compromise of 1850, asked, What is to become
of the public lands in the event of dissolution ? so no
member of the Convention of 1787 could fail to ask, in
his own mind, What is to become of the public lands in
case the States should not succeed in establishing a common government ?

After agreement on the points already mentioned had
been reached, though in no instance without severely
straining the patience of some among the delegates, if
not indeed greatly impairing their interest in the general result,* the work went swiftly forward. There still
remained many matters of important detail to be decided, such as the method of choice, the term of service,
and the eligibility of the chief Executive to re-election ;†
the provision for a Vice-President, the President's veto
upon legislation, the appointment of judges, the methods of amending the Constitution, should it be adopted,

* For example, Mr. Randolph, of Virginia, who himself proposed the
general plan which, with important modifications, had prevailed in the
Convention, declared in the debate over the navigation clause that the
scheme as it stood contained "so many odious features that he hardly
knew if he could agree to it." At a later stage, Mr. Mason, also of Virginia, one of the ablest and most influential members, expressed the belief that the proposed form of government would result in a monarchy or
a tyrannical aristocracy, and signified his intention to withhold his signature. On August 31st he declared that "he would sooner chop off his
right hand than put it to the Constitution as it now stands." Mr. Gerry,
of Massachusetts, spoke in the same vein.

† In its earlier stages the Convention fixed the term of the President
at seven years, and made him ineligible to re-election. When near adjournment, the Convention reduced the term to four years, and struck out
the provision of non-reëligibility.

the method of submitting the Constitution to the States, and the number of States whose ratification should suffice to bring the new government into being. On the last-named point the action of the Convention was most important. It was provided that the new Constitution should go into operation when ratified by nine States. This provision, eminently wise as it was, made the whole proceedings of the Convention revolutionary. The Articles of 1781 had provided for a " Perpetual Union ;" and it had been explicitly declared that no alteration should at any time be made in any of them unless such alteration should be confirmed by the legislature of every State. The Convention of 1787 had been called for the sole purpose of revising those articles ; but from the first its proceedings had been such as amounted to throwing the Confederation overboard and making a substantially new form of government.* The action taken regarding ratification was even more distinctly in violation of the principles of the Confederation. Instead of unanimous consent, the ratification of nine States was to suffice to set up the new government, while the States not consenting, be they one or two or three or four, were to be left out in the cold, having no part or lot with those whom they had helped to achieve independence, and with whom they had been closely associated ever since the Congress of 1774. Such a procedure was, as has been said, distinctly revolutionary in its character. The fundamental law,

Nine States sufficient for ratification.

* This change of purpose is indicated by Mr. Randolph's change in his first resolution. As originally drawn, this read as follows : " Resolved, That the Articles of Confederation ought to be so corrected and enlarged as to accomplish the objects proposed by their institution, namely, ' common defence, security of liberty and general welfare.' " This was subsequently modified by Mr. Randolph to read, " Resolved, That a national government ought to be established, consisting of a supreme legislative, executive, and judiciary."

as existing, was to be violated in the formation of the
new government. The dismemberment of the Confederation was to be made, if necessary—in fact was made
—a means to the creation of the union. The American
people, as they sprang to a higher political plane,
spurned away the support which had upheld them in
days of greater trial and weakness.

This fact of the revolutionary origin of the instrument
of 1787 is one of no little consequence to the student of
constitutional law. Those political writers
who have sought, lawyer-like, to trace an
uninterrupted descent from the Congress
which promulgated the Declaration of Independence,
through the Confederation of 1781, down to the first
Congress under the Union, have a difficult task to perform. Here, at the point we have now reached, yawns
an abyss which they can neither leap nor bridge. The
solution of continuity is complete. It is idle to seek to
derive the authority of the new government from whatever grants or concessions of power had been made to
the antecedent Confederation or to the revolutionary
Congress. But, even if the descent of the Constitution
from the Articles of Confederation, or from the acts
and proceedings of the Revolutionary Congress, had
been clear and uninterrupted, from the lawyer's point
of view, it would still have been true that the character
of the nation sought to be set up in 1787 was not to be
determined wholly by what was found in the Constitution as offered to the people. Governments are what
peoples by their acts make them. Even in the important step now taken, the real nature of the new government was to be determined, not wholly or mainly, by
the terms of the Constitution, but by the logic of events ;
by the fortunes of the nation ; by the growth of population ; the quickening of transportation ; the diversifi-

cation of industry ; the acquisition of territory ; by a
gradual process of evolution under the impulse or con-
straint of forces, some of which had not appeared in
1787 ; and, lastly, by act of war.

Even while the Convention was engaged in its constructive work, the Congress of the Confederation, on
July 13th, enacted the ever-memorable Ordinance regarding the territory northwest of the Ohio, which
comprised what are now the five States of Ohio, Illinois, Indiana, Michigan, and Wisconsin.   This vast
territory had been ceded to the United States * by the
acts of the several States making claim thereto under
their colonial charters.   By the Ordinance referred to,
Congress made provision, not merely for the The Ordi-
government of that territory in all ordinary nance of 1787.
civil respects and particulars ; but provided that there
should be formed out of it not less than three or
more than five States which should "forever remain a
part of this confederacy of the United States of America, subject to the Articles of Confederation, and to
such alterations therein as shall be constitutionally
made ; and to all the acts and ordinances of the United
States in Congress assembled, conformable thereto."

The Ordinance of 1787 is one of the monumental
charters of American constitutional history.   It not
only provided for building up great States Vast impor-
on that noble territory ; it also established tance of this
presonal liberty as the perpetual and inde- measure.
feasible law of those States, for it declared that slavery
and involuntary servitude, except for crime, should
never be known in that vast empire.   The honor of

---

* Virginia made exception of the proceeds of sales of certain lands in
Southern Ohio, which were needed to discharge her obligations to her
revolutionary soldiers; and Connecticut made the same exception as to
that portion of Northern Ohio known as the Western Reserve.

this enactment (which passed in a Congress of only eighteen delegates) has been claimed for several persons. It is most commonly given by fame to Nathan Dane, a member of Congress from Massachusetts, and to Dr. Manasseh Cutler, of the same State. It was another Massachusetts man, General Rufus Putnam, who was to lead the great enterprise of the practical settlement of the Northwest territory. The Ordinance of 1787 provided for the immediate establishment of a territorial government. It is interesting to note, as an evidence of the aristocratic political ideas of the time, that the governor was required to own a freehold of one thousand acres ; the secretary, judges, and members of the council, to have freeholds of five hundred acres each ; representatives to hold in their own right two hundred acres each ; while no resident should be a qualified elector who had not a freehold of fifty acres.

CHAPTER III

THE CONSTITUTION AS SUBMITTED TO THE PEOPLE

A National Form of Government—Organization of Congress—Rule as to Suffrage in National Elections : The Cause of this found in the varying Rules of the several States—The Powers of Congress—Acts Forbidden to Congress—Acts Forbidden to the States—Powers and Duties of the Executive—The Judiciary : Its Jurisdiction—Trials of all Crimes to be by Jury—Definition of Treason—Relations between Individual States and between the States and the United States : Mutual Faith and Credit, the Rule — New States — The Territories — Guarantee to the States of a Republican Form of Government—Future Amendments to the Constitution—Integrity of the Financial Obligations of the Confederation—The Constitution to be the Supreme Law of the Land—National and State Officers to be bound by Oath to Support the Constitution—The Ratification of Nine States sufficient to Establish the New Government.

As finally adopted by the Convention of 1787, and submitted to the people, the Constitution established a national legislature, a national executive and a national judiciary, each duly independent of the others. Of the seven Articles which made up the Constitution, the first provided for a Congress to consist of two houses, a Senate and a House of Representatives, following, in this division of the legislative authority, the example of most of the individual States. The House of Representatives was to be composed of members chosen every second year by the people of the several Organization States. In order not to impose a uniform of Congress. rule of suffrage upon the States, it was provided that those who in each State had the qualifications there

requisite for electors of the more numerous branch of
the legislature should be the electors of the representatives in Congress.   The number of representatives
in Congress was to be proportional to the respective
numbers of the several States, three-fifths of the slaves
being counted for this purpose.   The Senate was to be
composed of two senators from each State, chosen by
the legislature thereof for the term of six years, each
senator to have an individual vote.   The Vice-President
of the United States was to be President of the Senate.
It was provided that the time, place, and manner of
holding elections for senators and representatives should
be prescribed by the legislature of each State; but that
Congress might at any time make or alter such regulations, except as to the place of choosing senators.   The
purpose in this exception was that Congress should not
fix a place for choosing senators away from that in which
the State legislature, which was to choose the senators,
should by law be sitting.   Each house was to be the
judge of the elections, returns, and qualifications of its
own members; and might determine the rules of its
proceedings, punish its members for disorderly behavior, and, with the concurrence of two-thirds, expel a
member.   Neither house could, during the session of
Congress, without the consent of the other, adjourn for
more than three days, or adjourn to any other place
than that in which the two houses should be sitting.
Senators and representatives were to receive a compensation for their services, to be fixed by law, and to be paid
out of the treasury of the United States.   They were to
be in all cases, except treason, felony, and breach of the
peace, privileged from arrest during attendance and in
going to and returning from their homes; and it was
provided that they should not be questioned in any
other place—that is, in courts of law—for any speech or

debate.   The Senate should have the sole power to try all impeachments.   When the President of the United States was to be tried, the Chief-Justice should preside.   No person should be convicted on impeachment without the concurrence of two-thirds of the members present.   Judgment should not extend further than removal from office and future disqualification ; but the party convicted should still be liable to punishment at law.   Bills for raising revenue should originate in the House of Representatives, only, as the more popular branch ; but the Senate might propose or concur in amendments to such bills.   Bills which had passed both houses should become law only after receiving the approval of the President, except that Congress might, by a two-thirds vote of both houses, pass a bill which had been disapproved, or " vetoed," by the President.

The powers of Congress were expressed to be : To lay and collect taxes, duties, imposts, and excises, uniform throughout the United States, to pay the *The powers of Congress.* debts and provide for the common defence and the general welfare of the United States ; to borrow money on the credit of the United States ; to regulate commerce with foreign nations, among the several States and with the Indian tribes ; to establish a uniform rule of naturalization and uniform laws on the subject of bankruptcies ; to coin money and to punish the counterfeiting of the coin or current securities of the United States ; to establish post-offices and post-roads ; to provide for the granting of patent rights or copyrights for terms of years ; to define and punish piracies and felonies on the high seas and offences against the laws of nations ; to declare war, grant " letters of marque and reprisal," and make rules concerning captures by land and water ; to maintain armies and a navy ; to provide for calling out the militia, to execute the laws of the Union, suppress insurrections and repel invasion ; to organize and discipline the militia,* and to govern such of them as might be employed in the service of the United States ; to exercise exclusive jurisdiction over such district, not exceeding ten miles square, as might, by cession of particular States and the acceptance of Congress, become the seat of government ; and to exercise a like authority over all places purchased, with consent of the legislature of the State in which the same might be, for the erection of forts, magazines, arsenals, dock-yards, and other needful buildings ; *to make all laws which should be necessary and proper for carrying into effect the foregoing powers, and all other powers vested by the Constitution in the government of the United States or in any department or officer thereof.*

To Congress it was expressly forbidden : To prohibit the migration or importation of such persons (*i.e.,* blacks, imported as slaves) as any of the existing States might think proper to admit, prior to 1808 ; to suspend the writ of habeas corpus, unless when, in cases of invasion or rebellion, the public safety might require it ; to pass any bill of attainder or ex-post facto law ; to levy any capitation or other direct tax unless in proportion to population ; to lay any tax or duty on articles exported from any State ; to give preference, by any regulation of commerce or revenue, to the ports of one State over those of another.

Acts prohibited to Congress.

To the States it was expressly forbidden : To enter into any treaty, alliance, or confederation ; grant "letters of marque and reprisal ;" coin money ; emit bills of credit ; make anything but gold and silver coin a tender in payment of

Acts prohibited to the States.

* To the States was reserved the appointment of officers and the training of the militia according to the discipline prescribed by Congress.

debts ; pass any bill of attainder or ex-post facto law or laws impairing the obligation of contracts, or grant any title of nobility ; to levy, without the consent of Congress, any imposts or duties on imports or exports except what might be absolutely necessary for executing the inspection laws * of any State ; to lay, without the consent of Congress, any duty of tonnage ; keep troops or ships of war in times of peace ; or engage in war unless actually invaded or in such imminent danger as would not admit of delay.

In the Second Article, relating to the Executive, it was declared : That the executive power should be vested in the President of the United States, a natural-born citizen, who, with a Vice-President, should hold office for four years ; that the President and the Vice-President should be chosen by Electors, who, for each State, should be equal to the whole number of senators and representatives to which that State might be entitled in Congress—the time of choosing Electors and the day on which they should give their votes (uniform throughout the United States) being determined by Congress ; that, in case of the removal of the President from office, or of his death, resignation, or inability, the Vice-President should succeed, Congress being authorized to provide by law for a further succession ; that the President should be commander-in-chief of the military and naval forces ; and should have power to grant reprieves and pardons for offences against the United States, except in cases of impeachment ; that he should have power, by and with the consent of two-thirds of the Senate, to make treaties with foreign nations ; that he should nominate, and, by and

Powers and duties of the Executive.

* Such inspection laws to be subject to the revision and control of Congress ; and the net produce of all such duties and imposts to be for the use of the United States.

with the advice and consent of the Senate, appoint ambassadors, other public ministers and consuls, judges of the Supreme Court and all other officers of the United States whose appointment should not otherwise be provided for * and which should be established by law; that in the recess of the Senate the President should have power to fill all vacancies which might occur, such commissions to expire at the end of the next session; that the President should from time to time give Congress information of the state of the Union and recommend such measures as he might deem necessary and expedient; that the President should receive ambassadors and other public ministers; that he should take care that the laws be faithfully executed, and should commission all officers of the United States; that the President, Vice-President, and all the civil officers of the United States should be removed from office on impeachment for, and conviction of, treason, bribery, and other high crimes and misdemeanors.

The Third Article provided for the Judiciary. It was declared that the judicial power of the United States

The judicial power and jurisdiction.

should be vested in one Supreme Court and in such inferior tribunals as Congress might from time to time establish, the judges holding their offices during good behavior; that the judicial power should extend to all cases, in law or equity, arising under the Constitution, the laws of the United States, and treaties made under their authority, to all cases affecting ambassadors, other public ministers and consuls, to all cases of admiralty and maritime jurisdiction, to all controversies to which the United States should be a party, to controversies between two or more States, between a

---

* Congress having the power to vest by law the appointment of such inferior officers as they might think proper in the President alone, in the courts of law, or in the heads of departments.

State and citizens of another State, between citizens of different States, between citizens of the same State claiming lands under grants of different States, and between a State, or the citizens thereof, and foreign States, citizens, or subjects. In all cases affecting ambassadors, other public ministers, and consuls, and those in which a State should be a party, the Supreme Court should have original jurisdiction. In all the other cases before mentioned the Supreme Court should have appellate jurisdiction, both as to law and fact, with such exceptions and under such regulations as the Congress might make. The trial of all crimes, except in case of impeachment, should be by jury, such trial being held in the State in which such crimes should have been committed. Treason against the United States should consist only in levying war against them or in giving aid and comfort to their enemies : no person to be convicted of treason except upon the testimony of two witnesses to the same overt act, or upon confession in open court. In another place it was provided that Congress should have power to declare the punishment of treason ; but that no attainder of treason should work corruption of blood, or forfeiture except during the life of the person attainted.

The Fourth Article governed the relations between individual States and between the States and the United States. It was provided : That full faith and credit should be given in each State to the public acts, records, and judicial proceedings of every other State ; that the citizens of each State should be entitled to all the privileges and immunities of citizens in the several States ; that any person charged in any State with treason, felony, or other crime, who should flee from justice and be found in another State, should, on the demand of the executive authority of the State from

Relations between the States and with the United States.

which he fled, be delivered up ; that no person held to service or labor (apprentice or slave) in one State, under the laws thereof, escaping into another, should, in consequence of any law or regulation therein, be discharged from such service or labor, but should be delivered up on claim of the party to whom such service or labor was due ; that new States might be admitted into the Union ; but that no new State should be formed or erected within the jurisdiction of any other State, nor any State be formed by the junction of two or more States or parts of States, without the consent of the legislatures of the States concerned, as well as of Congress ; that Congress should have power to dispose of, and make all needful rules and regulations respecting, the territory belonging to the United States ; that the United States should guarantee to every State a republican form of government ; and should protect each of them against invasion, and on application of the legislature, or of the executive (when the legislature could not be convened), against domestic violence.

The Fifth Article provided for amendments to the Constitution, as follows : Congress, whenever two-thirds of both Houses should deem it necessary, should propose amendments to the Constitution, or, on the application of the legislature of two-thirds of the several States, should call a convention for proposing amendments, which in either case should be valid, as part of the Constitution, when ratified by the legislatures of three-fourths of the several States, or by conventions in three-fourths thereof, as the one or the other mode of ratification might be proposed by Congress ; provided that no State without its consent should be deprived of its equal suffrage in the Senate.

Amendments.

The Sixth Article declared : That all debts contracted and engagements entered into before the adop-

tion of the Constitution should be as valid against the
United States as under the Confederation ; that the
Constitution, and the laws of the United States made in
pursuance thereof, and all treaties made or to be made
under the authority of the United States, should be the
supreme law of the land ; and that the The Consti-
judges in every State should be bound there- tution the su-
by, despite anything in the constitution or preme law.
the laws of any State ; that the senators and representatives of the United States, and the members of the
several State legislatures, and all the executive and judicial officers, both of the United States and of the several
States, should be bound by oath or affirmation to support the Constitution ; but that no religious test should
ever be required as a qualification to any office or public
trust under the United States.

The Seventh and last Article provided that the ratification of the conventions of nine States should be
sufficient for the establishment of the Con- Ratification.
stitution between the States so ratifying the
same.

It has been said that Congress purposely avoided establishing a uniform rule of suffrage throughout the
Union. In the early settlement of the coun- The rule of
try the conditions imposed upon suffrage in suffrage.
the different colonies were of great variety. The New
England colonies generally seem to have regarded themselves, not as open communities into which anyone might
enter who chose to come and behave himself, but as
corporations in which regular members alone had any
share. Even in colonies more hospitable to foreigners,
the qualifications for suffrage were numerous and often
exacting. At the South, generally, no Indian or negro,
even if otherwise qualified, could vote. In at least two
colonies, Jews could not vote. The usual voting age

4

was twenty-one years; but in two colonies the age-limit was twenty-four years; while in two it was apparently fixed below the standard. Religious qualifications existed in many colonies. Quakers were excluded in a few colonies, and Roman Catholics in more. Property qualifications also were usual. At one time in Rhode Island not less than £400, or £20 annual income, was required. Sometimes land—say fifty acres—was necessary, with or without "a house twelve feet square." In other cases the qualification might be either land or money. In some colonies the estate must be in fee; in others, an estate for life sufficed; in others still, an estate for the life of the voter's wife would answer. The foregoing instances will give an idea of the extent and variety of the qualifications for full citizenship in the early colonies. By the time the Revolution broke out, these had been not a little reduced and simplified; but there remained differences enough to make it eminently desirable that the Constitution should avoid the imposition of an uniform rule of suffrage. This was effected by the adoption of the provision stated above.

CHAPTER IV

RATIFICATION AND THE INAUGURATION OF THE GOVERNMENT

Difficulties Attending Ratification—Pennsylvania and the Smaller States Promptly Accept the Constitution—Grounds of Opposition in the Larger States—Absence of a Bill of Rights—"The Federalist"—The Tories Support the Constitution—The Massachusetts Convention Ratifies, 187 to 168—Maryland and South Carolina Join the Union—New Hampshire, the Ninth State, Accedes—The Constitution Formally Accepted—Great Importance of Securing, also, New York and Virginia—The Conventions in those States—The Constitution Fiercely Opposed—General Consent to the Subsequent Adoption of Amendments in the Nature of a Bill of Rights—Virginia and New York Finally Ratify, the Latter, 30 to 27—North Carolina and Rhode Island Stay Out—The Government Organized—George Washington Chosen President—John Adams, Vice President—Congress Assembles, March 4, 1789 : No Quorum until April 6th—Inauguration of Washington, April 30th—The Beneficent Influence of Washington in the Establishment of the New Government—Extent of the United States : Population—The Western Colonies—The State of the Arts—Agriculture the Predominant Occupation of the People—Reasons for the High Productive Power of the United States : A Vast Breadth of Virgin Lands ; Popular Tenure of the Soil ; the Cultivating Class not a Peasantry—The Remarkable Mechanical and Inventive Genius of the People : The Genesis of this Trait Explained.

THE national principle had, as we have seen, triumphed in the Convention of 1787 ; but every one of its successive victories had lost the new Constitution some supporter in the Convention ; while, in the wider field of the country at large, alike the concessions made by the dominant party of the Convention and the most

characteristic features which they introduced into the
Constitution had alienated large numbers who, in a general way, were prepared to say that they were for a real
and permanent union, but did not relish one of exactly
this kind.   The question, whether the instrument presented to the States on September 17, 1787, could possibly secure the ratification of the needed nine States, was
Doubts as to enveloped in grave doubt : that a unanimous
ratification. ratification could be obtained no one probably imagined.   It is related, how truly one cannot say,
that Washington, on laying down his pen after signing the Constitution, remarked to those around him.
"Should the States reject this excellent Constitution,
the next will be drawn in blood."

Several of the States promptly accepted the Constitution : Delaware, the smallest State, first of all.   Penn-
The small   sylvania, under the lead of James Wilson,
States accede. who had contributed largely to the formation of the Constitution, came next, though here strong
opposition was manifested from the great interior high-
land district.   Then followed New Jersey, by a unani
mous vote ; then Georgia and Connecticut.   All but
one of the foregoing, it will be observed, were among
the smaller States, to which an immense concession had
been made in the matter of equal representation in the
Senate ; and which had, therefore, most to hope for and
least to fear under the proposed new government.   In
Georgia the argument for ratification had been greatly
strengthened by the fact that the larger part of the present State was held by powerful Indian tribes, whose ill-
repressed hostility made the existence of an effective
government very desirable for the white inhabitants.
Thus far the work of ratification had gone on swim-
mingly ; but all this proved nothing ; promised nothing.   The real struggle was to come.   Nearly all the re-

maining States were doubtful.   Many political reasons, many personal forces, opposed themselves to further ratification.   The more important of these will be sufficiently intimated in what will be said regarding individual States ; but one general ground of opposition requires to be stated.

Among the strongest objections, urged sincerely by some, urged by others as a cover to more real reasons, was the absence from the Constitution of a proper Bill of Rights, that is, a body of express provisions protecting the citizens from certain wrongs and abuses which had been made very familiar to the minds of Americans through the history of the mother country.   The traditions and modes of political thinking among our people were such as to make this omission from the Constitution, first, a real grievance, and, secondly and in a much higher degree, a taking popular objection.   The cause of that omission had been found partly in the fact that the members of the Convention had been engrossed in adjusting the conflicting claims and interests of the different States and sections : of the small, as opposed to the large, States ; of the Northern, as opposed to the Southern, States ; of the commercial, as opposed to the planting, States.   In part, also, the cause of the omission of the desired guaranties had been found in the opposition of the Southern States.   During the discussion in the convention of South Carolina, in justifying the absence of a Bill of Rights, General C. C. Pinckney said : " Such bills generally begin by declaring that all men by nature are born free.   Now, we should make that declaration with a very bad grace when a large part of our property consists in men who are actually born slaves."   In his "Journal of the Convention," Mr. Madison gives Maryland, Virginia, North and South Carolina, and Georgia as voting against a Bill of Rights. But although the Southern delegates largely took this position in the Convention, the absence of such provisions became one of the chief issues in the contest over the ratification, even in their own section. Such was one important obstacle which the Constitution encountered. Nothing could be more expressive of the good sense and good feeling of the American people than the fact that, while the absence of a Bill of Rights came to be more and more generally regretted and complained of as the debate over ratification progressed, this was not at last allowed to become a fatal objection. More and more it came to be understood and agreed that the omission should be supplied subsequently to ratification ; and, though some extremists sought to hold back the assent of their States until the desired guaranties should be secured, State after State waived its objections and accepted the Constitution upon the general understanding referred to.

The adoption of the Constitution was promoted, we cannot say in what degree, but beyond question very greatly, by a series of papers, conceived by Hamilton and by him mainly executed, though with great assistance from Madison and some also from Jay,* which have "The Feder- ever since been known as "The Federalist," alist." a body of essays which, though written for what in these days we should call "campaign" purposes, has not only become a classic in our national political literature, but is the repository of the best, and, apart from judicial decisions, the most authoritative, expositions of the extensive text of the Constitution. That, in a task like this, Hamilton, the great coming leader of the Federalists, at least on the intellectual side,

* Forty-six of the papers are attributed to Hamilton ; twenty-nine to Madison, in some of which Hamilton probably had a share ; and five to Jay.

should have been able to write in such harmony of views with Madison, who was destined to be Jefferson's chief lieutenant in the organization and control of the Republican-Democratic party, shows how well the Convention had done its part, in laying down the main lines of the Constitution ; how well the Committee on Detail had done its part, in working out the subordinate features of the scheme ; how well the Committee on Style and Revision, through Gouverneur Morris, had done its part, by putting the Constitution into clear and simple language ; more than all, how closely the two leading authors of " The Federalist " had worked together at Philadelphia, how thoroughly they understood each other's views and notions, how strong was their common interest in the triumph of their cause.

Another and very curious feature of the contest over the Constitution deserves to be mentioned. This was the general accession of the Tories of the Revolution to the party of ratification. These persons, still to be found in great numbers in some States, notably in Massachusetts, New York, Maryland, and South Carolina, were strongly drawn toward the proposed form of government by the persecutions to which they continued to be subjected. They thought they saw, in the establishment of an effective government for the whole country, a safeguard against the malignity of their immediate neighbors. It is also to be said that the Tories comprised many men of wealth and prosperous merchants, who favored an efficient government on commercial and financial grounds.

Tories support the Constitution.

Let us now return to the separate acts of ratification. Five States had accepted the Constitution when the Convention met in Massachusetts, to determine what the State whose people had been foremost in resistance to the encroachments of the Crown would do with that government which was the outcome of so much toil, treasure, and blood. The elements here opposed to the Constitution were most formidable. On the side of ratification were arrayed the lawyers, the clergy, the mercantile class, and the men of property, generally, with the almost unanimous support of the officers of the late Continental army. All these classes believed in a strong and efficient government, which should pay the debts of the Revolution, put a stop to paper-money, secure the country against domestic disturbances, and make the nation powerful at home and respected abroad. The Constitution was opposed very largely by the less favored classes; by the advocates of paper-money; by the promoters of Shays's Rebellion, of whom a number found their way into the Convention; by some of the old Revolutionary leaders, soured at finding themselves "back numbers" in the general movement of American life; by many small politicians, who feared they should lose influence under a really national government; by the delegates from the District of Maine, who were disposed to hold that their chances of separate Statehood would be better without the new Constitution than with it; and, finally, by some patriotic and able men who sincerely believed that the proposed government was too aristocratic in its organization, and that it would be used to crush out the rights and interests of the States, if not, also, the personal liberties of the people.

With the parties for and against ratification thus made up, the issue of the struggle was looked for with intense interest by the whole country, particularly in view of the fact that Massachusetts lay between two other doubtful States, New York and New Hampshire. John Hancock, President of the Congress which had promulgated the Declaration of Independence, presided over the Massachusetts Convention ; and his attitude aroused much apprehension.   Samuel Adams, the popular agitator of the pre-Revolutionary period, The Massa- was understood to be opposed to ratification, chusetts Convention. like his great ally in those burning days, Patrick Henry, of Virginia.   Elbridge Gerry, who, as a delegate to the Philadelphia Convention, had refused to sign the Constitution, was also present.   At last, on the strength of nine amendments formally proposed to the proposed Constitution, mainly in the nature of a Bill of Rights, the vote for unconditional ratification was carried, February 7, 1788, by the small majority of 187 to 168.   Thus was one perilous stage safely passed, though by an escape so narrow that, even now, we hold our breath in contemplating it.

In Maryland, the last State to join the Confederation in 1781, the opposition was led with great ability and much acrimony by Luther Martin, who had been one of the chief figures of the Convention ; but that State, its former objections regarding Western lands having been removed, handsomely acceded to the new form of government on April 28th.   South Carolina followed on May 23d, by a large majority.   Eight States had now ratified the Constitution.   In the New Hampshire Convention so doubtful, at first, was the outlook that the friends of the Constitution consented to an adjournment, rather than take the chances of an adverse or of a too close vote ; but the action of Massachusetts turned the scale, and New Hampshire fell into line on June 9th.

Technically this completed the union, since the ratification of nine States had been made sufficient, as between the States ratifying ; but the strain and anxiety were yet far from over.   While it would have been lawful to set up the government with as many as four

States outside, including both New York and Virginia,
it would yet have been little less than hopeless to do
The States outside. so. A government established under these
conditions would have been looked upon
with the gravest apprehension of disaster. At least one
more from the missing States, and that one of the two
just named, was, if not constitutionally, at least politically, essential to a fair trial of the Constitution. All
eyes were therefore turned to New York and Virginia,
whose conventions met during the month of June, and
were for a few days simultaneously in session.

In the latter State the result was long doubtful.
Virginia had called the Convention at Philadelphia ;
The Virginia Convention. and it had been her delegation which offered
the National plan of government, adopted in
preference to the Federal plan from New Jersey. Virginia might, therefore, have been looked to for an early
and enthusiastic ratification. But, on the other hand,
as the largest State, Virginia had been deeply alienated
by the adoption of the principle of equality in the Senate, which placed her on a par in that respect with
Delaware and Rhode Island, as well as by many other
things which occurred in the course of the Convention :
so that, in the result, two of her leading delegates,
George Mason and Edmund Randolph, refused to sign
the Constitution. When that instrument was laid before the people, great popular opposition was developed. The belief was expressed that the navigation of
the Mississippi, in which Virginia, and especially the
sons of Virginia across the mountains, in the present
State of Kentucky, were vitally interested, would be
sacrificed to the commercial selfishness of the North and
East. The absence of a Bill of Rights was also made
the subject of strong objections ; and, finally, we have
the same painful feature that was exhibited in Massa-

chusetts, namely, a great orator of the ante-revolutionary period, opposing what was the only possible fortunate issue of the Revolution. Patrick Henry was among the ardent opponents of the proposed government; and threw himself into the contest with all the vehemence of his impulsive nature. Fortunately, Mr. Randolph had repented of his refusal to sign the Constitution, and appeared as the advocate of ratification.

Mr. Madison was there, sagacious, politic, plausible, adroit, perhaps the very best person to counteract such opposition as that of Mr. Henry. He knew his case better than any other man in the Convention; and, though destitute of eloquence, in the unfortunate American sense of that word, was a clear reasoner and an effective debater. The very defects alleged by the opponents of the Constitution were artfully wrought by Mr. Madison into an argument which made that instrument appear fair and rational to the "average mind." The proposed government, he said, was neither federal nor national; it had a mixed character, in some parts federal, in others national. The parties to the government would be the people; but the people as composing thirteen sovereignties, not as composing one great society. Its mixed character is also shown by the mode of ratification prescribed. If purely national, the assent of a popular majority would suffice. In fact, it must be adopted by the States; yet within each State it is not the State legislature, but a convention of the people, which gives assent. The mode of possible amendment also shows that mixed character. A majority of the States cannot amend the Constitution, which is a departure from a national plan. Nor is the assent of all the States necessary for amendment, which is a departure from the federal plan. The rule of representation, finally, shows

Mr. Madison's advocacy of the Constitution.

the mixed character of the new government, since the members of the first house are to be in proportion to population, which is a recognition of the national character ; while the members of the second house are to be elected by the States in their equal capacity, which is a recognition of the federal character.   This complex character, Mr. Madison urged, was necessary in order to secure at once power and liberty ; and it was hoped thereby to exclude the evils of absolute consolidation on the one side, and those of mere confederation on the other.   To a people of English blood such a line of argument could not fail to commend itself.

In Virginia, as in almost every other State, the progress of the discussion steadily strengthened the friends of the Constitution ; and at last, on June 25th, the Convention, by a small majority, gave in the adhesion of that State.   But it was still exceedingly important to secure New York, alike on account of its geographical position, its commercial importance, and the distinguished character of its political leaders.   The Convention here met on June 17th, and the great debate was at once opened.   Hamilton advocated ratification with all his marvellous eloquence and personal influence.   He was ably seconded by Jay and Livingston.   The opposition was led by Melancthon Smith, no unworthy antagonist, supported by Yates and Lansing, who had been Hamilton's colleagues at Philadelphia, and had refused to sign the Constitution.   More, perhaps, than all, George Clinton, the War Governor of New York, was a bitter and seemingly irreconcilable opponent of the Constitution.   But the friends of ratification now enjoyed one tremendous advantage.   So many States had already acceded that it was beyond a doubt the necessary number would soon be had to inaugurate the new Government.   It was,

The New York Convention.

therefore, pertinent to ask—and the question was put with overwhelming force—not, do you altogether like the Constitution? but, is New York to stay out of the Union and become a foreign State? Soon arrived news that New Hampshire had joined, the ninth State. The debate still continued, but the tone of discussion was somewhat changed. The question now was, not of adoption or rejection, but of securing amendments. The friends of ratification were ready to afford every assurance that amendments should be passed as soon as the new government came into operation. The opponents still held out for conditional ratification or for postponement pending amendment; but their strength was continually failing, alike under the unceasing assaults of the friends of the Constitution and under the relentless logic of events. At last, by the slow despatches of those days, came the news that Virginia had joined. The opposition vainly tried to keep up the fight. Though they started out with claiming forty-six of the sixty-five delegates, they were clearly beaten. After some more tedious weeks spent upon proposals to amend, ratification was finally carried on July 26th, though only by a majority of thirty to twenty-seven; and the great constitutional battle was won.

North Carolina and Rhode Island still remained outside. It was, however, so desirable that these should be won over, and withal so evident that they *The recalcitrant States.* must sooner or later come in, that, though they were technically foreign States, their vessels were for the present put on the same terms as regards tonnage duties with those of the United States; and all goods, the growth or manufacture of these States, were exempted from import duties. Without waiting for their accession, the eleven States already in the Union proceeded to organize the Government under the Constitution. The

first Wednesday in January, 1789, was fixed for choice
of presidential electors ; the first Wednesday in February
for their balloting ; the first Wednesday in March, the
4th, for inaugurating proceedings under the Constitution.

For the presidency no name but that of Washington
had been suggested or was considered by the electors.

Washington
chosen President.

It had generally been agreed that John
Adams, of Massachusetts, should, both from
considerations of "locality" (so potent in
American political affairs) and also with reference to his
long and eminent services to the cause of American independence, before and during the Revolution, be chosen
Vice-President ; * but in the electoral colleges of the several States there was a wide scattering of the votes for
this office ; and Mr. Adams actually came in by one less
than a majority of the total vote.   For this Mr. Adams
and his friends blamed Hamilton, charging that the result had been effected by his intrigues, for the purpose
of impairing Mr. Adams's prestige and influence.   Congress assembled, pursuant to appointment, at New York,
on March 4, 1789 ; but such were the vicious traditions
of the old Confederation, that a quorum of both houses
could not be obtained for several weeks.   "The States
most convenient," wrote Mr. Madison, "are among the
defaulters."   At last, on April 6th, members had arrived in sufficient numbers to transact business.   On
April 30th the President was inaugurated.   The election of Washington had been, as we have said, unanimous.   Even if party spirit had already arisen, it would
have been hushed in that majestic presence.   Assuredly
no man was ever more truly "first in war, first in peace,
and first in the hearts of his countrymen."   The grate-

* The peculiar and highly objectionable method of choosing the Vice-
President, under the Constitution as it went into operation, will be described in connection with the third presidential election.

ful nation recognized him as its saviour in a long and wasting war ; the new Constitution, inaugurated with so many hopes, was in no small measure due to his influence.   John Adams said of him : " Were I blessed with powers to do justice to his character, it would be impossible to increase the confidence and affection of his country or to make the smallest additions to his glory.   If we look over the catalogue of the first magistrates of nations, whether they have been denominated presidents or consuls, kings or princes, where should we find one whose commanding talents and virtues, whose over-ruling good fortune have so completely united all hearts and voices in his favor ; who enjoyed the esteem and admiration of foreign nations and fellow-citizens with equal unanimity." The closing sentiment of this extract is unqualifiedly just.   It is not American partiality which exalts the name of Washington.   To-day all nations revere our first President as the finest and noblest character of political history.   But, while the position and prestige of Washington were such as to have commanded for him the election without reference to political opinions or predilections, parties could not be said to exist.   It was not doubtful that they would soon arise ; nay, sentiments of attachment or repugnance had already pretty clearly marked out those who would be found on one side and on the other of the political division when it should take place ; but as yet the questions of the national life had not come into shape, and all sections and classes, including men of all tastes and predilections, stood in suspense until the issues of our politics should be defined.

Before proceeding to the administration of Washington, let us for a moment consider the extent and population *

* In the statistics immediately following we use the figures of the first census, taken in 1790.

of the country. The States were thirteen in number. Of these, two still remained out—North Carolina, with a population of 393,751 ; Rhode Island, with 68,825. The geographical relations of these States, however, were sufficient to give assurance of their ultimate accession to the Union, which, in that case, would embrace a population of 3,929,214. Vermont, with 35,691, was, formally, a part of New York ; Maine, with 96,540, a part of Massachusetts. With the exception of about one hundred and twenty-five thousand souls, all the population was found east of the Appalachian chain. Two important colonies only had been planted at the West, upon territory belonging to Virginia and North Carolina. Of these, the District of Kentucky had a population of 73,677. Tennessee had 35,691 inhabitants. Central New York was still an almost unbroken wilderness, as was Western Pennsylvania, though some not inconsiderable settlements had been made around the junction of the Allegheny and Monongahela rivers. At the South, the line of white occupation was almost parallel to the Savannah River, and distant therefrom a short distance ; the remainder of the State of Georgia was occupied by powerful and not over-friendly Indian tribes. The population of Philadelphia was 42,-520 ; of New York, 33,131 ; of Boston, 18,038 ; of Charleston, 16,359 ; of Baltimore, 13,503 ; of Richmond, 3,761. The total value of the exports and of the imports of the United States was about twenty million dollars each. The shipment of American cotton had as yet hardly begun, the export of 1791 only reaching 19,200 pounds, the equivalent of forty-eight modern bales. The exports from the Southern States at this time were mainly tobacco and rice, with some indigo, and also "naval stores," viz., tar, pitch, and turpentine.

Extent and population of the United States.

As we begin this story of the life of the American nation during the first years of its accomplished and recognized independence, it is appropriate to State of the call the reader's attention to the fact that he arts. is contemplating the experiences of a people born, bred, and living under conditions, many of them now gone forever; belonging to a time earlier by a century than our own; a time when arts familiar to us were unknown and unthought of; when chemistry had as yet wrought not one of its marvels,* the discovery of oxygen, by Priestley, having taken place near the beginning of our narrative; when electricity was recognized only through its terrific and destructive agency as lightning; when biology, with its wondrous revelations of natural life and its not less startling lights cast on social and political philosophy, was still deeply buried under ignorance, prejudice, and superstition. It was an age in which many of the ordinary phenomena of physics met the eye of peasant and gentleman, alike, either as miracles, due to direct, immediate, particular intervention of divine power, or as matters of course, as completely outside the relations of cause and effect as they appear to the ox in the furrow. Though the expansive power of steam had been already adapted in some small measure to forms of manufacture then practically unknown in the United States, it had not yet been applied to transportation, either by land or by water. In agriculture the implements were hardly a whit improved from those in use twenty-five hundred years before. Medicine, though stripped of its mediæval elements of charlatanry and imposture, was still barbarous in its cautery, its surgery, its blood-letting, its dosing. History as a science was not known; what was called by that name being but a collection of fables, of heroic and sentimental legends,

* Perhaps we ought to say, except gunpowder.

5

of unauthenticated traditions, of records half-read or misread. But, on the other hand, political philosophy, which in logical order should have awaited the birth of history, had already attained a robust manhood, through the splendid virile efforts of the English, French, and German peoples to achieve a practical political freedom ; and the art of constructing constitutions and framing laws had been developed to great perfection through errors and mistakes innumerable and of infinite consequence to untold numbers, through speculations daring and profound, through experiments in which the lives of millions had been distilled into policies.

Agriculture was the chief occupation in the United States at the achievement of independence ; and even with the rude implements and the defective knowledge of the time, our people had, through certain fortunate conditions, and also through the possession of a faculty which, in degree and almost in kind, distinguishes them from all other peoples on the face of the earth, attained a marvellous productive power. The fortunate condi-

Causes of the remarkable productive power of American agriculture.

tions referred to were, first, a vast breadth of virgin lands, which required only the cultivation of the best soils, and, even upon these, exempted the occupier from the tremendous tax which, in the agriculture of all old countries, has every year to be paid to keep up the fertility of the land ; secondly, the popular tenure of the soil and excellent laws for the registration of titles and the transfer of real property ; and, thirdly, the fact that the agricultural class, unlike the body of cultivators in every country of Europe, except only Switzerland and perhaps also Scotland, had never constituted a peasantry, in any proper sense of that term. The men who tilled the soil here were the same kind of men, precisely, as those who filled the professions or were engaged in commercial or mechanical pursuits. Of two sons of the same mother one became a lawyer, perhaps a judge, or went down to the city and became a merchant, or gave himself to political affairs and became a governor or a member of Congress. The other stayed upon the ancestral homestead, or made a new one for himself and his children out of the public domain further west, remaining through his life a plain, hard-working farmer. This state of things made American to differ from European agriculture by a wide interval. There was then no other country in the world, there is now no other considerable country, where equal mental activity and alertness have been applied to the soil as to trade and industry.

But more even than the total effect of the fortunate conditions which have been indicated, American agriculture in those days owed its really remarkable productive power to a special, almost a technical, quality of our people, namely, mechanical insight and invention. It is difficult to write of this subject without producing the impression of exaggeration. There is only one nation in the world to the mass of whose population this form of genius can be attributed. That nation is our own. In other countries it is only picked men, a select few, who possess mechanical insight and aptitude, the power of instantaneously, because instinctively, seizing upon mechanical relations, together with a high degree of native efficiency in the use of tools. With us the rule is the other way: there are few Americans of American stock, at least throughout the Northern States, who have not mechanical insight and aptitude in a measure which elsewhere would make them marked men. As a great organ of English opinion has said, "Invention is a normal function of the American brain. The American invents as the Greek chiselled,

The mechanical genius of the American people.

as the Venetian painted, as the modern Italian sings."
By some persons the wonderful mechanical developments of our history have been attributed to our patent laws.   But there is reason to believe that the power
to invent was created altogether irrespective of and long
antecedently to that system of legislation.   It was with
us an inheritance ; and it is fairly a question whether
this inheritance has not been impaired rather than increased during the period covered by our patent laws.

Why was it that the American of the time of which we
write possessed this quality in such a remarkable degree ?   It was not because of long training in manufactures.   On the contrary, the jealous and repressive
Not due to policy of England had prevented the de-
manufactures. velopment of technical industry.   In 1699
Parliament declared that no wool, yarn, or woollen
manufactures of their American plantations should be
shipped, or even laden in order to be transported from
thence to any place whatsoever.   In 1719 the House
of Commons declared that the erecting of manufactures
in the colonies tended to lessen their dependence on
Great Britain.   In 1731, in consequence of numerous
complaints from interested persons, among whom the
London Company of Hatters were conspicuous, Parliament directed the Board of Trade to inquire and
report with respect to laws made, manufactures set up,
or trade carried on detrimental to the trade, manufactures, or navigation of the mother country.   The
immediate outcome of this investigation was an Act of
Parliament, in 1732, which not only prohibited the export of colonial hats to a foreign port, but forbade,
under severe penalties, their transportation from one
British plantation to another.   Eighteen years later,
the griefs of another body of British manfacturers
called for remedy from Parliament ; and an act of

1750 prohibited the erection or continuance of any mill or other engine for slitting or rolling iron, or any plating forge to work with a tilt-hammer, or any furnace for making steel, throughout the colonies. And every such mill, engine, forge, or furnace was declared to be a " common nuisance ; " and colonial governors were required to cause the same to be "abated." But while the Americans of the days before the Revolution were thus forbidden to practise any branch of industry which might interfere with the market for British produce, the foundations of future greatness were being laid where the power of Parliament and all the armies of the king could not reach them. In a very high sense, the history of American manufactures reaches back beyond the Revolution, for it was in that period that the peculiar industrial character of our people was developed.

In inquiring into the genesis of this truly national trait we note, first, that the country was settled predominantly by men of the great inventive Teutonic race ; and that, of this race, it was the most ingenious branch, the English, which furnished by far the largest part of the population of the Atlantic coast. Secondly, the early settlers constituted, in the main, a picked population. The possibilities of improvement which reside in breeding from the higher, stronger, more alert, and aggressive individuals of a species are well recognized in the case of the domestic animals ; but there have been few opportunities for obtaining a measure of the effect that could be produced upon the human race, by excluding from propagation the weak, the vicious, the cowardly, the effeminate, persons of dwarfed stature, of tainted blood, or of imperfect organization. The inhabitants of the English colonies, especially in New England, constituted a population which was more truly selected, in the respects of mental vigor, intellectual inquisitiveness, enterprise, and self-reliance than any other considerable population which history knows. Thirdly, upon a community thus constituted were laid the severe requirements of existence under an exceptionally rigorous climate. The first settlers brought with them from the old country all the desires, tastes, and ambitions proper to a highly advanced society; while yet there was but small means for their gratification. It was not, at least after the first few winters, the dread of physical privation, but wants of the higher nature, which afforded the most acute stimulus to the scheming, devising, calculating faculty in early American life, out of which in the course of generations was developed that inventive power of which we write. To make shifts; to save time; to shorten labor; to search out substitutes for what was inaccessible or costly; to cut corners and break through barriers in reaching an object; to force one tool to serve three or four uses, and to compel refractory or inappropriate material to answer urgent needs — this was the constant occupation of our ancestors. Life was no routine, work was no routine, to them, as it is to the peasantry of every country of Europe, as it is fast coming to be among us. Then, everywhere and at all times, it was possible, by thought and care and pains, to save something from labor, to add something to comfort and social decency. Originality of conception, boldness in framing expedients, and fertility of resource grew by constant exercise in father and mother, and were transmitted with increasing force to sons and daughters, until invention came to be " a normal function of the American brain," the American inventing as the Greek chiselled, as the Venetian painted, as the Italian sings.

This wide popular appreciation of mechanical forces and relations was later to constitute a most important element in the development of American manufactures ; but down to the time of which we are writing it had been mainly applied in promoting the rapid, effective settlement of the country and in increasing the productive power of the American farmer. It was not merely or mainly that the mechanical genius of the whole people secured the progressive improvement of all the known tools and implements of husbandry, so that the American axe, the American spade and shovel, the American plough, and the American farm-wagon early became the best of their kind in the world, being little less than marvels of combined lightness, efficiency, and strength. It was not merely or mainly that this mechanical genius of the whole people gave the widest possible, indeed a universal, application of every agricultural tool, improvement, and invention to its appropriate work, though this constituted an enormous advantage. " Experienced mechanicians," says Professor Hearn, "assert that, notwithstanding the progress of machinery in agriculture, there is probably as much sound, practical, labor-saving invention and machinery unused as there is used ; and that it is unused solely in consequence of the ignorance and incompetency of the working people." Such a remark would utterly fail of significance if applied to the United States in the time of which we are writing. It was because mechanical insight and aptitude were found throughout the whole mass of the American people, that every product of invention and skill was speedily made of service on petty farms all over the land, even in the most remote districts.

Influence of mechanical genius upon American agriculture.

But it was neither through the invention and improvement of agricultural tools and implements, nor through the wide application of every such invention or improvement, that the peculiar and extraordinary mechanical genius of the American people made its largest contribution toward increasing the national capacity for agricultural production. In the daily use of this faculty throughout the pioneer period, and in some degree through every subsequent stage of settlement and cultivation, the American farmer, a natural

Influence of mechanical genius in promoting settlement.

mechanic and a natural engineer, derived from this source an advantage beyond estimation. The way in which the pioneer of New England birth or blood, stopping his cattle in the wilderness, and tumbling axe and spade, bundles and barrels out upon the unbroken ground, set about the task of providing shelter for his children and his animals, clearing the ground and getting a first crop out of the soil, was not admirable merely as an exhibition of courage, faith, and enterprise, but, if we look at the results accomplished for the time and labor expended, it constitutes a triumph of mechanical, we might fairly say of engineering genius. We shall have occasion at a later period to refer again to this quality of the American people as promoting, and indeed alone making possible, the extraordinary progress of population westward over new lands, enabling vast tracts to be brought yearly within the frontier of settlement, and building up empires in a decade. At present we make use of it mainly as explaining the high degree of comfort, and even of comparative luxury, in which our people lived within their more familiar seats. Beside any other agricultural population on the globe, the Americans of the close of the last century were rich and prosperous. The exceptions to agriculture as the general occupation of the time were found in the commerce of New York and in the commerce and fisheries of New England.

CHAPTER V

WASHINGTON'S FIRST TERM

THE acts and events of Washington's first term will
not be considered in chronological order, except so far
as the succession of one upon another was significant;
but will be grouped according to essential relations, or
for the greater convenience of consideration or recol-
lection. And first let us speak of those which may be
regarded as completing the Union of the States and
closing the career of the antecedent Confederation.
Most important of these was the accession of North
Carolina and Rhode Island. The causes of
delay in these States need not be dwelt upon.
In Rhode Island much of the opposition had
arisen from the paper-money party, although a curious
conservatism, characteristic of the people of this State,
and due to causes appearing in the course of its history,
has also been adduced in explanation. In North Caro-

lina Mr. Madison attributed the opposition to " the influence of the minority in Virginia which lies mostly in the southern part of the State and to the management of its leader." The leader referred to was Patrick Henry, who had with all his soul resisted ratification in his own State, and whose influence was very great throughout the parts of North Carolina contiguous to his own home. The opposition is also largely attributed to a fear that the free navigation of the Mississippi, in which the State's western colony, Tennessee, was vitally interested, would be sacrificed under the new government. It has been stated that the first Congress of the Union kept open a place for the two recusant States, going so far as to admit their ships and productions to equal benefits with those of other States. North Carolina succumbed on November 21, 1789. Rhode Island came in on May 29, 1790.

It was shown that the adoption of the Constitution was impeded, if not indeed gravely imperilled, by the absence of a Bill of Rights. A few of the features proper to such a bill had, it is true, been incorporated in the Constitution—such as the provision against the extension of attaint beyond the offending person, even by sentence of court; the immunity of senators and representatives for speech or debate; the prohibition of the suspension of habeas corpus in times of peace and order; the prohibition of ex post facto laws and legislative bills of attainder; the requirement of trial for offences to be held in the State or district where the offences were committed; the definition given to treason, and the limitation placed upon the evidence necessary to convict of this crime. But all these together fell far short of making up what was deemed essential to the due security of popular rights and personal liberty. We have already said that

Amendment of the Constitution.

by many this defect was considered an insuperable objection, some of the State conventions seeming prepared to make the incorporation of such provisions a condition of acceptance, or even to postpone action altogether until this should have been effected ; but that, as the great debate went on all over the land, it became so generally conceded that the necessary amendments would be proposed and ratified that the most backward were at last satisfied they might safely leave the matter to subsequent action. That trust was not misplaced. Among the acts of the first Congress was the submission of twelve amendments, of which ten were ratified by the requisite three-fourths of the States. Of the two which were rejected, the first established limits within which Congress might reapportion the membership of the House of Representatives. The second prohibited any change in the compensation of members of Congress until an election of Representatives should have intervened, a provision, which, if adopted, would have prevented the several " back-pay " scandals of our history. The amendments adopted provided, in effect,

(Article 1.) That Congress should make no law respecting an establishment of religion or prohibiting the free exercise thereof ; or abridging the freedom of speech or the press, or the right of the people peaceably to assemble and petition for the redress of grievances. The ten Amendments.

(Article 2.) That the right of the people to keep and bear arms should not be infringed.

(Article 3.) That no soldier should in time of peace be quartered in any house without the consent of the owner ; or in time of war, except in a manner prescribed by law.

(Article 4.) That the right of the people to be secure in their persons, houses, papers, and effects, against unwarrantable searches and seizures should not be violated ; and that no warrant should issue except for probable cause, supported by oath or affirmation, and particularly describing the places to be searched and the persons or things to be seized.

(Article 5.) That no person should be held to answer for a capital or otherwise infamous crime unless upon the presentment or indictment of a grand jury, except in cases arising in the land or naval forces or in the militia when in actual service in time of war or public danger ; nor should any person be subject to be twice put in jeopardy for the same offence, or be compelled in any criminal case to be witness against himself, or be deprived of life, liberty, or property without due process of law ; nor should private property be taken for public use without just compensation.

(Article 6.) That in all criminal prosecutions, the accused should enjoy the right of a speedy and public trial by an impartial jury of the State and district wherein the crime was committed, which district should have been previously ascertained by law ; to be informed of the nature and cause of the accusation ; to be confronted with the witnesses against him ; to have compulsory process for obtaining witnesses in his favor ; and to have the assistance of counsel.

(Article 7.) That in suits at common law where the value in controversy should exceed $20, the right of trial by jury should be preserved ; and that no fact tried by a jury should otherwise be examined in any court of the United States than according to the rules of common law.

(Article 8.) That excessive bail should not be required, or cruel or unusual punishments inflicted.

(Article 9.) That the enumeration in the Constitution of certain rights should not be construed to deny or disparage others retained by the people ; and finally,

(Article 10.) That the powers not delegated to the United States by the Constitution, or by it prohibited to the States, should be reserved to the States respectively or to the people.

A great deal of persistent popular misconception regarding our government and the liberties and immunities of the American people has been due to the fact that the foregoing amendments do not explicitly state that the things therein enjoined or prohibited are enjoined upon or prohibited to the United States only, and not also upon or to the several States.* Thus, where the amendment says the right of the people to bear arms shall not be infringed, most persons suppose that this binds the several States; whereas it is only a prohibition to the United States. Similar misconceptions have existed in the public mind regarding the effect of nearly every other provision of these amendments. Again, it is to be regretted that these ten amendments were treated as amendments, and were not declared to be a part of the original Constitution and incorporated into its body and substance. When a student of our history is told that there have been fifteen amendments, he necessarily forms a greatly exaggerated idea of the amount of change which has been wrought in that instrument. The first amendments having been, virtually, a condition of ratification, there have been but five real amendments, namely, those numbered from 11 to 15. A statement like this would give a much more just idea of the extent of the alterations which our organic law has undergone during a hundred years of actual trial. In fact, there was a period of more than sixty years during which not an amendment was adopted.

These Amendments bind only the general government.

---

* See Barron *vs.* Baltimore, 7 Peters, 243.

The reader will recall the statements made regarding the distress and dishonor into which the Confederation was plunged by its inability to meet the demands of foreign and domestic creditors. The Union inherited from its predecessor an enormous burden. The foreign debt, including arrears of interest, amounted to nearly twelve millions, due mostly in France and Holland, on account of loans which had been made to us during the Revolution from political friendship and sympathy. The domestic debt exceeded forty-two millions, of which nearly one-third represented unpaid interest. In such a condition it is small wonder that the value of government certificates had sunk to one-eighth of their face value. Moreover, there was outstanding, as estimated, seventy-eight to eighty millions of " continental currency," the history of which is significant of the whole philosophy of fiat-money. In March, 1778, a dollar of coin had been worth $1.75 in paper ; in September of the same year it was worth $4 ; in March, 1779, $10 ; in September of the same year, $18 ; in March, 1780, $40. At the last stage, Congress provided for funding the money at $40 to $1. About two hundred millions were so funded. The new certificates themselves, however, soon depreciated to about one-eighth of their face value. Such was the body of indebtedness, the legacy of the war of the Revolution, for which the new government was called to provide.

The funding of the debts of the Confederation and the assumption of State debts.

In regard to the necessity and propriety of discharging fully and promptly the foreign debt, no difference of opinion existed. This was well, though we cannot accept the reason for making a distinction between the foreign and domestic debt given by Mr. Jefferson. The claim that Congress was, in the case of the domestic debt, the representative of both

The foreign debt.

parties to the contract, and could therefore alter the terms of the transaction, provided only "substantial justice" was secured, is unfounded, immoral, and destructive of national credit. The slightest departure from the exact terms of a contract must be sanctioned, if at all, by the plea of absolute necessity overriding all law, an exigency which leaves no room for choice, the same exigency which would justify the taking of private property without compensation.

To the payment of the domestic debt at the par value of the certificates, vehement opposition was made, on the ground that these certificates had long The domestic been depreciated and had been so largely debt. transferred, at less than par, that the present holders were not entitled to be paid in full. It was said that the wrong done to the original subscribers or to intermediate holders was irremediable ; while to pay the debt at par was to throw the money away upon speculators who had bought the stock for a song. On the other hand, Hamilton argued in favor of paying the holders of the debt, in full, as follows : "Whatever necessity the seller may have been under, was occasioned by the Government not making a proper provision for its debts. The buyer had no agency in it, and therefore ought not to suffer. He is not even chargeable with having taken an unfair advantage. He paid what the commodity was worth in the market, and took the risks of reimbursement upon himself." The act, as finally passed by Congress, authorized the borrowing of not exceeding twelve millions for the payment of the foreign debt [this, unanimously], the money to be reimbursable within fifteen years. It also authorized a loan for the domestic debt : two-thirds of the principal to draw interest at six per cent. from January 1, 1791 ; the remaining one-third at the same rate, from 1800 ;

arrears of interest to be funded at full value, but to draw interest at only three per cent., from July 1, 1791, and to be redeemable at the pleasure of the Government. Subscriptions to the loan were to be payable in certificates of the national debt, or in continental paper-money at 100 to 1. Nonsubscribing creditors were to take their chances out of any surplus in the treasury. The action of Congress in paying the Revolutionary debt as nearly in full as was done has been strongly approved by posterity. After such a career of financial distress and dishonor as had prevailed between 1777 and 1789, there are always a plenty of good rascally reasons for "cutting away the broken mast of the public credit," to use the striking phrase of Sir James Graham ; but the considerations advanced by Hamilton will always be sufficient for the statesman and ought to satisfy every true lover of his country.

But the measures regarding the public debt were not yet complete. The proposition was made to assume the State debts occasioned by the war. To this the most passionate objections were made.

Assumption of the State debts.

It was argued : (1) That the amount of the State debts was unknown ; (2) that assumption would be unjust as between States, giving advantage to such as had most freely contracted debts during the war, in place of raising money by taxation, and doing a double wrong to those which had made the greatest exertions since the war to pay off their debts, which some had already done to nearly the extent of one-half, while others had done nothing ; (3) that it would be a usurpation of powers not conferred by the Constitution ; (4) that it would make necessary a resort to internal taxation. Assumption was finally carried in a qualified form, $21,-500,000 being apportioned among the several States, according to a schedule incorporated in the law, Massachusetts and South Carolina receiving $4,000,000 each ; Virginia, $3,500,000 ; and so on, down to $200,000, each, for Rhode Island and Delaware. Even this was not effected without a good deal of artifice and outside pressure. Jefferson afterward bitterly complained of having been cheated by Hamilton into favoring a measure which he misunderstood ; while it is admitted that the friends of assumption made a distinct bargain with the advocates of another measure, hereafter to be mentioned, by which a joint support was given to both bills. Hamilton had triumphed in his comprehensive scheme for funding the debts of the Revolution ; he had placed the credit of the new nation on a secure foundation ; and he had won to the support of Government the whole power of the capitalist and commercial classes. But he had aroused, almost to madness, the opponents of his financial measures ; and he had created throughout large sections of the country a deep distrust and dislike of federal authority. Let us now pass to consider the other financial measures of Washington's first term. These related to the mint ; the national bank ; tonnage duties ; custom duties ; excise duties.

By an early resolution of the First Congress, steps were taken toward the establishment of a national mint. Under an act of 1792, the mint was set up in Philadelphia, the distinguished mathe- The mint. matician and astronomer, David Rittenhouse, being appointed director. The coinage provided for was to be both of gold and of silver, at the legal ratio of 15 to 1, an under-valuation of gold according to the market ratio of the time. The gold coins were to be the eagle ($10), the half-eagle, and the quarter-eagle, the silver coins being the dollar, half-dollar, quarter-dollar, dime, and half-dime. It is worth noting that the bill, as first reported, provided that upon one side of the coins

6

should be an impression or representation of "the head of the President of the United States for the time being." This proposition aroused the sharpest objections, which rose into furious denunciation. Some who took part in the debate talked as though only this was necessary in order to establish an absolute despotism. An amendment was offered to make the image on the coin that of Washington only ; but this did not satisfy the objectors. After a severe contest, in which the houses of Congress came for a time to a "deadlock," both refusing to yield, the offensive provision was stricken out, and "an emblematical figure of Liberty" was substituted. To this conclusion we owe the image, emblematical or enigmatical, as one chooses to consider it, but in either view exceedingly ugly, so long presented on our national coins.

A bank had been incorporated by the Congress of the Confederation in 1781. It was a comparatively small affair ; and had, at the time of which we are writing, gone under a charter from the State of Pennsylvania. There is a very common assumption that it contributed largely to independence. That theory has been combated by Mr. William M. Gouge, who argues that the bank did not go into operation until after the capitulation of Cornwallis ; and that the net advances made by it to the government were of the most petty character. However this may be, it is certain that the popular opinion as to the services of the bank during the Revolution did much toward establishing a bank in 1791.

The National Bank.

The project was opposed by Mr. Madison for financial reasons, and also on the ground of unconstitutionality, a power to grant charters of incorporation having been proposed and defeated in the Convention of 1787. Mr. Hamilton was the main champion of the measure, pressing it with the full force of his personal influence and his official position. His Report on the Bank is one of his masterpieces. The bill passed the House of Representatives, 39 to 20. The division was highly sectional. All, except one, who voted in the negative were from the Southern States. All who were present from the Northern States, except one from Massachusetts, voted in the affirmative. Before signing the bill Washington took the advice of his cabinet on the question of constitutionality. Jefferson, Secretary of State, and Randolph, Attorney-General, both from Virginia, were adverse. General Knox, Secretary of War, supported Hamilton in his view that the right of Congress to charter a bank was carried by the "implied powers" of the Constitution. This doctrine of implied powers was to become a mighty *The doctrine of implied powers.* weapon in the hands of those who desired to magnify the general government and to make the United States more and more a nation. As that was the first occasion on which the doctrine had come strongly into view in an important issue, Washington hesitated, but finally accepted it and afterward stood strongly by it.

The capital stock of the bank was to be $10,000,000, one-fifth to be owned by the United States: four-fifths to be subscribed by individuals. Of the subscriptions three-fourths were to be paid in *Organization of the bank.* gold and silver. The corporation was not to own property exceeding $15,000,000 or to owe (exclusive of deposits) exceeding $10,000,000. It might sell any part of the public debt composing its capital; but not purchase any public debt, or trade in anything but bills of exchange and gold and silver bullion, or take any rate of interest higher than six per cent. It was to be a bank of deposit and discount. Its notes were to be payable in specie and receivable in all payments to the United

States. No loan was to be made to the United States exceeding $100,000 ; or to any State, exceeding $50,000 ; or to any foreign prince or state, in any amount. The bank was to be located in Philadelphia, with power to establish in other places offices of discount and deposit, only. Eight branches were, in fact, established. The charter was to be in force twenty years, that is, from 1791 to 1811. No other bank was to be established by Congress in that time.

By an act framed at the first session of Congress, discriminating duties were laid on tonnage : six cents per Tonnage du- ton on American and fifty cents per ton on ties.   foreign ships. Duties on goods imported in American bottoms were to be one-tenth less than on goods imported in foreign bottoms. Mr. Madison argued strongly in favor of discrimination, as building up an American navy. The objection came mainly from the extreme Southern States, on the ground which was indicated in the discussion of the two-thirds vote question in the Constitutional Convention, viz., that Georgia and the two Carolinas, while they furnished a vast amount of freight for export, built and owned few ships, and would thus have to pay the higher rates of freight without a proportional benefit. But the opposition was not violent, the acts of England adverse to American trade having made the idea of building up an American marine highly popular.

Congress had not been organized seventy hours when the question of taxing foreign imports for revenue was introduced ; and the question of indirectly favoring American manufactures came under discussion. Mr. Madison brought forward the tariff bill in the House of Representatives. He professed himself what would be called a free-trader, although the preamble of the bill contained the phrase, "for the encouragement and protection of manufactures." Mr. Hartley of Pennsylvania, was the principal advocate of "protection." The bill contained certain specific and certain ad valorem duties ; and imposed a uniform tax of five per cent. on all other articles imported. The purpose of affording encouragement to domestic manufactures is nowhere conspicuous, revenue being chiefly considered. The social question, *i.e.*, the American rate of wages and the American standard of living, had not yet come out in the discussion of protection. So far as the encouragement of domestic manufactures was then sought, it was for the purpose of making the United States independent of foreign nations in the supply of necessary articles.

Customs, duties: protection.

The imposition of customs duties had incurred no passionate objections from any quarter. It had been distinctly understood and agreed that the government would raise its revenue largely from foreign goods imported. But the imposition of excise duties, that is, duties levied upon articles grown or produced within the country, or duties, like stamps and licenses, upon the occupations and business of the people : these were an altogether different thing. It is true, the word "excises" was contained in the grant of powers to Congress ; but this did not prevent a large party, especially at the South, from strenuously maintaining that the power should be exercised very rarely and only in extreme necessity. This party held that the States should be allowed to obtain their revenue from excises, according to the needs and feelings of their own peoples. Moreover, it is historically true that excise taxes arouse far more popular discontent than do customs or tariff duties. What is paid by great merchants at the ports of entry is, speaking generally, added to the price of the goods without being seen or

Excise duties.

scarcely felt by the consumer ; but when a government undertakes to raise a revenue by internal or excise taxes it is obliged to interfere with private business in a very annoying way, to exercise espionage and supervision, and to collect its money often at the most inconvenient times and by the most irritating methods.

Mr. Jefferson was the leader of those throughout the United States who objected most strongly to the use of this power in any degree by Congress. It was his idea that the American farmer, the American mechanic, the American laborer, should never see a tax-gatherer of the United States. But Mr. Hamilton's extensive scheme for funding the national and State debts had made a large revenue necessary ; and consequently Congress, by The whiskey act of March 3, 1791, imposed heavy duties tax. upon spirits distilled in the United States. The selection of that article as the subject of taxation was justified by many reasons ; but the conditions of the manufacture at the time were such as to render this tax peculiarly galling and odious. At present a comparatively few vast distilleries produce nearly all the spirits made in the country. In such a case the payment of even high duties is a matter of little consequence ; the distillers are men of large capital, and immediately add the tax to the price of their product. At the time of which we are writing, however, there was an immense number of petty distilleries spread all over the country. It was estimated that there were three thousand in Pennsylvania alone ; and small stills abounded equally in Virginia and the Carolinas. To the proprietors of these, the payment of a tax, in advance of marketing their product, or personally consuming it, as was quite commonly the case, constituted a great hardship, and aroused the most bitter feelings of indignation. Moreover, there was another feature of the situation which has not been sufficiently dwelt upon. The enterprise characteristic of the American people had carried tens and hundreds of thousands far away from the Atlantic coast, and even from navigable waters, to build up homes for themselves and their children. With the rude and inadequate facilities for transportation existing, the grain which these pioneers raised upon the soil would not "bear transportation" to market. If, however, the grain could be reduced, both in bulk and weight, to the form of spirits, the cost of transportation would be greatly diminished and the price of the product greatly enhanced. Yet, since the Constitution prescribed that all taxes, duties, imposts, and excises should be uniform throughout the United States, it was necessary to tax the whiskey of Western Pennsylvania or of Kentucky at the same rate as that imposed upon spirits distilled along tide-water or upon the banks of navigable streams. We shall, a little later, see how the whiskey tax of 1791 not only aroused great opposition throughout the country, but led to armed resistance, and even open rebellion.

CHAPTER VI

WASHINGTON'S FIRST TERM—CONTINUED

Formation of Executive Departments—Development of the Cabinet—The Constitution Silent on this Subject—Congress Establishes the Departments of State, of Treasury, and of War—Also Provides for the Appointment of an Attorney-General—Practice of the Early Presidents Regarding the Function of the Cabinet—Should Cabinet Officers Sit in Congress, or Occasionally Meet with Congress, or Communicate with that Body Only in Writing?—The Last Procedure Adopted—Washington's Cabinet: Jefferson, Hamilton, Knox, Randolph—Parties Under the Constitution not yet Formed—Antagonism Developed between Jefferson and Hamilton—State's Rights *vs.* National Aggrandizement—Washington Consents to Re-election—Opposition of Antifederalists to Mr. Adams—Organization of the Supreme Court—Washington's Appointments strongly Federalist—John Jay, Chief Justice—The Foreign Relations of Washington's First Term—Weakness of the United States Abroad—Washington's Policy of Neutrality, especially as between France and England—Rising Passion of Antifederalist Sympathizers with French Revolutionists—Colonialism in American Public Life—War with the Miamis—The Indian Policy of the United States—The Permanent Seat of Government—The District of Columbia and the City of Washington—The First Census and the Redistribution of Representation in Congress—The Fugitive-Slave Law—Admission of New States—Influence of the States beyond the Alleghanies upon the Growth of American Nationality—Difficulties Arising at the West from the Spanish Control of the Mississippi—Unanimous Re-election of Washington—Adams Re-elected by a Smaller Vote.

WE continue the narrative of the first term of Washington's administration. Let us now consider the formation of executive departments, and the relation of the cabinet to the President and to Congress. It is a curious, though excellent, feature of the Constitution that it prescribes nothing regarding executive departments. In the Convention it was proposed to form a Council of State, to be composed of certain high officers, to assist, and in a measure control, the President in the discharge of his duties. This project having failed, it would have been natural that the Convention should provide at least for a cabinet to surround and support the President in his office, to be composed of the principal officers of state. Even this it failed to do, only inserting a provision which gives the President power to " require the opinion, in writing, of the principal officer in each of the executive departments, upon any subject relating to the duties of their respective offices." It will be seen from this that, not only did the Convention not constitute a cabinet, but that all the intimation there is regarding the subject in the Constitution goes rather the other way, the President being contemplated as consulting the heads of departments separately regarding the duties of their several offices, and not as assembling them together for consultation concerning matters of general interest to the administration.

When Congress met under the Constitution, it at once proceeded to form three executive departments, viz., State (at first called Foreign Affairs), Treas- *Executive departments.* ury, and War. The head of each department was to bear the title, Secretary. Provision was also made for the appointment of an Attorney-General ; but this officer was not the head of an executive department; nor did he become so until 1870, when the Department of Justice was established.

In creating these high offices a most important question arose, viz., whether heads of departments could be removed by the President alone, or the concurrence of

the Senate should be necessary, as in their appointment.
Mr. Hamilton, in the *Federalist*, had taken it for granted

*Power of re-
moval.*

that such concurrence would be essential to
removal in the case of all officers, and had argued that this would contribute to the stability of administration ; but when Congress came to deal with the
matter, the question above stated came under active discussion.   Mr. Madison, Hamilton's colleague in the
Federalist, strongly argued that the President should
have the sole power of removal.   The opposite side was
taken by Messrs. Sherman and Gerry.   Congress decided
in favor of conferring on the President the power of removal.   This result was of beneficial and far-reaching
consequences.   Had the decision been the other way,
heads of executive departments would have been able,
by cultivating personal and political relations with the
Senate, to intrench themselves against the President and
to defy his power.   Only mischief could have ensued.

Executive departments having been constituted, it
became a question for the President whether he should

*The cabinet
under Wash-
ington and
Adams.*

for his own purposes bring the heads of these
departments together into a cabinet ; or
should deal with them separately, as the
Constitution seemed to contemplate.   We may anticipate results so far as to say that the practice varied during the first few administrations.   President Washington
was in the habit of taking the opinions of his secretaries
in separate consultations or by letter ; while upon occasions of greater importance he assembled them for oral
discussion in the form of a council.   Having heard the
opinion of each, he decided upon the course to be pur-
sued.   The second President, Adams, followed substantially the same practice, though we shall see that the members of his cabinet were disposed to put forward something
like a claim to an integral share in the executive office.

"The third President, Jefferson," says Mr. George Ticknor Curtis, "adopted a somewhat different practice. When a question occurred of sufficient magnitude to require the opinions of all the heads of departments, he called them together, *Mr. Jefferson and his Cabinet.* had the subject discussed and a vote taken, in which he counted himself as but one. But he always seemed to have considered that he had the power to decide against the opinion of his cabinet. That he never or rarely exercised it was owing partly to the unanimity of sentiment that prevailed in his cabinet and to his desire to preserve that unanimity, and partly to his disinclination to the exercise of personal power. When there were differences of opinion, he aimed to produce a unanimous result by discussion, and almost always succeeded. But he admits that this practice made the executive, in fact, a directory." Later in our constitutional history the cabinet was more fully recognized in practice, though still not known to the Constitution ; its meetings were more regular and frequent ; and its function of at once advising the President, checking his impulses, and bringing to the administration the support of the different sections of the country, became of more and more importance in the real, as distinguished from the written, government of the United States.

So much for the relations of heads of departments to the President. It was quite another question whether these officers should sit in Congress and present their measures, or occasionally meet *Relation of the cabinet to Congress.* Congress for that purpose, or communicate only with Congress as a whole by writing, leaving their personal communications to be made to individual Congressmen or to committees, as is at present done. A great deal has of late been written in advocacy of a cabinet government for the United States, like that which

has been so successfully carried on in England. This
would involve a change in the Constitution, by which
the President should be obliged to select his heads of departments from among actual members of Congress, in
one or the other house. Taking it for granted that
such a change in the Constitution would be impracti-
cable, it has thereupon been urged that the heads of executive departments should still be authorized by law to
sit in Congress, having a voice but no vote, so that they
might present, explain, and defend their proposed
measures in person. The matter is perhaps worth
further discussion ; but it appears extremely doubtful
whether cabinet officers occupying seats by sufferance,
having no vote as members, would attain to anything
like the authority and influence which the advocates of
this scheme expect. It would even be something to be
dreaded, lest, with the rude parliamentary manners of
our country, these officers might be so treated in speech
and debate as to impair their dignity and influence.
Assuming, then, that under existing constitutional
provisions, it is not desirable that heads of executive departments should regularly sit in Congress, the question
arises why they should not meet that body upon important occasions, for the presentation of reports or the
advocacy of measures. No constitutional objection is
known to exist ; and it would appear that we came very
near having this established as a recognized form of
procedure. Mr. Hamilton, early in the first administration, expressed his desire to present to the House of
Representatives certain financial measures. Had this
been done, it would probably have passed into precedent
and been extensively followed. But the opponents of
Mr. Hamilton, jealous of his rising fame, or fearful of
his eloquence and personal influence, secured a decision
adverse to his wishes in this specific instance ; and that

decision, though purely individual and personal, became a precedent * unrevoked to this day, so that, ever since, the heads of our executive departments have communicated with Congress only in writing or by personal conference with committees.

We have already named the distinguished citizens who were appointed to the highest offices at the beginning of Washington's administration, and who became his cabinet, in the modern American sense of that term. It is now appropriate to speak of the cabinet as a whole ; and of the relations of its members to each other, to the President, and to the issues which were beginning to emerge from the surface of American political life. It is customary to say that Washington's choice of his cabinet officers was nonpartisan. This is strictly true ; but those who say it sometimes explain their meaning by adding that he took men of both political parties. This is not true. The only political division, as yet, had been as to the adoption or rejection of the Constitution ; and we have seen how large and formidable was the minority on this question. When Washington came to make up his cabinet, he selected the members wholly from those who had supported the Constitution. So that, in one sense, that body was purely partisan. It is true that the four men chosen for his chief advisers constituted two groups, Jefferson and Randolph, Hamilton and Knox, having

*It appears that President Washington, accompanied by General Knox, Secretary of War, went once into the Senate, in the days of the first Congress, and suggested that General Knox should explain to the Senate the provisions of a pending Indian treaty. The Senate would seem to have put the matter off, at the time, for the purpose of getting rid of the President and the Secretary. Inasmuch, however, as the question at issue was the ratification of a treaty, by the Senate alone, and that in executive session, we have chosen not to consider this as an instance of a cabinet officer offering himself to assist in the legislation of Congress.

widely different and strongly antagonistic views as to what should be done under the Constitution ; as to the degree in which the powers of the new government should be called into action for the general good ; as to the relations of the new organization to the States and to the people. But parties did not then exist throughout the country ; the issues upon which citizens were to range themselves, on the one side and the other, had not been defined, had not even arisen.

No prescient mind, however, could fail to discern the signs of an early and a deep division of the people on questions of vital interest. It was evident that Jefferson would soon be at the head of those who favored a strict construction of the Constitution, a close limitation of the powers of the general government, and the reduction of federal agency to a minimum ; while Hamilton would become the recognized leader of those who wished to make the nation powerful and imposing. At first the relations of the several members of the cabinet were friendly and harmonious. All rejoiced in the establishment of a union of the States ; all respected the great leader who had carried the country triumphantly through its war of Independence, who had become the head of the new nation in peace, and who was now their official chief. Hamilton had even been able, as recited, upon Mr. Jefferson's somewhat late arrival from his post of duty as Minister at Paris, to draw that astute politician into the support of the measure for funding the State debts. But, as Hamilton's financial measures developed his purpose to build up commerce and manufactures, to make the national debt a means of both financial and political power to the government, and in other respects to magnify the Nation in comparison with the State, Jefferson, who was not only a strong States Rights man,

The coming parties.

but was also a protectionist of a peculiar type, disliking commerce, and favoring manufactures only as developed in small groups around the plantation and the farm, became first alienated and then angry. With Hamilton's successive triumphs he became furious. There was another very marked difference between these two great leaders. Hamilton was essentially an aristocrat, distrusting the impulses of the masses of the people, believing in the absolute necessity of a leadership by men of wealth and education, and regarding it as good government to build up powerful interests within the commonwealth which should support law and to a great extent influence political action. He had even, in the Constitutional Convention, frankly professed his preference for monarchical institutions ; and he still believed it to be desirable to break - up and make - over the existing States. Jefferson was a democrat of democrats ; with all his mind and soul he believed in the honesty, intelligence, and patriotism of the common people ; he disliked vested interests, estates, or powers within the commonwealth ; he favored primitive and simple habits of life, and primitive and simple forms of government ; he held strongly to the perpetual integrity of the existing States.

Between two men with such conflicting views, each of the highest intellectual power, not even the presence of Washington could long keep peace ; while the commanding influence of each leader soon rallied a great following from out a people exhibiting the widest diversities of political and social conditions, thoughts, and feelings. The party of Hamilton became known as " Federalists," a term previously applied to those who sup- The Federalists. ported the Constitution, as against those who opposed ratification. To this party belonged Mr. Adams, the Vice-President, who was, indeed, in many respects, more truly its leader than Mr. Hamilton himself, possessing a degree of confidence, on the part of vast numbers of that general way of thinking, which was withheld from the more showy and brilliant champion of federal ascendency. In his general views and political predilections President Washington inclined strongly toward the Federalists ; though in his high office he held the scales with so much of dignity and impartiality that Jefferson was able afterward to deny that Washington was, in any true sense, a Federalist.

Within his own party, which at first was known only by the name of Antifederalists, Mr. Jefferson enjoyed such pre-eminence that he was and remained to the end without a rival, and swayed his vast and growing constituency almost at his will. But while Mr. Jefferson found no one who could dispute his claim to leadership, he possessed a remarkably good second in Mr. Madison, then a member of the House of Representatives from Virginia. Madison was a man much calmer than his great chief, much more sensible and practical in matters of detail, a strong and judicious speaker and writer. No general ever had a more useful lieutenant. The division of the people was still, as in the Convention, largely sectional. While Adams and Hamilton had not a united North behind them, the South from the first took position overwhelmingly * in support of Jefferson. The warmth of feeling and of expression characteristic of the latter section tended to widen the breach. "I am unable," wrote Mr. Wolcott, "to form any opinion as to the real condition of the Southern States. Were the representatives of the northern country to express the same sentiments and oppose the projects of the government with the same vehe-

Jefferson and the Antifederalists.

* The most marked exception being in South Carolina, where a strong Federalist district surrounded the commercial city of Charleston.

mence, I should imagine the people were on the eve of a rebellion." The antagonism thus developed culminated at the close of Washington's first term. For a while it was uncertain whether he would consent to serve again ; indeed, he had expressed his purpose not to do so ; and the prospect of a succession brought sharply and strongly out the relations of party. When Washington consented to re-election, the opposition to what was considered the dominating influence of the administration turned itself to advocating the choice of another Vice-President in place of Mr. Adams. The Antifederalists now began to call themselves " Republicans."

The Constitution had provided for a Judiciary ; but the effect of that provision had been but faintly apprehended, even by the most sagacious of those who took part in framing it. The third article was, in truth, the "sleeping lion" of the Constitution, not because its phraseology was obscure, but because no one had been able to lift himself high enough to see the full scope of that terrific power which should decide alike laws of Congress and the acts of State Legislatures to be contrary to the Constitution ; which should sit in judgment alike on measures and on men, from highest to lowest ; which should become the " supreme arbiter " between State and Nation ; which should, in the result, determine, in spite of nullification, secession, and rebellion, what kind of a government ours was to be. Whatever Jefferson may say about Washington not being a Federalist, the appointment of Justices of the Supreme Court affords a test which will satisfy most minds on which side the President stood. His choice for Chief-Justice was John Jay, of New York. Judge Jay was one of those rare men who, with clear views and strong convictions, are yet capable of being absolutely fair, just, and right-minded. Though

Organization of the Supreme Court.

7

not a very great judge, from the juridical point of view, his lofty character, his fervent patriotism, the nobility of his aims, the simplicity of his mind, with a fair store of learning, made him a better Chief-Justice than a much greater lawyer might have been. The Associate Justices were John Rutledge, of South Carolina; William Cushing, of Massachusetts; Robert H. Harrison, of Maryland; James Wilson, of Pennsylvania; John Blair, of Virginia. During his first term, Harrison and Rutledge resigning, the President appointed in their places James Iredell, of North Carolina; and Thomas Johnson, of Maryland.

It has been stated, in connection with the establishment of the Mint, that the proposition to place the head of the President, for the time being, upon the national coins, gave rise to an embittered contest, in which that proposition was finally defeated. Other matters relating to the degree of state to be assumed by the chief executive or affecting his relations to Congress and to the people, called forth an almost incredible amount of feeling during the administration of Washington; and this, we may believe, had not a little to do, Official eti-quette and the not, indeed, with the formation of parties manners of the executive under the constitution, but with the party mansion. affiliations of large numbers of citizens. Many leading Federalists were disposed to hold that the President should assume a great deal of state in the administration of his office; they desired that he should have high-sounding titles,* like those given to potentates of the old world; that his intercourse with the public

* The Senate Committee reported in favor of addressing the President as "His Highness the President of the United States and the Protector of their Liberties." The House of Representatives, however, contented itself with addressing him solely as the President of the United States, and this mode of address fortunately passed into precedent.

should be marked by a distinct reserve ; and that the executive mansion should take on somewhat the aspect and air of a court. This, in general, was not distasteful to Washington, who was of a highly aristocratic turn of thought and feeling ; who shrank instinctively from indiscriminate contact and approach ; who wore a sword at his inauguration and upon important occasions ; who did not object to having his birth-day celebrated like the King of England's ; and in all respects bore himself as a great man among men. The Antifederalists, or Republicans, were strongly opposed to this sort of thing, both from their ordinary way of thinking and, particularly, from the influence of the extreme democratic, or "levelling," ideas then prevalent in France, from which country Mr. Jefferson had recently returned thoroughly imbued with a distaste for all titles, even for one so harmless as Esquire, and with a passion for that plainness of dress and that freedom of intercourse which subsequently gave rise to the expression "Jeffersonian Simplicity." The political literature of the time abounds in slurs and sneers regarding the manners of the executive mansion ; and there is reason to believe that the popular dislike of the little, harmless, pomp and pageantry there displayed had much to do with re-enforcing the ranks of opposition to the dominant influences of the administration.

Let us now proceed to contemplate the foreign relations of Washington's first term. The inauguration of the government found these in a most unsatisfactory condition. The United States had not acquired by war so much reputation among the nations of Europe as we are apt to imagine. The alliance with France had, indeed, been subsequent to the surrender of Burgoyne at Saratoga ; but the long interval of despondency which followed, and the achievement of the victory at Yorktown so conspicuously through the aid of the French army and the French fleet, had not unnaturally tended to produce abroad the belief that the colonists owed their independence more to the prowess of their ally than to their own strength. Nor was French deli-cacy likely to disparage the services of Rochambeau and de Grasse. Regular troops serving with militia and volunteeers, even of their own nationality, never do justice to them ; much less are they likely to do so when of another race and another speech. If such had been the division of honors be-tween the allies in the closing scenes of the struggle which we denominate the War of the Revolution, the conduct of our foreign affairs under the Confederation, from 1781–89, had not been of a character to exalt our national credit. Enough has been said of the weakness of that government in its foreign aspects. That weak-ness had made more bitter the enmity of England ; had come nigh to alienating fast friends, like France and Holland ; and had inspired contempt for the young re-public among the neutral and indifferent nations of Europe. Toward England we were delinquent in fail-ing to comply with provisions of the treaty of peace which provided for the payment of debts due to British merchants by American citizens, and which looked to the restitution of the estates of royalists confiscated under State laws. Toward France and Holland we were delinquent in respect to moneys borrowed in our neces-sity. With Spain we had a standing quarrel regarding the boundary of Florida and the navigation of the Mis-sissippi. Toward other powers our attitude was merely that of a weak confederation, without means of enforc-ing its decrees upon the constituent members, even in a matter so purely federal as a treaty of commerce.

Such were the difficulties under which the new nation,

Weakness in foreign relations.

with its new Constitution, entered upon its career as one of the powers of the world. But those difficulties were only such as the United States might reasonably hope to overcome by steady adherence to the policy of avoiding entangling alliances, of cultivating carefully its financial credit, and of devoting its energies in peace to the development of its marvellous natural advantages and resources. In his view of the needs of his country at this time, Washington was wisest among the wise, and patriotic above all. In 1795 he wrote to Morris, " My policy has been and will continue to be, while I have the honor to remain in the administration, to maintain friendly terms with, but to be independent of, all the nations of the earth; to share in the broils of none; to fulfil our own engagements; to supply the wants and be the carriers for them all; being thoroughly convinced that it is our policy and interest to do so. Nothing short of self-respect and that justice which is essential to a national character ought to involve us in war; for, sure I am, if this country is preserved in tranquillity twenty years longer, it may bid defiance in a just cause to any power whatever; such in that time would be its population, wealth, and resources."

Washington's policy of neutrality.

We shall see how the progress of the revolutionary movement in France and the tremendous wars which arose out of that event, in spite of the warnings and the influence of Washington drew the young republic of the western world into their own mad turmoil, and, if they did not engulf the untried bark with its untried crew, at least kept the politics of the United States in agitation for twenty years, diverting the attention of the nation from its own true interests. But in the first term of Washington's administration, of which we now speak, these things had not taken place; nor were they yet evident, in anything like their full extent, even to the most prophetic eye. We need here only note that the government during the first four years of its existence steadily improved its position abroad.

But while the revolution in France had not yet disturbed the foreign relations of the United States, it had gone far to intensify the bitterness of parties here, and to draw deep lines across the face of the republic. The new Constitution of France had been adopted after the inauguration of our own government ; but before the close of 1792 revolutionary frenzy had proceeded to the point of abolishing monarchy, soon followed by the murder of the king. The intensity of interest with which these events were watched in the United States French sym- can scarcely be understood in this generation. pathizers. Two explanations are necessary before we can see how it was that the Republicans, so called, of that day could give themselves to the French cause with such passionate eagerness. The first is that the world had not yet learned by sad experience that revolution makes no people free. The painful and humiliating spectacle of nations building up liberal constitutions and professing the noblest political sentiments, only to fall into anarchy on the one hand, or into tyranny on the other, had not then been repeated so often as to teach mankind that popular government is a thing of slow growth, and that those institutions only can be durable which have their roots deeply in the past and have grown into close and intimate adaptation to the needs, feelings, habits, and aspirations of their people. It was an age of political optimism, when it was believed that nations might spring with a bound into liberty ; and that the execution of a king or the massacre of a privileged class would open the way to peace and order.

The second explanation of the state of feeling which

existed at the time of which we are writing is found in
the wretched colonialism which tainted our social life,
degraded our politics, and prevented the formation of a
national literature during the first fifty years of our
separate existence. Colonialism is the disposition of a
country, be it great or small, to look abroad for its
standards of action, thought, or manners ; not to be
satisfied with the approbation of its own taste, judgment,
and conscience ; to be forever craving recognition, no
matter how patronizingly given. Colonialism, which,
in other words, is simply want of self-respect in a
community, was the curse of our earlier politics, as it
was of our earlier society. The States which had become independent in government were still unduly dependent in thought and feeling upon the old world,
from which they had cut themselves off by the Declaration of July 4th. In spite of the prophetic warnings of
Washington, the whole nation acted as though America
was of necessity to be a tender to one of the American
two great powers which disputed the suprem- colonialism.
acy of Europe. Few and faint are the traces of anything like a true respect for the position and future of the
United States which we find in the political literature of
the times ; while the conduct of both parties was equally
far from making good that high-sounding declaration,
" We hold them, as we hold the rest of mankind, enemies in war, in peace friends."

Certain other events and measures remain to be considered before we can take leave of Washington's first
term. Foremost among these is the war with the
Indians northwest of the river Ohio. The policy of
the whites, from the first settlement of the country to
the inauguration of the Constitution, had generally
been to postpone contests with the Indian tribes ; to
evade the inevitable issue ; and, by playing off one

chieftain against another, one tribe against another, to reduce the strength of the savages without engaging in a distinct struggle for supremacy. The War of the Revolution had incidentally destroyed the prestige and almost the existence of some of the most formidable tribes ; and the concentration of the fighting power of the nation in a single hand, together with the ownership by the general government of the western lands formerly held by the several States, had tended to produce a greater readiness to meet the issue frankly and at once. Accordingly, we find much less of a disposition to resort to indirection in accomplishing the settlement of the country contiguous to the range of hostile tribes. The occasions for conflict were not far to seek. Kentucky and Tennessee were already partially occupied ; and population was pushing across the Alleghanies into the fertile lands of the Ohio and the Wabash. The beginnings of the future State of Ohio had already been made at Marietta. Murders by the savages were continually reported to influence the public mind ; and early in 1790 a powerful expedition under General Harmer was despatched to subdue the Miamis and to chastise their confederates. This expedition met a severe repulse at the junction of the Great Wabash and the Wabash of the Lakes. Early in the next year Colonel Scott, with a mounted force, pushed into the Indian country, and by rapid movements achieved some partial successes ; but in the fall of that year General Arthur St. Clair, with a powerful army, was routed with terrible slaughter by this determined confederacy. His defeat led to the appointment of General Anthony Wayne, the hero of Stony Point, who had ten years before distinguished himself in battle against the Creeks of the South. General Wayne was destined to become the pacificator of this vast region ;

War with the Miamis.

but his preparations carried the war over into the second term of Washington, the final defeat of the Indians taking place in 1794, and the treaty by which they ceded their lands bearing date 1795.

It may be asked, Why should, how could, the United States make "a treaty" with some of its own inhabitants ? The answer to this question will serve to indicate the highly peculiar position which, from the beginning of the government down to 1871, was held by the Indian tribes within our domain. This position was that of "domestic dependent nations," in the phrase of Chief-Justice Marshall. Their exclusive right to occupy the land they had inherited from their ancestors, until such time as they should voluntarily cede it to the United States, was fully recognized in the policy of the government, in annual acts of Congress, and in numerous treaties ratified by the Senate. Of course they could not cede their land to any foreign government. Residing thus upon their territory, the Indian tribes which were not within the limits of any State were, as a rule, left to govern themselves as to all internal affairs, according to their own laws and traditions, or as their own interests and passions might dictate. The right of the United States to intervene, at any time, in the punishment of crime was fully asserted ; but, as a matter of policy, the United States forebore to assume the responsibility for the administration of justice between Indian and Indian in the same tribe. The "Agent" appointed to any tribe was at once a sort of pension-agent, to disburse the annuities provided for by treaty or the supplies voted by Congress out of charity, and a sort of minister-resident at the court or in the camp of a domestic, dependent nation, which, so long as it kept the peace, Congress chose to indulge, or perhaps felt it

right to entrust, with self-government.   To this policy
there had been a certain reservation to the effect that a
tribe might " become so·degraded or reduced in numbers " (Justice McLean, 6 Peters, 593, 594) as to fall
out of its high estate and become fully subject to the
ordinary control of the law.

In pursuance of this policy the United States made,
as I count them, three hundred and eighty-two treaties
Indian trea- with Indian tribes, down to the time when,
ties.   in 1871, Congress declared that, " Hereafter
no Indian nation or tribe within the territory of the
United States shall be acknowledged or recognized as an
independent nation, tribe, or power with whom the
United States may contract by treaty."   These would
have seemed bold words, the very tallest of " tall talk,"
to Anthony Wayne.   Times had, indeed, changed ; and
men's minds had naturally changed with them.   But,
in the period with which we are here dealing, it was
not deemed derogatory to the national honor and dignity to make treaties with the Indian tribes ; and the
government was, in general, only anxious about getting
the better of the bargain.

Recurring to the Miamis, it is curious to observe that
the Federalists and the Antifederalists, while agreed as
to the necessity of war, found opportunity for antago-
nizing each other, in preparing for the conflict, as to
the use of militia or of "regulars."   The first suggestion
of enlarging the army for this purpose brought up again
to Mr. Jefferson's eager mind " the corrupt squadrons
in Congress " which had filled his vision during the
progress of Mr. Hamilton's funding measures.   " The
least rag of Indian depredation," he writes, " will be an
excuse to raise troops, for those who love to have troops
and for those who think the public debt is a good
thing."   The same question arose in connection with

all the early Indian troubles ; and Mr. Jefferson's party invariably opposed the organization of regular troops for the purpose, and demanded the use of local militia. While government was thus en-gaged in desperate contest with Indians in the North-west, the people of Georgia became embroiled with the Creeks, who still held a large part of the territory now embraced in that State ; but the earnest efforts of Washington to prevent an outbreak here were for the time successful.

Regulars vs. militia.

Congress first met under the Constitution at New York. The struggle as to the permanent location of the seat of government was marked by an inten-sity of feeling which found expression in a bitter sectional strife. The southern mem-bers proposed the banks of the Potomac ; and this sug-gestion was very grateful to Washington, whose own home was Mount Vernon. The northern members de-sired to have the capital in their section. It seems to have been generally agreed that the capital must be on some river, because Rome was on the Tiber ; and nearly half the rivers of the country were, first or last, brought into the debate. The question, finally, was made a part of a parliamentary bargain. The advocates of the as-sumption of State debts adroitly got the two issues joined together, and, finally, by that most dangerous form of political corruption known as "log-rolling," * both measures were carried together. The result was that Congress was to meet for ten years at Philadelphia, and afterward have its home on the Potomac. Maryland and Virginia made cession of a district, ten miles square, on both sides of the Potomac, to become the seat of govern-ment. The Virginia portion was subsequently retro-

The perma-nent seat of government.

---

* " You help roll my log, and I will help roll yours."

ceded, as not needed for the purpose. The Maryland cession is known as the District of Columbia.

In providing for the election of the First Congress, the Constitution apportioned the total number of Representatives—sixty-five—among the States, according to certain rude estimates of numbers.
The first census having been taken in 1790, the number was fixed at one hundred and five ; and these were reapportioned among the States according to their ascertained population, three-fifths of the slaves being included in the schedule, according to one of the compromises of the Constitution. The population of the country had been ascertained to be 3,929,214. The four largest States were, in order, Virginia, Massachusetts, Pennsylvania, New York. The three smallest, Georgia, Rhode Island, Delaware.

Redistribution of representation.

Under the provision of the Constitution that "no person held to service or labor in one State, under the laws thereof, escaping into another shall, in consequence of any law or regulation therein, be discharged from such service or labor, but shall be delivered up on claim of the party to whom such service or labor may be due," Congress, on the 5th of February, 1793, passed the first Fugitive Slave Law. The measure at the time aroused little opposition, and indeed attracted slight attention, though it will appear in a later volume of this series that the Fugitive Slave Act of 1850 set the nation on fire. The change was mainly in the times. While the later law contained some features which were very objectionable from a purely legal point of view, it is questionable whether that of 1793 was not worse. Under it gangs of slave-hunters perpetrated a great amount of most brutal kidnapping of colored persons on whom no master had even a shadow of a claim.

The first Fugitive Slave Law.

Two States were admitted to the Union during Washington's first term : Vermont, March, 1791, with a population, by the census of 1790, of 85,425 ; Admission of new States. Kentucky, June, 1792, with 73,677 inhabitants, of whom 11,430 were slaves. Vermont was formed from territory long disputed, under royal grants, between New York and New Hampshire, but undoubtedly belonging to New York. Kentucky was formed from territory belonging to Virginia.

The admission of Vermont introduced no new element into the Union. The admission of Kentucky marks the first operation of a force which was to exert a tremendous and always increasing influence upon the destinies of the republic, and even upon the nature of the government itself. It does not seem too much to say that but for the growth of great communities upon the western territory, and their admission, one after another, as new States, the least probable result of the formation of the Union in 1789 is that it would have continued to our time. Massachusetts, New York, Virginia, South Carolina, had existed as separate communities before confederation had been practically accomplished. Each had its laws and social institutions, its consciousness of statehood, its definite character, its history. When these communities entered into the Union, it was, even for those most strongly federalist in feeling, inevitably with large reservations of pride, interest, and affection ; with some grudging as to every grant of power to the new government ; with much of hesitation, jealousy, and suspicion regarding the motives and actions of its allies. How different the case in respect to the States which, during the next twenty or fifty years, were to be introduced into the giant league from the territory beyond the Alleghenies ! What is about to be said of them was not wholly true of Ken-

tucky, because of the close relations of that colony with
Virginia ; but in general it may be asserted that they
came into the Union with vastly less of reservation, both
of purpose and of feeling, than was possible to any of
the original members. They had grown up, as weak
and isolated communities, upon territory belonging in
fee to the United States, and under the protection of its
military power. They had been governed, while in a
territorial condition, directly by the United States, with
such concessions as to local self-government as might
seem to Congress for their good. They had learned,
from the very first, to look to the general government
for protection against the Indians, for the means of
opening their rivers to navigation, for the survey of
their lands. If, in their zeal for " the old flag—and an
appropriation," something of greed mingled with the
impulses of patriotism, this was yet all for the increase
of national feeling and the strengthening of the bonds of

Influence of
the West upon
American na-
tionality.

Union. No one can rightly read the history
of the United States who does not recognize
the prodigious influence exerted in the direction of unreserving nationality by the growth of
great communities beyond the mountains, and their
successive admission as States of the Union.

Such, as we now, after the fact, regard it, was the influence of the Great West upon the fortunes, and even

Fears of the
West in the
Convention of
1797.

the fate, of the republic. The forecast of
that influence by the men of the Constitutional Convention had been less favorable, if,
indeed, it may not be said to have been gloomy in the extreme. At various stages of the debate, apprehensions
were expressed regarding the power of the new States
which were to be formed within the public territory.
To prevent the Eastern States from being ultimately
overwhelmed from this source, it had even been pro-

posed to limit the number of Representatives in Congress which should ever be allowed, in the aggregate, to States beyond the Alleghenies.

But while the opinion we have expressed regarding the influence of the West upon the main point of the stability and the integrity of the Union is thus highly favorable, it should be added that two dangers, one temporary, the other more permanent, came from this quarter. The transient danger alluded to is that which arose, during the first fifteen years under the Constitution, from the passionate desire of the settlers beyond the mountains to secure the free navigation of the Mississippi. To this end these hardy pioneers were ready almost to sacrifice their allegiance to the Union. That a foreign power should keep its grasp upon what was, to them, of vital importance, seemed intolerable; and we can hardly blame them for their impatience, though a keener appreciation of the difficulties of the new government in attaining that object would have been more creditable to their patriotism. On the other hand, it must be admitted that the first administration, and especially Washington and Judge Jay, showed a singular obtuseness in dealing with the eager demands of the West upon this point. Washington, having penetrated as a surveyor beyond the mountains, even before the outbreak of the French War, had become so deeply interested in projects for opening up communication between the West and the seaboard as to be almost infatuated with that idea, believing that, in the matter of transportation, all would thus be effected which the West could reasonably ask. Jay, on his part, held, with the utmost sincerity and disinterestedness, that the benefits which would result to the whole country from favorable commercial treaties with Spain, would be so great as fairly to justify the government in asking the western people to submit, for twenty-five years longer, to restrictions upon the navigation of the Mississippi. There are few things more instructive than the fact that men like Washington and Jay could have been so far wrong in such a vital matter.

The second and more permanent danger arising to the country from the influence of the Western States, has been through the aversion of the people of that region to measures proposed in the interest of financial integrity, commercial credit, and the national honor. The opposition from this quarter to proper laws regarding bankruptcies, and the predilection there manifested for cheap money, have been a constant menace and a frequent cause of mischief. This, however, we may regard as due to the stage of settlement and civilization reached. As fast as manufactures, commerce, and banking have made their way into that section, the communities concerned have become sound and conservative.

Financial unsoundness of the West.

The consent of Washington to be a candidate for reelection put at rest all thoughts of a contest for the presidency in 1792. Faction had not raised itself so high as to dispute his pre-eminent claims to the confidence and respect of his countrymen. Not only did his position and reputation make it vain for any body of men, if so disposed, to assail him ; but his impartiality, his truthfulness, and his singleness of patriotic purpose had enabled him so to mediate between the embittered factions in his cabinet and in Congress that each by turns was ready to accept his action in all important cases as wise and just. It was fortunate for the young republic that its great leader still lived and gave to its councils his benign presence, thus securing a short interval of comparative repose. The contests between the Federalists and the Republi-

The second presidential election.

cans had become so bitter and furious that, had either controlled the executive office in the critical times of 1793–97, the results might have been disastrous to our destinies. "Monocrats" was the mildest term which Jefferson could find whereby to characterize the party of Hamilton, Adams, and Jay, while the Federalists hurled back the epithet "Jacobins," in allusion to the crazed and bloodthirsty revolutionists of France. Neither party was content to charge the other with less than disloyalty to the Constitution.

The consent of Washington to be a candidate took the life out of the election of 1792, although the Republicans made an ineffectual and perhaps not very sincere effort to capture the vice-presidency by "running," in the phrase of our modern politics, George Clinton, the "War Governor" of New York, and still the incumbent of that office, a man of great natural powers, a hard fighter and a bitter hater, who had made himself peculiarly obnoxious to the Federalists, not only by his opposition to the ratification of the Constitution, but by his conduct and bearing upon all occasions. He received 50 votes, viz., all 21 of Virginia ; all 12 of New York ; all 12 of North Carolina ; all 4 of Georgia ; and 1 from Pennsylvania. Adams received 77 votes. Five were "scattering." Washington received an unanimous vote, 132 in all ; and the new government was inaugurated March 4, 1793. Clinton's vote is scarcely to be accepted as showing the actual strength of the opposition. The fact that the Republicans were precluded from nominating a president distinctly of their own side, was calculated to prevent their putting forth much effort to capture an office comparatively insignificant. Their power would be better measured by the result of the elections to the House of Representatives, in which that party secured a major-

8

ity. The Senate, however, from the fact that the popular strength of the Republicans was, as yet, chiefly in the large States, as well as from the longer duration of the senatorial term, remained strongly Federalist. We have thus, only four years from the beginning, that distinct opposition of the two branches of the legislature, the possibility of which many persons regard as largely neutralizing the advantages of our form of government.

CHAPTER VII

WASHINGTON'S SECOND TERM

Foreign Relations—The Genet Episode—Difficulties with France
—England and France Vying with each Other in Wrong to the
United States—With which should We go to War ?—The
Whiskey Insurrection—The Militia Called Out—Democratic
Societies—The Funding System—The Admission of Tennes-
see—Oliver Ellsworth becomes Chief-Justice—The Eleventh
Amendment to the Constitution—The Disruption of the Cabi-
net and the Movement of Parties— Jefferson's Commercial Re-
port—New Cabinet Appointments—Randolph Retires from
Office under a Cloud—Hamilton Resigns : His Services to the
New Government—Knox is Succeeded by Timothy Pickering
—Washington's Last Cabinet : Painful Decline in Ability—
Party Divisions go Rapidly Forward—The Third Presiden-
tial Election : John Adams Chosen—Jefferson becomes Vice-
President, though of the Opposite Party—Defective Method of
Choosing President and Vice-President.

LET us speak of the foreign relations of Washington's
second term, and first, of the Genet episode. Early in
1793 France proclaimed war against Great Britain and
Holland. It is not necessary to go into the reasons, or
pretexts, put forward to justify her act. On April 22d,
as in duty bound, President Washington issued a proclamation of neutrality. Close upon this occurred an extraordinary series of events, which we have chosen to
call the Genet episode. The Federalists, indeed, insisted
that the acts of Genet were under instructions from his
government and constituted a part of its policy. But
as it appears that much of what Genet did was the
result of his own Jacobinical fanaticism, his extrava-

gance, and bad temper, we prefer to isolate all those things which were not unmistakably chargeable to the French government, and to style them the Genet episode.

Mr. Edmond C. Genet, or "Citizen Genet," as he was called, under the frivolous democratic impulse in France The Genet (imitated, for a time, more frivolously in the episode. United States) to abolish all titles, having been appointed minister from France to this country, arrived at Charleston, S.C., on April 8th. With an extraordinary contempt for the authority to which he was accredited, he immediately set about enlisting American citizens for service against Great Britain, and fitting out and commissioning vessels against the enemies of France. From Charleston to Philadelphia, after a considerable delay, he journeyed in a sort of Jacobinical procession, receiving ovations from the admirers of the French Convention, and declaiming against those who should seek to restrain the United States from active co-operation with France : all after a fashion derogatory to our national dignity and compromising our neutral position.

After Genet's arrival in Philadelphia he made direct issue with the government on several points which were decided against him, even Mr. Jefferson repudiating his claims ; and had the astonishing impudence to appeal to Congress and the country against the administration. He insisted upon his right, under the treaty of 1778, to arm vessels and to try and sell prizes in American ports.* In spite of expressed prohibitions, the consuls of France, at his instigation, exercised admiralty powers in holding courts and in condemning and selling prizes. His insolence only grew by contradiction, until, encouraged by the democratic frenzy aroused in many parts of the United States by the progress of the French Revolution,

---

* It was not in dispute that French privateers and prizes were entitled to shelter in American ports.

which had now proceeded to a Reign of Terror, and by the formation here of "Democratic Societies" for the purpose of giving sympathy and support to the revolutionary movement in Europe, Genet broke all diplomatic bounds. He insulted the President and his advisers; set on foot within our territory military expeditions against the Spanish dominions; issued commissions for enlistment; and, in the case of the Little Sarah, a prize that had been fitted up as a privateer, openly defied the government. It is not to be wondered at that, after such acts, the French consul at Boston, M. Duplaine, should have dared to rescue a vessel by armed force out of the hands of a United States marshal. M. Duplaine was, however, made to learn the difference between an ambassador and a consul in point of privilege. His exequatur was promptly revoked.

These outrageous acts of Genet at a very early date called for remonstrance by our government with France; and, the fanatical minister still persisting in his acts of contempt, his recall was requested. A successor was appointed by the government of France, which, as the party to which Genet belonged had already fallen from power, was at no pains to spare *Genet retires.* its minister humiliation. Genet, having reason to fear he might be made to taste the sweets of liberty in the arms of La Guillotine, wisely concluded not to return home. He remained in the United States; married a daughter of Governor Clinton; became a citizen, and left children and grandchildren who were Americans by birth.

Stripped of the extravagance and folly of Genet's demonstrations, the claims of France upon us were two. First that, by a stipulation in the treaty of alliance (1778), the United States was expressly bound to guarantee against all enemies the French possessions in

America. Of the cabinet, Hamilton and Knox maintained that this guarantee was applicable only to a defensive war ; and hence was not binding in the present war, which was commenced by France. Jefferson and Randolph, without touching the latter point, recommended the issue of the proclamation of neutrality spoken of above. The question of guarantee Jefferson regarded as reserved to the meeting of Congress, which alone could, in his opinion, properly judge of the effect of the treaty. Secondly, the French government claimed that the United States was bound to give the French government, in case of war, peculiar facilities for fitting out privateers within our ports, and for the trial and condemnation of prizes. This claim was based upon the article by which the parties agreed not to permit the enemies of either to fit out privateers in their ports. The express prohibition of this privilege to enemies the French considered as implying a promise to the parties themselves. This claim the United States peremptorily denied ; and there can be little question of the rightfulness of that position. No nation ought to allow itself to be dragged into war, against its wishes and its interests, by a stipulation of such doubtful significance. Nothing but the extravagant sympathy of the Republicans with the French cause could have made an accession to this proposal possible. On the other hand, perhaps nothing but the effrontery of Genet and the stern, calm decision of Washington would, against the Jacobinical frenzy of the hour, have prevented such a lamentable result. But, whatever may have been the claims of France upon us, as her ancient ally and by virtue of the treaty of 1778, she soon forfeited all right to peculiar consideration by ordering that neutral vessels containing goods belonging to her enemies should be captured, and also by laying an embargo upon our

The dispute with France.

shipping at Bordeaux, and by other acts in distinct violation of that treaty.

With England our difficulties were of a more substantial, and, for the present, serious character. England still held our western posts, under the plea that the conditions of the treaty of 1783 had not been fulfilled on our part ; and the same *Difficulties with England.* political forces which had in vain urged an alliance with France, for the sake of France, urged, with more reason and with more prospect of success, a war against England (which would have amounted to the same thing), for the sake of vindicating our national rights and dignity. But that arrogance which has always marked the commercial policy of England did not long leave us this as the only cause of war. In June, 1793, that power ordered that the goods of neutral nations, if consisting of provisions for the enemy, should be captured or bought up, unless shipped to a friendly port. This was followed by an order that all vessels laden with produce of a French colony, or with supplies for the same, were lawful prize. More than all, Great Britain claimed and exercised the right to impress into her service seamen of British birth, wherever found, and for this purpose to stop and search the ships of the United States.

Measures so outrageous made war, in the then feeling of the nation, imminent and seemingly inevitable. More than all others, the United States had come, by force both of tradition and of interest, to represent and champion the rights of neutral trade. Our "carrying" business was very large ; and our people were fully determined to protect it, not only from motives of gain but from sentiments of national pride. A temporary embargo upon American ports was voted in March, 1794, in order that our ships might not be caught at sea in the event of war. A bill was passed for fortifying certain rivers and harbors, and a report was adopted largely increasing the army. War would have been justifiable, but the great interest of the nation was peace. So Washington saw it ; so we now see it to have been, and in spite of clamor, in the face of passion, the president determined upon a last effort for a peaceful solution of the difficulties. To this end he selected Chief-Justice Jay, a Federalist, and therefore esteemed by the opposition a friend of England, but a man of the loftiest character and the most fervent patriotism, to proceed to England and open negotiations. In November, 1794, Judge Jay concluded a treaty ; and in June, 1795, the Senate ratified the same.

The Jay treaty.

We should despair of giving the reader an idea of the intensity of the indignation with which the Republican party opposed the mission of Jay and denounced the outcome. The debates on the " British Treaty " are among the most memorable of the Senate, while the agitation in the House of Representatives, which was Republican, and throughout the country, was wholly unparalleled. Then it was that the House struck out the phrase " undiminished confidence " from an address to the president ; then it was that Virginia, by her legislature, refused to declare her trust in Washington ; then it was that vituperation spared not the august chief who had conducted the States thus far in war and in peace with the universal acclaim of his countrymen. Anti-treaty mobs filled the streets of New York and Boston ; Jay was burned in effigy ; Hamilton stoned.

Opposition to the treaty.

Looking back calmly at this series of events we can say that, while the treaty sacrificed no American rights, it granted far less than our people were entitled to claim ; and was therefore open to criticism. The western posts were, indeed, to be surrendered, and indemnity granted to the sufferers by search or capture. A few concessions, also, were made to American commerce. But, in the main, the British government maintained its commercial system in full rigor, and by no means renounced the right of search and impressment on the high seas. Those great questions the Jay treaty still left to be decided later, as it proved, by the arbitrament of war ; but we cannot doubt that the United States were fortunate in attaining a postponement of that contest until twenty years more had nearly doubled their population and had compacted the national strength.

It will be observed that the United States were brought by these differences with France and with England into a very singular and most embarrassing position. From each of the two antagonists we were receiving both insults and injuries. With which should we go to war ? or, should the young republic defy both these powerful nations, and assert its rights and interests against each in turn ? Of this dilemma Jefferson afterward wrote : "The difficulty of selecting a foe between them has spared us many years of war, and enabled us to enter into it with less debt, more strength and preparation.   France has kept pace with England in iniquity of principle, although not in the power of inflicting wrongs upon us." The usurpations of Bonaparte had by that time cured Mr. Jefferson of an admiration which the "Reign of Terror" did not abate ; so that he could write : "As for France and England, with all their prominence in science, one is a den of robbers and the other of pirates." It is worth while to note here that the acts of Congress necessary to carrying into effect the Jay treaty gave rise to a struggle in which the House of Representatives asserted the claim to have a voice in the adjustment of international relations under

Two enemies at once.

the form of treaties, a claim frequently reappearing in the course of our constitutional history.

But if the Jay treaty settled provisionally the difficulties with England, the negotiation and ratification of that treaty proved a grave offence to France; and angry remonstrances and threats of war came from Paris, where Mr. Monroe was representing the United States, not at all to the satisfaction of Washington. The French government in 1796 declared the alliance with the United States under the treaty of 1778, which had ceased to be of importance to France when our government refused to be drawn by it into hostilities with England, to be at an end, by reason of the fact that the United States had, in the treaty with Great Britain, abandoned the principle that "free ships make free goods," while naval stores and provisions were rendered contraband of war. This France insisted, not without some reason, was a hardship to her; and for a time Spain and Holland seemed determined to make common cause with her to compel the United States to protect the property of their citizens when in American vessels. Spain, which on October 27, 1795, had concluded a treaty with the United States, negotiated by Thomas Pinckney, our minister to that country, most favorable to our claims in respect to the navigation of the Mississippi and the boundary of Florida, now refused to make good the stipulations of that treaty. Mr. Monroe's conduct of affairs at Paris being increasingly unsatisfactory to the administration, that gentleman was recalled, and Charles C. Pinckney was appointed in his place. Mr. Monroe returned home in great dudgeon, and the French government (to which Mr. Monroe had been highly "grateful") refused to receive Mr. Pinckney, declaring that it would not again recognize a minister from the United States until reparation had been

France resents the Jay treaty.

afforded for the injuries which the French nation had suffered. So in clouds of war set the sun of Washington's administration.

It now seems incredible that, not only our own people, but the proudest and most warlike nations of Europe should long have paid tribute to the corsairs of Algiers, Tripoli, and Tunis, who claimed the sovereignty of the Mediterranean ; yet such was the fact. We shall later see by what acts of heroic daring our young navy freed the republic forever from this shameful dependence. It is only necessary here to refer to the treaty of 1795 with the Dey of Algiers, who, on condition of large payments, consented to release the crews of American merchantmen who had for years been held by him in captivity, and thereafter to respect our commerce. *The pirates of the Barbary States.*

Let us now turn to the internal affairs of Washington's second term. The year 1795 witnessed the successful conclusion of the Indian War in the Northwest, against the Miamis and their confederates, and the cession of what is substantially the present State of Ohio. *The Indian War.*

In noticing the passage of the excise law, which imposed duties on spirits, in Washington's first term, reference was made to considerations which rendered that tax peculiarly odious and obnoxious, especially at the West. From the first, grave trouble had been experienced in collecting the revenue ; and soon actual resistance began to be offered by the persons directly concerned, while large districts became highly inflamed. The measures of resistance were, as usual in such cases, compounded of acts wholly outrageous and unlawful, mingled with remonstrance, petition, and protest from citizens of character and standing. The movement soon became *The whiskey insurrection.*

a really capital parody of the proceedings prior to the Revolution ; and there is little doubt that the prestige which had long attended such acts as the "Boston Tea Party" and the riotous intimidation of the stamp collectors in New Haven, Charleston, and elsewhere, encouraged the opponents of the whiskey duty to defy the law and to commit outrages on the revenue officers. Certain it is that many of the leaders of the Republican party manifested no small sympathy with the mobs ; and gave their breath to ridiculing the militia called out to vindicate the authority of the government, rather than to denunciation of incipient rebellion. As early as 1792 the President had found it necessary to issue a proclamation, calling on his fellow-citizens to support the law. But in 1794 opposition rose to such a point that collectors of revenue were driven from their homes, government mails seized, and the United States Marshal fired upon in the course of his duty. The culminating point of the Rebellion was at Pittsburg. We have already referred to the conditions which rendered the tax a peculiar hardship to the people of this region ; but there was something in the character of the people themselves which made rebellion easy, on such a theme. Just prior to the outbreak of the Revolution, there had been an extraordinary immigration of Irish, who settled in large numbers at the junction of the Allegheny and Monongahela rivers. Hatred of excise and skill in evading duties on whiskey had been among the virtues of the Irish peasant at home ; and among the promoters of opposition to the tax in western Pennsylvania the men of this race were conspicuous. In August, 1794, an armed convention met on Braddock's Field, to denounce the law and defy the government. The secretary of the meeting was none other than Albert Gallatin, a Swiss immigrant, afterward Secretary of the Treasury. Such acts satisfied both the President and Governor Mifflin, of Pennsylvania, that the time for vigorous measures had come.   Fifteen thousand militia were called out ; but were preceded by commissioners with offers of general amnesty on condition of The militia peaceable submission.   It was, however, called out. only by the actual presence of the troops that quiet was restored and the authority of the government vindicated.   The enactment of the whiskey tax was unquestionably one of the most serious political mistakes of the Federalist party ; but the result of this legislation which we have least to regret was the energetic action of the executive in putting down resistance to the law. The Republican leaders might, as many of them did, sneer at the militia who marched to western Pennsylvania ; but the rioters themselves and the country at large made no mistake about the matter ; they understood that, at last, there was a government in the United States which could not be defied.   The learning of this lesson was worth all it cost.

So manifestly had the " Democratic Societies," which had been formed very generally throughout the United States on the abolition of the monarchy Democratic in France, contributed at once to foreign in- Societies. solence, as in the case of Genet, and to domestic disturbance, as in the case of the whiskey insurrection, that Washington, in his annual message of 1794, strongly denounced these organizations as unpatriotic and dangerous.   It must be confessed that the President's position was somewhat weakened by the fact that he himself was, and had long been, the head of the Society of the Cincinnati, an organization of officers of the Revolutionary army which, as then organized, was charged with a strong aristocratic tendency.   With the fall of Robespierre, however, of whose clubs they were an imitation, the Democratic Societies rapidly declined, more probably from that cause than from the effect of Washington's deserved denunciations.

During the summer of 1793 yellow fever broke out with frightful violence in Philadelphia, then the seat of the general government. For months terror reigned in the devoted city. Over four thousand interments took place from August to November, the first month of frost. It is said that, at the time the panic was at its height, seventeen thousand citizens were absent from their homes, seeking safety among the mountains or in the rural districts. The pestilence extended southward to Charleston, and as far north even as Boston and Newburyport; but Philadelphia remained the greatest sufferer. The same dread scourge reappeared in 1797 and 1798, though working far less mischief, probably because of a better knowledge of the evil and its remedies.

Yellow fever in Philadelphia.

Upon a report of Mr. Hamilton, the last of his "Reports," so called, Congress proceeded to make permanent provision for the debt of the United States. The principal feature of this scheme was the establishment of a sinking fund, consisting of the surplus revenues, of the bank-dividends payable to the government, of the proceeds of the sale of public lands, and of the taxes on spirits and stills until 1801. This measure may be regarded as a creditable one in its conception, though the praise awarded for it to Hamilton is hardly deserved, since it was largely in imitation of Mr. Pitt's English system.

The funding system.

In June, 1796, Tennessee was admitted as a State of the Union, from territory ceded by North Carolina. The population of Tennessee in 1790 was 35,691; in 1800, 105,602. Judge Jay, having

The State of Tennessee.

been elected Governor of the State of New York, resigned his office as Chief-Justice. The Senate having
refused to confirm * John Rutledge, of South
Carolina, whom President Washington nomi-   The change
nated, and Judge Cushing, of Massachusetts,   in the Chief-
                                                Justiceship.
having declined, the office was conferred upon Oliver
Ellsworth, of Connecticut.

It was said that apparently not a member of the Constitutional Convention of 1787 adequately appreciated
the tremendous powers with which the judiciary had
been invested ; and it was intimated that, should the
courts of the United States actually be permitted to exercise the jurisdiction granted them by that instrument,
a really effective national government could not fail to
result, subject only to those liabilities to insurrection
or rebellion which beset all governments, of whatever
type. The Constitution had not been long in operation,
however, when it was ascertained that, at least in one
instance, the Supreme Court would not be permitted
to exercise that jurisdiction. In the case of Chisholm
vs. the State of Georgia, the party defendant refused to plead except to the jurisdiction of the court.
Georgia declared, through its legal representatives, that
it could not be brought into the courts as a defendant ;
and challenged the construction given to the first clause
of the second section of the third Article of the Constitution by the law officers of the government. The
court, Chief-Justice Jay presiding, maintained its jurisdiction ; † but the excitement caused by the case, and a
general sense of the impropriety of thus bringing a

* Largely on account of extraordinary and intolerable language used
by Rutledge in connection with the Jay treaty.

† It is interesting to note that, in the debate in the Virginia Convention over the adoption of the Constitution, John Marshall, afterward the
great Chief-Justice, declared that, under Article 3, a State could not be
sued by a citizen of another State.

State into court, led Congress, on December 2, 1793,
to propose the Eleventh Amendment of the Constitution—which was, in fact, the first real amendment of that instrument—providing that the
judicial power of the United States should
not be construed to extend to any suit in law or equity,
commenced or prosecuted against one of the United
States by citizens of another State, or by citizens or subjects of any foreign State. This amendment, having
been duly ratified, became a part of the organic law.
It is to be said that this amendment made no important
breach in our constitutional system. It has, indeed,
enabled some of the States to do very rascally things in
the way of repudiating debts or neglecting obligations ;
but enough remained of the jurisdiction of the United
States courts to enable them to perform their great part
in the making of the nation.

The Eleventh Amendment of the Constitution.

We have seen that Washington began his administration, in 1789, with a cabinet comprising some of the
most illustrious men of the republic, yet containing
within itself elements of discord and even of strong antagonisms. The cabinet remained intact during the
whole of Washington's first term ; but in the very year
of his second inauguration it began to go to
pieces. Jefferson had felt outraged, to the
very depths of his being, by what he regarded as the corrupt and dangerous financial measures of Hamilton and by the general tendency
of the government toward consolidation and monarchy.
The course of the administration, as between France
and England, had been very painful and not
a little mortifying to him. On December
16, 1793, Mr. Jefferson made a special report
to Congress on the commercial relations of the United
States ; and, within a day or two thereafter, retired

Disruption of the cabinet and the movement of parties.

Jefferson's commercial report.

from the State Department.   His report was regarded
by the Federalists as ingeniously designed to embarrass
the administration he was leaving.   Upon its reception
by the House of Representatives, Mr. Madison offered
resolutions for carrying out the principles of the report.
These were opposed by the Federalists, led by Mr.
Smith, of South Carolina, on the ground that the measure was designed to punish England and to favor
France.   Mr. Jefferson's allegations were denounced
as false and misleading.   The Federalists declared that
our commerce was as much favored by England as by
France ; while our relations with the former country
were vastly more important.   Messrs. Jefferson and
Madison were taunted with having forgotten to be free-
traders in their eagerness to injure England.

Upon Mr. Jefferson's retirement from the State Department, Mr. Randolph was transferred from the office of Attorney-General to succeed him.   Mr.   Randolph's
Randolph's course while in office had been   error.
marked by the same indecision and vacillation which
characterized his actions regarding the formation and
ratification of the Constitution.   He had appeared desirous to " trim " between the two parties, and in consequence had not won the support of either.   He was
not destined to remain long in his new office.   In August, 1795, he resigned, in consequence of the publication of a very compromising letter from Mr. Fauchet,
the French minister, which forfeited for him the confidence of Washington.   Charges of corrupt action were
then and subsequently made against Mr. Randolph.
The results of recent investigation have disproved these
charges, though they have not restored Mr. Randolph
to the historical rank of a great statesman.   He was
succeeded in the State Department by Timothy Pickering, of Pennsylvania, formerly of Massachusetts.

9

In June, 1795, Mr. Hamilton retired from the Treasury Department, where he had won such fame as has never been even approached by any of his successors, though that office has been filled by many men of remarkable ability. For good or for ill, according to one's political predilections, it is admitted by all that Mr. Hamilton had done more to give form to the new government, to fill its veins with life-blood, and to inspire its actions with energy, than any other man of his time. Much of what Mr. Hamilton did could, in the nature of the case, never be undone; and by consequence he must be regarded as having been a great creative force within the government. He was succeeded in the Treasury by Oliver Wolcott, Jr., of Connecticut, who had filled the office of Comptroller. General Knox retired from the War Department toward the close of 1794, and was succeeded by Colonel Pickering, who, as we have seen, was soon transferred to the State Department, being succeeded by James McHenry, of Maryland. William Bradford, of Pennsylvania, who had succeeded Randolph as Attorney-General, died in August, 1795; and Charles Lee, of Virginia, was appointed in his place.

Hamilton retires; his services to the new government.

At the close of Washington's administration, therefore, the cabinet consisted of the following members: Timothy Pickering, Secretary of State; Oliver Wolcott, Jr., Secretary of Treasury; James McHenry, Secretary of War; Charles Lee, Attorney-General. One cannot let his eye fall on this list without being painfully struck with the decline which had taken place in so short a time in the dignity and authority of the cabinet. Three of the gentlemen named were of good abilities and character; but not one of them approached the rank of his predecessor; nor was this change the result of accident. In some

Washington's last cabinet.

part, it was undoubtedly due to the expenses of living
for a cabinet officer at Philadelphia in this time, which
were far in excess of the means of all but wealthy citizens.   But in still greater part it was due to a lack of
respect for the office, arising from the obloquy and
abuse which had been heaped upon Washington's earlier advisers ; from the quarrels and antagonisms which
had developed among them ; and from the fact that the
position of cabinet officer in the government had not
yet been properly distinguished and emphasized to the
public mind.   Mr. Adams states that Washington offered the post of Secretary of State, between 1795 and
1796, to four persons whom he names, and to three
others whom he does not recall.   He adds : "He has
not been able to find anyone to accept the War Office."

During the whole period of which we have been writing, the division of the country into two parties had
steadily gone forward.   Little by little those Progress of
who had been doubtful in sentiment, or who party feeling.
had been disposed to find something good in the principles of either party, had ranged themselves definitively upon one or the other side of the dividing line.
The parties themselves had come to recognize their
natural leaders, to fall into order, and to acquire discipline.   This, of itself, was not a thing to be regretted.
Indeed, the existence of a formulated opposition, at the
outset of the new government, was essential to bringing
out the true theory of the Constitution.   Without two
parties closely watching and strongly opposing each
other, things might have come to be lightly done, from
lack of criticism and objection, which would have been
mischievous in their ultimate results.   But the altogether unnecessary and unreasonable animosities which
were developed by public measures exerted a most prejudicial influence.   Party differences cut deep into so-

cial life and personal relationship. Our people were politically raw and unformed ; they had not learned to hold their beliefs temperately and to respect the convictions of others. Even political morality had as yet been but vaguely outlined in the public thought ; and things were done by men of good standing which would be universally reprobated at the present time.

Upon the conclusion of his second term Washington declined re-election, setting a precedent which there is reason to believe will never be departed The third presidential from. Certainly no man can ever again have election. such claims upon his countrymen, or be so necessary to his country, as was Washington when he declined a third term. John Adams, of Massachusetts, was nominated by the Federalists ; Thomas Jefferson, of Virginia, by the Republicans. The latter had been the author of the Declaration of Independence ; the former, its great champion on the floor of Congress. They had long been associated in friendship ; but personal ambition and party strife had made deep division between them. Many years afterward, when the battles of their lives had been fought, they were again, by an accident, to be brought into friendly relations ; and, in the leisure of declining years, to gossip together, in long, old-fashioned letters (impossible forevermore in these days of telegraph and postal cards), about their early achievements, their common friends and foes, and even about the very events which once made them speak so disparagingly and harshly of each other.

A word concerning the manner in which nominations to the presidency were made. The National Convention, made up of delegates of the voting members of the party and giving forth a " platform " of principles and selecting candidates for the support of the people, was then unknown. " A caucus, as it is called " (Gibbs, ii., 347) of the members of Congress acting together on national issues was held before a presidential election; and, with as little machinery as is now used for the nomination of a sergeant-at-arms, the party ticket was made up. It must not be inferred, however, that, because the nomination was simple, the system was a desirable one. Undoubtedly it encouraged congressional intrigue, to a degree not now experienced; and tended toward a dangerous confusion of the parts of government. This is the place, too, in which to speak of the system first established by the Constitution for the choice of President and Vice-President. The electors chosen by the several States were to vote, each, for two persons, without designating either for the office of President or Vice-President. The person receiving in the aggregate the largest number of electoral votes became President; the person receiving the next largest number of votes, whether of the same party or not, became Vice-President. A more senseless arrangement could hardly have been devised. Should each one of the electors of the victorious party vote for both persons nominated by his party, each of these would receive the same number of votes; and there would be nothing to determine who should be President and who Vice-President. Neither would have been elected to office; and the election would thus be thrown into the House of Representatives, as was done in 1801. In order to avoid such a result, it would be necessary that one or more electors should throw away his second vote; but, as this would be a difficult matter to arrange, especially in those days of slow communication, and as there would always be a danger of treachery in the matter, a considerable number of electors might throw away their second votes, to prevent a tie. In this case it might happen that one of the can-

Method of nominating the President and Vice-President.

didates of the other party would be brought in as Vice-President. Just this, as we shall see, occurred in 1797.

Let us now return to the candidates at the third presidential election. In addition to the advantages which
Jefferson's strength. Mr. Jefferson derived from the definitive retirement of Washington from public life, from the unpopularity of many of the measures of the closing administration, and from the growing democratic spirit of the country, he possessed an immense source of power in the fact that he was the sole possible candidate of his party and its universally recognized leader. No man stood near him for the nomination ; no rival divided with him the confidence and support of the Republicans of the United States. On the other hand, Mr. Adams was only one of three great leaders of the Federalist party. Hamilton and Jay came also within the possible range of nomination. Each of them had hosts of followers, who held Mr. Adams in less esteem. Jay, however, just at this time, was an undesirable candidate, on account of the British treaty ; and his own support of Adams was loyal and hearty ; but between Adams and Hamilton was mutual distrust, while the soaring ambition of the younger statesman and his consciousness of vast powers made him unhappy at seeing another preferred to himself, mainly on the ground of revolutionary services. Adams had always been disposed to charge Hamilton with the responsibility for the large reduction of his vote in 1789 ; and in 1796 he fully believed that, at the election then impending, Hamilton was not indisposed to secure his defeat, even at the cost of bringing in Jefferson. But while the Republicans thus entered upon the third presidential election with greatly increased force, the time had not as yet been long enough completely to wear away the hold which the Federalist party had, at the beginning,

upon the mind of the country. It was to require four years more to break down Federalist supremacy and give the leadership to the party which Mr. Jefferson had been so assiduously and astutely building up.

Mr. Adams triumphed ; but it was only by the narrowest majority. He received seventy-one votes in the electoral college ; Mr. Jefferson, sixty-eight. Even this hairbreadth escape was due more to personal than political reasons. "A single voice in Virginia and one in North Carolina," writes Mr. Charles Francis Adams, "prompted by the lingering memory of revolutionary services, had turned the scale." Had these two electors consented to forget how John Adams stood up for American liberty in the days of the Stamp Act and the Boston port bill ; how he urged on the cause of Independence and defended the Declaration upon the floor of the Revolutionary Congress, Jefferson might have been elected in 1797, for those two votes would have just brought him in. The narrowness of his majority could not have been pleasant to Mr. Adams. He jocosely called himself "a President of three votes," but there is reason to believe that he took the matter in his heart more seriously. It would even appear that the Republicans made an attempt, or at least put out "feelers" in that direction, to draw Mr. Adams, in his natural irritation at the manner in which he had been dealt with, over to themselves ; but if they really thought that this was possible, they did know their man, who was as sturdy, sincere, and loyal, as he was vain, dogmatic, and obstinate.

In the same connection we see the evil consequences of the peculiar provision we have recited regarding the choice of Vice-President. Thomas Pinckney had been nominated for this office with Adams ; but, in fact, he received fewer votes than Mr. Jefferson, who thus, though the Republican candidate for the presidency, be-

came Vice-President under a Federalist chief, a result
conducive neither to his own dignity and pleasure, nor
to honest politics and good government. The
reason for " cutting " Mr. Pinckney had
largely been the fear of the Federalist electors
that there might be a tie between him and Adams.

*Jefferson
becomes Vice-
President.*

On retiring from public office, Washington issued an
address to the American people, of whom he had for
twenty-two years been the leader, alike in
war and in peace. This Farewell Message
is among the most precious of the nation's
many legacies from its great men of thought and action.
Written simply and without rhetorical artifice, it is
dignified in form, earnest in tone, clear in statement,
effective in argument, impressive in admonition, powerful in appeal. As was natural on such an occasion, the
address deals less with policies and with positive recommendations than with the dangers to which the new
nation, so strangely and curiously composed, would
surely be subjected in the days of its trial and experi-
ment; less with precepts than with warnings. Chief
among its themes are the evils of entangling alliances
with foreign nations and of sectional animosities and
jealousies at home. On these two points the address
dwells with a fulness which reveals how strongly the apprehension of them had taken possession of the great
patriot-chieftain's mind and heart. In the most solemn
terms he adjures his fellow-citizens to be Americans
above all things and in all things, cherishing the interests
of their whole country with equal affection, and knowing no foes and no friends, politically, but the foes
and friends of the United States. Respect for law, the
sacredness of national credit, moderation in party feeling, public and private virtue are all made the subjects
of earnest admonition and argument.

*Washing-
ton's Farewell
Address.*

CHAPTER VIII

THE ADMINISTRATION OF JOHN ADAMS

President Adams Retains Washington's Cabinet—Foreign Affairs—
Difficulties with France Aggravated—A Special Mission sent
—Envoys Insulted—War Imminent—Federalist Enthusiasm—
Washington appointed Commander-in-Chief — Schemes of
Hamilton and Miranda—Spanish Possessions to be Seized—
President Adams sends a New Mission—The French Treaty
—The Spoliation Claims—Taxation in this Administration—
Stamp Duties arouse Opposition—The Direct Tax—Inefficiency
of this Tax in the United States—Resistance to the Law—
Conviction of the Rioters—Fries Pardoned—Anger of the Fed-
eralists—What Constitutes Treason ?—Navy Department Cre-
ated—Alien and Sedition Laws—Furious Opposition by the
Republicans—Nullification Resolutions of Virginia and Ken-
tucky—Responses of Federalist States—Madison's Defence—
—Congress Meets in the New Capital—The First Bankruptcy
Law—The Second Census—Death of Washington—Split in the
Cabinet—Secretaries Intrigue against the President—Hamilton's Opposition to Adams—His Pamphlet—The Fourth Presidential Election—Adams Defeated—Jefferson and Burr receive an Equal Vote—Contest in the House—Federalists take
up Burr—Jefferson finally chosen President—Causes of the
Defeat of the Federalists—Marshall becomes Chief-Justice.

UPON his inauguration, March 4, 1797, Mr. Adams
retained in office the cabinet of Washington. This,
as we shall see, became the cause of much
trouble to him. The Senate was still strongly Federalist ; but many of its members were not well
disposed toward the President.

The importance of foreign affairs under this administration seems to require that we should deal first with

The Cabinet.

them. It has been said that France deemed itself in-
jured by the British treaty ; and that General Pinckney
was notified that the French government would receive
no minister from the United States until reparation
should be made. Soon news arrived that Pinckney had
been ordered out of France. French cruisers were
already seizing our ships, under a decree of their government authorizing the capture of neutral vessels having
on board any of the productions of Great Britain or of
any of her possessions. War seemed * imminent ; and
Congress was convened for a special session. It met

War with France immi-nent. with an administration majority in both branches. In his opening message, Presi-dent Adams used language so strong that it
was resented by the French Directory as an additional
grievance. Having effected its organization, Congress
proceeded to make provision for defence.

Mr. Adams, however, was resolved to make one more
effort to secure a peaceful settlement ; and, with this

The mission to France. in view, nominated to the Senate as envoys to France, Charles C. Pinckney, Elbridge
Gerry, and John Marshall—Gerry being a Republican
but an intimate personal friend of Adams. Time would
fail to describe the ludicrous and shameful incidents of
that embassy. Suffice it to say that, the French Directory being composed of low and irresponsible persons,
the negotiations soon degenerated into an attempt to
fleece the American envoys, apparently for the benefit
of covetous individuals in the Directory. After our
representatives had been for some time kept waiting,
certain " strikers " (in the phrase of modern municipal

---

* Whether, in the result, France, engaged, as she was, in a deadly
struggle, would have carried matters so far with us, may now be doubted ;
but that was the way in which it appeared to the statesmen and people
of the time.

politics), known in our diplomatic records as Messrs. X., Y., and Z., made their appearance and offered to secure an audience and promote the objects of the embassy, upon the condition of ample payments. At last, after very humiliating rebuffs, the Directory refusing to give an audience except through Messrs. X., Y., and Z., or to communicate officially in writing, Messrs. Pinckney and Marshall left Paris, the former going to the south of France for his daughter's health, the latter returning home. Gerry still remained in Paris. For this he was at the time severely blamed. On June 21, 1798, President Adams transmitted to Congress a letter from Gerry, which enclosed correspondence with Talleyrand, the French minister. In his letter of transmittal the President said, "I will never send another minister to France without assurance that he will be received, respected, and honored as the representative of a great, free, powerful, and independent nation." In his message upon the meeting of Congress, in December, 1798, he further said, "To send another minister without more determinate assurances that he would be received, would be an act of humiliation to which the United States ought not to submit. It must, therefore, be left with France (if she is, indeed, desirous of accommodation) to take the requisite steps." To these declarations the country responded heartily.

It was the failure, as charged by his opponents, to duly observe this laudable resolution, which brought Mr. Adams's griefs upon him and went far to wreck the Federalist party forever. Meanwhile the armament of the country went forward. The publication of the correspondence had caused a great outburst of popular indignation, and had for the time immensely strengthened the administration. At the South, particularly, there were large accessions to the Federalist party. This was the period of the Black Cockades and the composition of "Hail, Columbia!" The land forces were increased, Preparations ships of war were built, and the defence of for war. ports and harbors provided for. Vessels of the United States were prohibited from going to the domains of France, or being employed in trade with or for persons residing therein, upon penalty of forfeiture of vessel and cargo. French vessels were not allowed to enter or to remain in the United States without passports, except in cases of distress. War being considered inevitable, Washington was solicited to take command of the army, and with much reluctance accepted the appointment of Lieutenant-General, with Hamilton as Inspector-General and second in rank. The last fact constituted another of President Adams's grievances against his distinguished rival. He alleged that Washington had been induced by an intrigue to demand Hamilton's appointment and his promotion over the gallant revolutionary veteran, Knox, who, in consequence of that indignity, declined his own appointment as Major-General. The ultimate object of the intrigue was supposed to be that, in Washington's infirmity and advanced age, Hamilton would take command of the armies in the field, and thus have an opportunity to prove himself as great in war as he had shown himself in finance.* The President could, of course, refuse no demand of Washington under the circumstances ; but he complied only with the deepest resentment against those whom he believed to have promoted this result.

It would at first seem that a war with France must have been a naval war mainly. But the plans of the

* " Military glory appealed strongly to a sweeping intellect and powerful nature like Hamilton's ; and we may readily believe that he dreamed of extensive conquests and great deeds of arms."—Lodge's Hamilton.

leading spirits among the fighting Federalists were more
far-reaching.   It was upon the possessions of Spain,
along our southern border, that their eager
eyes were fixed.   Spain, to be sure, was at   *Secret de-*
peace with us, but that did not greatly   *signs of the*
                                             war party.
matter; she was an ally of France; and it would be
easy to bring at once to a point the long-standing disputes we had with her regarding the Florida boundary,
the "right of deposit" at New Orleans, and the navigation of the Mississippi.   But not even such extensive
conquests could satisfy the ambition of those who were
now urging on the war with France.   The South
American provinces were believed to be an easy prize.
A restless adventurer, of the true Latin type, Francisco
de Miranda by name, had long cherished the project of
drawing England and the United States into an invasion
of that continent, in which case, it was assumed, the
Spanish dominion there would speedily fall to pieces.
The thought was one well suited to fire Hamilton's
mind; and his soaring plans soon came to embrace this
as at least among the possibilities of the situation.   He
entered into confidential correspondence with Miranda;
and his agents in Mr. Adams's cabinet became all agog
with the notion.   The United States and Great Britain
were not to be allies exactly in this matter.   But there
was to be "co-operation" between them.   The latter
country was to loan the ships to convey the expedition, and to keep open the communications by sea;
the former was to furnish all the land force required—
this last, in order that England might not be in a position to keep too large a share of whatever might be
gained.   Such was the precious scheme in which the
war-federalists proposed to throw to the winds that
neutrality which Washington had so highly valued, and
to embark the new nation in a career of glory and con-

quest.   All of this, however, had not appeared upon the surface.   Ostensibly the object of the government was to resent and resist the encroachments of France.

But a very remarkable change was soon to take place. Though no declaration of war had been made, engagements had occurred at sea and many captures made of American merchantmen, when France unexpectedly intimated, in a very roundabout and hardly decent manner, a willingness again to receive envoys from the United States.   It was what the Federalists, eager for war, regarded as the President's undue haste in the matter, and his choice of envoys especially acceptable to France, which, as we shall see, broke up both his cabinet and the party which had elected him.   We have now, however, only to do with the negotiations thus reopened. In February, 1799, President Adams nominated Mr. Murray as envoy to France ; and subsequently joined The new mission to France. with him in the mission Chief-Justice Ellsworth and William R. Davie, of North Carolina.   Before, however, the embassy could reach Paris, another revolution had taken place ; and a new Directory had obtained control.   After delays, vexatious enough anyway, and certainly not calculated to remove the discredit attaching to previous negotiations, the envoys succeeded in framing a treaty, September 30, 1800, of which the following were the principal stipulations :

The binding force of the old treaties and the mutual claims for indemnities were reserved for future negotiations.

All public ships and all property captured by either party and not yet condemned were to be restored.

All government and individual debts due were to be paid.

The vessels of either party were to enjoy, in the ports

of the other, equal privileges with those of the most favored nation.

The rule of the old treaty, that free ships should make free goods, was retained, except as to articles properly contraband of war.

Provision was also made for the security of American commerce in the future.

On being laid before the Senate, in December, opposition was made by Federalist Senators who were inimical to the President, because the payment of indemnities and the renunciation of the old treaties were not provided for. The result was the adoption of an article limiting the term of the treaty to eight years, as a substitute for the article which referred to indemnities and the former treaties.   When the amended treaty came to be submitted to Bonaparte, then ruling France, he added a proviso that the expunging of the article relating to indemnities, etc., should be considered as a relinquishment of all claims to indemnity.   In this form the treaty was ratified by our government ; and thus France obtained a new treaty without indemnities.   Herein was the origin of one of the most vexed questions of our history, the French Spoliation Claims, which was destined to recur, at intervals, through a period of ninety years.

The French treaty.

Such was the famous French treaty, which was to the administration of Adams, in large measure, what the British treaty had been to the administration of Washington. Of its effects upon the fortunes of Adams and the fate of the Federalist party, we shall speak hereafter. With other countries our relations were generally pacific ; and we were making progress toward a good international position.   A mission to Prussia was created in 1797 ; and John Quincy Adams, the able and accomplished son of the

Other foreign relations.

President, afterward himself the sixth President of the United States, was with general approbation transferred to this post from The Hague, where he had been minister. Near the close of the administration an appropriation was made for the payment of debts due to British subjects from American citizens, which had remained unpaid, in defiance of treaty obligations, by reason of State laws obstructing or denying payment.

The imminence of war with France created fiscal necessities which render important the history of taxation in this administration. To provide necessary funds for national defence, an act was passed at the special session, laying duties on stamped vellum, parchment, and paper. These "Stamp Duties" were graded according to the purposes for which the paper was used or to be used. For example, a piece on which a certificate of naturalization was to be written or printed, was taxed five dollars; a license to practice law, ten dollars; a paper containing the seal of the United States, four dollars; receipts, notes, and other ordinary business instruments, from twenty-five cents to one dollar, according to the amounts for which they were given. Insurance policies, inventories, and protests were all liable to duty. This act proved very obnoxious, its title and its provisions unpleasantly recalling the impositions of Great Britain, against which the colonies had made war. So far is the human mind subject to prejudice! The Stamp Act of George III. had been resisted, not because it was a bad form of tax, but because the patriots denied the right of George III. to levy any kind of tax upon them. If money is to be raised, stamp duties are a very cheap and effective mode of doing it. But men are largely the creatures of names, appearances, and traditions; and the Americans of Adams's administration resented stamp duties enacted

by a Congress of their own choosing, just because their
fathers had in 1765 opposed stamp duties enacted by
the British Parliament. It would have been as reasonable to oppose the issue of stamps for postage. The
President signed the stamp-duties bill with reluctance,
not from any objection to this form of tax, but on account of certain provisions of the bill which he regarded
as intended to make the Secretary of the Treasury his
rival in influence and authority. In the original organization of that department a remarkable variation had
been introduced, by which the Secretary was to report
directly to Congress, instead of to the President as in
the case of other departments. The Stamp-Duties Act
further magnified the authority of the Secretary of the
Treasury, with the purpose, as Mr. Adams conceived, of
diminishing the proper influence of the President.

The proceeds of the stamp duties not proving sufficient, an act was passed at the regular session, 1797-98,
for laying a direct tax of $2,000,000 on The direct tax
real estate and slaves. The enactment of of 1798.
this law, and, still more, the experiences of the Treasury
in collecting the tax, brought out strikingly one of the
principal defects of our revenue system. We have already seen, in reciting the inhibitions of the Constitution, that the United States can lay no duties on exports ; so that here one large source of possible revenue
is struck off at a blow. The Supreme Court having decided that income-taxes are not direct taxes, within the
meaning of the Constitution, this source of revenue is
left to the general government, though it is difficult for
the lay mind to apprehend the reason for the decision
referred to. The provisions of the Constitution regarding direct taxes, again, are such that it might just about
as well have been declared that such taxes should not be
imposed at all. The difficulty in this case is that Con-

10

gress is permitted to levy direct taxes only in proportion to the population of the several States. But since, in a country growing and extending itself as ours has done during the past hundred years, some States, viz., those newly or sparsely settled, will always possess very little accumulated wealth and have very little ready money, the condition referred to practically destroys the value of a direct tax. If the amount of tax were to be made large enough really to bring out the resources of the older and richer States, the newer and poorer States could not pay their share. If, on the other hand, the amount is kept so low as to be within the means of the frontier States, the proceeds for the whole country will be insignificant. This is the dilemma which has always confronted Congress in the enactment of a direct tax. Three times has the general government undertaken to levy such a tax ; but in each case the amount raised was small in proportion to receipts from other sources. In each case the collection of the tax excited bitter opposition. In each case large portions of the tax were left uncollected, after the lapse of years. It would not be a very hazardous prediction that the United States government will never again resort to this mode of raising revenue.

Let us now recur to the direct tax of 1798. The amount, $2,000,000, was apportioned among the States, beginning with Virginia, at $345,489, and going down to Tennessee, the youngest State, at $18,806. Time will not serve to give the details of this tax. A year later, open resistance was made to the law in Pennsyl-

Resistance to the direct tax.

vania, where the measurement of houses was violently opposed. A number of the rioters were arrested, but were rescued by a party of armed horsemen under a man named Fries. Thereupon the President issued a proclamation and made requisition upon the Governor of Pennsylvania for a military force. Fries was tried and convicted of treason. Others were convicted of misdemeanor. All were pardoned, to the great discontent of the Federalists, who demanded that an example should be made. Some of the cabinet were vehement in insisting upon the execution of the sentence against Fries, and deeply resented the President's course.

A case like that of Fries brings up the question, What is fairly to be considered treason in our country ? The Constitution says : "Treason against the United States shall consist only in levying war against them or in adhering to their enemies, giving them aid and comfort." Are riotous acts, in a state otherwise one of peace, aimed only at a particular law or done in resistance to particular acts of executive power, and not seeking the destruction of the government or the dismemberment of its territory, rightly to be considered treason, under the definition of the Constitution ? Such a construction seems to be without reason. Yet we have a series of judicial decisions, by which acts like that of Fries, or even less outrageous, have been declared treasonable. The party in power has always favored the straining of the law ; and the ingenuity of judges has been heavily taxed to make out a case. During the times of anti-slavery excitement, the doctrine of Constructive Treason was invented. It would certainly seem that penalties upon riotous resistance to the law, coupled with full accountability for any deaths occurring in consequence of such acts, could be made sufficiently severe to vindicate the authority of government, without forcing the definition of treason so wisely incorporated in the Constitution.

The preparations for the anticipated contest with France led to the establishment of the Navy Department. During the Revolution, Washington had been command-

er-in-chief of both services ; and the officers of our war-
vessels had been commissioned as officers in the United
States Army. The division of the two ser-

The Navy. vices—the army and the navy—between independent departments, is according to the example of
most nations ; but there are not a few reasons for doubt-
ing its expediency. Benjamin Stoddert, of Maryland,
was appointed Secretary of the Navy. Toward the close
of the second session of the Sixth Congress provision
was made for a naval peace establishment. Apprehensions of a war with France having subsided, the President was authorized to sell all vessels except thirteen.
With President Adams a navy had always been, as he
himself expresses it, a hobby-horse. Jefferson strenuously opposed the formation of a navy. We shall later
see how, in his own administration, he undertook to
deal with the problem of protecting our coasts against
the fleets of Great Britain.

Party spirit had now proceeded to the most extravagant abuse and vituperation. Ferocious denunciations of
the government were heard on every side. Charges and
challenges were hurled across the political arena with a
fury which exceeded the bounds of sanity. The intem-
perance and extravagance of controversy were greatly
enhanced by a few imported foreign editors and pam-
phleteers—Duane, Collot, William Cobbett, and others—
who seemed to find the air of this western continent
peculiarly stimulating. The revolutionary madness of
France, now held firmly in check at home by the masterful grasp of Napoleon, appeared to have overflowed
into England and the United States, to try the utmost
that could be done to defy law, order, and decency. Instead of looking at these ebullitions of democratic frenzy
as a mere passing stage of political development, the
conservative element of both the Anglo-Saxon countries

saw in them the beginning of anarchy, and proceeded to deal with them in the spirit of repression. The Federalists of the United States imitated the Repressive legislation. methods of the Tories of Great Britain, and, by their ill-advised efforts to gag the foul mouth of partisan vituperation, prepared the way for the destruction of their own party. By no instigation of the President, Congress, in 1798, passed two laws, known as the Alien and Sedition Acts, to deal with these abuses.

The Alien Act * was to continue in force two years. It authorized the President to order all such aliens as he should deem dangerous to the peace and The Alien Law. safety of the United States, or should have reasonable grounds to suspect were concerned in any treasonable or secret machinations against the government, to depart out of the country within a given time. Any alien, so ordered to depart, who should be found at large after the time limited, and not having obtained a license to reside in the country, or having obtained such a license had not conformed thereto, was liable to imprisonment not exceeding three years.

The Sedition Law was to expire in 1801. It provided for the punishment, by fine and imprisonment, of persons convicted of combining or con- The Sedition Law. spiring together to oppose any measures of the government directed by proper authority, or impede the operation of any law of the United States, or to intimidate or to prevent any officer under the government from performing his duty ; and secondly, for the punishment, by fine or imprisonment, of any person who

---

* Another Alien Act, passed at about the same time, related to "alien enemies," that is, citizens of countries with which the United States might be at war. This act is still in force Its provisions are unexceptionable. It permits the President in time of war or invasion, after suitable proclamation, to restrain or remove all natives, citizens, denizens, or subjects of governments at war with the United States.

should write, print, utter, or publish, or aid therein, any
false, scandalous, or malicious writing against the government, Congress, or President of the United States,
with intent to defame them, or to bring them into disre-
pute, or to stir up sedition, or to excite unlawful com-
binations for opposing or resisting laws of the United
States, or any act of the President done in accordance
with those laws.   Now, all these offences were already
punishable at common law, in the State courts.   Wherein, then, consisted the obnoxious character of this measure ?   We answer, the statutory enactment of a com-
mon-law principle emphasizes it, renews it, and gives
vigor to the enforcement of what may perhaps have been
for an indefinite period practically obsolete.   In this
case the Sedition Law was understood and accepted by
the opposition as showing the determination of the party
in power to break down the free discussion of its measures and to provide new federal agencies apt and efficient
to that end.   While we admit that, so far as the offenders themselves were concerned, nothing would have been
too bad, considering the foulness of the abuse in which
they indulged, we must assert that repressive measures of
such a character are unworthy of the statesmen of a free
government.   If political blackguardism will not cure
itself, it will never be cured by fines and imprisonment.
As Mr. Jefferson well remarked in his inaugural address,
nothing is more impotent in public affairs than libel.

The blunder of the Federalists in enacting the Sedition Law was not an accidental one.   On the contrary,

The blunder
of the Feder-
alists.

it was thoroughly characteristic.   It sprang
out of a distrust of the masses ; a belief that
the people must always be led or repressed ;
a reliance on powers, estates, and vested interests within
the commonwealth ; a readiness to use force—all of
which were of the very essence of the aristocratic poli-

tics of the last quarter of the eighteenth century. It should be said, however, that, as President Adams had taken no part in making this law, beyond affixing his signature to the bill after it had passed both branches of Congress, so he showed little interest in having the offenders under it prosecuted. The number of cases brought to trial was insignificant, only about six in all.

The Alien and Sedition Laws were generally approved throughout the Federalist districts ; but aroused the most intense opposition on the part of the Republicans, which culminated in the famous Nullification Resolutions of Virginia and Kentucky. The draft of the Kentucky resolutions, which were presented in the legislature of that State by Mr. Nicholas, is known to have been made by Mr. Jefferson. The Virginia resolutions were drawn by Madison, then out of office and living at home. Mr. Madison had Mr. Jefferson's draft of the Kentucky resolutions before him ; but, with his more conservative temperament, modified considerably the declaration of nullification which it contained. Both sets of resolutions occupied themselves at length with the special cases of the Alien and Sedition Laws ; but their importance in our constitutional history is chiefly due to the doctrine enunciated in each, of the right, on the part of any State, to declare and make void within its own limits any law of Congress which it may deem unconstitutional. The language of the Virginia resolutions on this subject is as follows :

" That, in case of a deliberate, palpable, and dangerous exercise of other powers, not granted by the said compact [*i.e.*, the Constitution], the States, who are parties thereto, have the right, and are in duty bound, to interpose, for arresting the progress of the evil and for maintaining, within their respective limits, the authorities, rights, and liberties appertaining to them."

The Kentucky legislature, with less reservation, declared : " That, whensoever the general government assumes undelegated powers, its acts are unauthoritative, void, and of no force . . . that this government created by this compact [*i. e.*, the Constitution], was not made the exclusive or final judge of the extent of the powers delegated to itself, since that would have made its discretion, and not the Constitution, the measure of its powers ; but that, as in all other cases of compact among parties having no common judge, each party has an equal right to judge for itself, as well of infractions * as of the mode and measure of redress."

It must have been a great stress of party passion which could bring two statesmen who had done so much toward the foundation of the republic to put forward views of the Constitution which, if accepted and made good, would have rendered a real nation forever impossible. Mr. Madison, indeed, afterward claimed that there was nothing like nullification in these resolutions ; and spent no little time, during his declining years, in arguing against the construction once universally given to them. But the American people, from Maine to Georgia, were not likely to be mistaken in such a case ; and no student of constitutional history can fail to see in the resolutions of 1798–99 not only the spirit but the full-grown body of the demon, nullification.

The Virginia resolutions were sent, by the legislature which had passed them, to the other States, but met Nullifica- a generally cold reception, while certain of tion repudiat- the State legislatures took the occasion to ed by the other States. denounce their doctrines in most vigorous terms. The Senate and House of Representatives of Delaware contented themselves with declaring : "That they consider the resolutions from the State of Virginia

* That is, as to the fact of an infraction of the Constitution.

as a very unjustifiable interference with the general
government and constituted authorities of the United
States, and of dangerous tendency, and, therefore, not
fit subject for the further consideration of the General Assembly." Rhode Island, however, condescended
to argue the question raised in the nullification resolutions, and in so doing hit the nail squarely on the head
by declaring : " That, in the opinion of this Legislature, the second section of the third article of the Constitution of the United States, in these words, to wit,
' the judicial power shall extend to all cases arising under the laws of the United States,' vests in the Federal
courts, exclusively, and in the Supreme Court of the
United States ultimately, the authority of deciding on
the constitutionality of any act or law of the Congress
of the United States." Other States responded in the
same vein.

The resolution of Rhode Island contains the true constitutional doctrine of the relations of the State and the
nation. When Mr. Jefferson, through the Kentucky
resolutions, declared that State and Nation had "no
common judge," he denied to the Supreme Court of the
United States that great and beneficent function, the
exercise of which has made this country what it is, and
through the continued exercise of which alone can
American nationality be sustained. In a report made to
the Virginia legislature, Mr. Madison, who had then
become a member, probably for that purpose, sought to
break the force of the hostile r sponses from the other
States by declaring, first, that it had not been proposed
that nullification should be resorted to for trivial reasons, but only in case of long-continued and outrageous
violation of the reserved rights of the States ; and, secondly, that nullification should only be resorted to in
cases where the Supreme Court itself had joined with

Congress in approving such violations. Mr. Madison was logically correct in assuming that a situation might conceivably arise in which the Judiciary should join with Congress in flagrant and outrageous invasions of the rights of the States ; and he was also logically correct in stating that, in such a situation, if redress became hopeless, the right to resist these invasions must exist somewhere. But Mr. Madison was both logically and politically in error when he pointed to nullification as the proper resort. In such a situation as he describes, the right to redress wrongs done under the Constitution would lie with the people who established the Constitution which had thus been perverted, and who might, for sufficient reasons, destroy it. The true remedy, then, is not nullification, but rebellion. The latter right always exists ; and no political writer in these days would venture to deny that, if any government, whether a monarchy or a republic, becomes thoroughly and hopelessly perverted from its proper office of serving the interests and the liberties of its people, the people may rise and put it down. This is the doctrine of the Declaration of Independence ; it is the doctrine of modern freedom, the doctrine of common-sense. To inject nullification into a perverted political situation would be to add anarchy to tyranny.

True remedy against usurpation.

The battle over the resolutions of 1798–99 went against the advocates of nullification. That heresy, indeed, was not stamped out. It was even yet to reappear in our politics ; but the great debate which has been hurriedly described destroyed its prestige and greatly crippled its malignant power. When, long years after, it was again asserted, during the fierce contest over the tariff of 1832, it found a people who had been educated to regard the Supreme Court of the United States as " the common judge "

Fatuousness of the resolutions of 1798–99.

between Nation and State. But more remains to be said regarding the resolutions of 1798–99. Had the special friends of the general government been permitted to choose the occasion on which the doctrine of nullification should be put forward, they could not have found another which was so well suited to bring that doctrine into contempt. The Alien and Sedition Laws had furnished the grievance which led Kentucky and Virginia to take this most doubtful and dangerous position ; yet each of these laws was to expire by limitation within three years ; and, in fact, before that term closed, a Congress and a President had been elected intensely hostile to the principles of this legislation, thus putting the renewal or continuance of those laws out of the question. It was against alleged abuses so brief and transient that Jefferson and Madison would have invoked the evil spirit of nullification, which would make stable government and a permanent union impossible. Rather than bear with patience and manly fortitude a wrong, however severe, during a space so short, these two statesmen of the Revolution would have had the nation submit to anarchy in the immediate instance, with civil war in the background.

There remain to be considered certain other acts and events of this administration which had not much to do with the movement of parties and the development of politics, but which still require to be considered. In 1798 was formed the so-called Mississippi Territory, comprising substantially the present States of Mississippi and Alabama ; and, in 1800, the Indiana Territory, comprising substantially the present States of Indiana, Illinois, Michigan, and Wisconsin. The word Territory had now come to be used with a perfectly definite signification, to characterize a region which had not yet become ripe for Statehood ; but which was organized

provisionally, for political purposes, by act of Congress. As such a territory became more densely settled,
it might either be admitted entire, as a State,
with a constitution framed by a convention
of its own people ; or the nearer and more
populous part might be admitted, the remainder being
still left in a territorial condition, to become in time
itself a State.

New territorial organizations.

Congress met in the new capital, on the banks of the
Potomac, November 17, 1800. The name of Washington was given to the permanent seat of government, which had been laid out as a city
by Major l'Enfant, a French engineer in the employ of
the United States. The plan had been drawn on such
an immense scale that Washington was destined to remain for sixty years " a city of magnificent distances,"
with dreary and desolate intervals, and with bad and at
times almost impassable streets. But as, in the wonderful growth of the nation, the outlines of the city
were filled in with comely dwellings and splendid public buildings, Washington was to become one of the
most beautiful capitals of the world.

The new capital.

Congress in 1800 enacted the first bankruptcy law of
the United States. The passage of this law was due to
the fact that the Federalist party comprised
the greater portion of the commercial and
capitalist interests of the country. We shall
see how quickly, when the Republicans came into power
under Jefferson, this law was repealed.

The first bankruptcy law.

In 1800 was taken the second census of the United
States. The total population was ascertained to be
5,308,483. The gain since 1790 had been
thirty-five per cent., a rate of increase which
would allow population to double in twenty-two or
twenty-three years.

The second census.

On December 14, 1799, Washington died at Mount Vernon, after a brief illness. Although definitively retired from public life, his presence with his countrymen had been a force continually operating for union, peace, and harmony. His removal was a blow to the new nation, which needed his influence hardly less in those stormy times than in some of the more manifest crises of our history. It does not need to be said that the death of Washington moved the country profoundly, and that he was mourned by all classes and all sections.

Death of Washington.

Our narrative from this point has to deal with ever-deepening divisions among the Federalists; and first let us speak of the split in the cabinet. It has been stated that Mr. Adams retained the Secretaries who had been left in office by Washington. This fact proved to be the spring and fountain of un-numbered woes. It was distinctly bad policy. A new President should have a new cabinet all his own, each member owing his place to the distinct preference of his chief. Men left over from a former administration can-not be expected to be as loyal and single-minded as if they had been called to office fresh from the people or from congressional life. But the objection to the reten-tion of the members of a previous cabinet rises to a maximum where the late President has been of tran-scendent fame and power, like Washington. In such a case the retained Secretaries, being human, could hardly fail to feel as if the traditions of the government were in their keeping, and as if the fact that they had been the confidential advisers of such a man gave them a cer-tain authority and influence above what belonged to them personally. We might have supposed that Mr. Adams retained his predecessor's Secretaries, not so much out of deference to Washington as on account of

An inherited cabinet.

the scarcity of "cabinet timber" (Washington having been, at the last, not a little troubled to get anybody at all to serve in this capacity), were it not that Mr. Adams has himself stated that at the beginning he had no objection to any of these officers and entertained no thought of removing them.* Mr. Adams afterward came to consider this the great mistake of his administration. His subsequent troubles he attributed largely to the members of his cabinet, whom he regarded as disposed not only openly to domineer over him, but secretly to intrigue against him.

That at least three of Mr. Adams's cabinet were, during the greater part of his term of office, in close correspondence with a person whom Mr. Adams regarded as his rival, if not his enemy; that they communicated to that person and to others information which Mr. Adams did not desire communicated, and which was intended to be used against him; and that his Secretaries did frequently invoke, as the means of restraining him in his fixed purposes, influences which Mr. Adams deprecated as prejudicial to his interests and disparaging to his dignity: these things cannot be questioned. It does not need to be said that nothing would justify such action except some great emergency involving the safety of the nation. Circumstances may, indeed, be conceived where cabinet officers would rightly deem it their duty to "stick" (as Senator Sumner wrote to Secretary Stanton), and to perform such an odious and offensive part as the sole means of checking designs immediately dangerous to the liberties or the life of their country. Such an emergency, for instance, existed in the last year of Mr.

The secretaries intrigue against the President.

---

* Before his inauguration he had written: "Pickering and all his colleagues are as much attached to me as I desire. I have no jealousies from that quarter."

Buchanan's administration, while the war of secession was impending. But no claim of this kind can be put forward in behalf of Mr. Adams's Secretaries. The President was as honest and brave a man as ever lived ; he was deeply devoted to the interests of his country.

But while nothing can justify the actions recited, several things may be adduced to qualify the condemnation to be pronounced. In the first place, these gentlemen had an overweening sense of their own importance from having been the advisers of Washington, and regarded themselves as being, in a certain sense, the depositories of the first President's opinions, wishes, and plans. Had they been greater men themselves, they would probably have been less puffed up by that relationship. In the second place, they appear to have been much influenced by a view of their official position which made them out to be, not the President's confidential advisers and supporters, bound to be loyal to him so long as they remained in his cabinet, but as persons having a claim upon a share of the executive office. In the third place, they were all deeply under the influence of Mr. Hamilton ; looked up to him as the great light of their party and its true leader ; and deceived themselves into a feeling that their allegiance was to him rather than to Mr. Adams, whom they regarded as smashing the Federalist crockery by his bungling obstinacy. Finally, it should be said that the traditions of the government were then unformed, and the ethics of cabinet office were not well understood. Nowadays such a course would be impossible in the case of any man of character.

This matter of the relations of President Adams to his cabinet would not justify so much attention, were it of personal interest only ; but the condition of things we have recited became no inconsiderable part of the causes which transferred the control of the country to the opposition party and changed the history of the United States. Mr. Hamilton had been profoundly disaffected by the action of the President in seeking to avert war with France. He sincerely believed that the time for war had fully come; but it was his own personal ambitions which drove him on to thwart and injure Mr. Adams in Congress and before the country. Hamilton had no thought of his own election; that was clearly impossible. But he believed that by joining with Mr. Adams in the nomination * some moderate Federalist of high standing who should be unobjectionable to any of the party, he might then, by influencing the votes in the Electoral Colleges, throw Mr. Adams out. For this purpose he selected General Charles C. Pinckney, of South Carolina, of whom it is sufficient to say in a word that he was entirely incapable of being a party to such an intrigue. In furtherance of his plan Mr. Hamilton, in 1800, made a tour through New England, where he found the people little disposed to sacrifice Mr. Adams.

Hamilton's opposition to Adams.

It was at about this point that the President became sufficiently aware of the situation to determine him to part with two of his Secretaries. Mr. Mc-Henry, the head of the War Department, had been, on all accounts, the least satisfactory member of the cabinet, while he had been very active in the intrigues of Hamilton. Colonel Pickering was a man of far higher ability; but his antagonism to the President's policy had become so pronounced that Mr. Adams sought and obtained his resignation also. Mr. Wolcott, however, still remained in office, the President entertaining no doubt of his fidelity. The charge of suspiciousness,

Disruption of the cabinet.

---

* It is to be remembered that, at this time, each elector voted for two persons, without designating which he intended to make President.

so frequently made against Mr. Adams, seems almost ludicrous in view of the fact that he had for years retained in his "political family" three men who were in immediate communication with his great rival. The place of Colonel Pickering was taken by John Marshall, of Virginia, soon to become Chief-Justice ; and that of Mr. McHenry by Samuel Dexter, of Massachusetts. Both of these appointments were of a high order. Had Mr. Adams possessed such advisers from the first, his administration might have had a different issue. Mr. Wolcott held on until November, in the meantime furnishing confidential information to Mr. Hamilton, for the express purpose of its being used against Mr. Adams. Upon his resignation Mr. Dexter was transferred to the Treasury ; and, a little later, Roger Griswold, of Connecticut, was made Secretary of War.

Finding himself foiled in his efforts to secure, in advance, by personal and private communications and arrangements, the substitution of General Pinckney for Mr. Adams in the coming election ; irritated at some of the rebuffs he had received ; made doubly angry with Mr. Adams because there was so little that could be alleged against him ; borne on by his overweening ambition, Mr. Hamilton proceeded to the extraordinary step of issuing a pamphlet against the President, just on the eve (October, 1800) of the election, in which Mr. Adams was to be the candidate of his own party. The pamphlet was entitled, " Letter from Alexander Hamilton, concerning the public conduct and character of John Adams, Esq., President of the United States." It severely reflected upon the President for his pardon of Fries and for his initiation of the new mission to France, matters certainly within the discretion of the chief magistrate of a nation. For the rest, the pamphlet contained little more than accusations against Mr. Adams of an im-

11

practicable spirit, of an inordinate vanity, of imperfections of temper. Even so, Mr. Hamilton did not reach the result of advising his countrymen to vote against Mr. Adams. A more "lame and impotent conclusion" was never seen. The publication was an act of spite and angry impatience

Hamilton's fatuous pamphlet.

and aimless rage, which are only matter of sorrow when one remembers the services of the author to the cause of American independence and union, and his transcendent abilities. A little more of the greatness of soul which lifted Washington and Jay so high in the esteem of their countrymen, would have prevented this painful exhibition.

It was under auspices so unfavorable, with internal divisions and intrigues so discreditable, that the Federalist party went into the fourth presidential election, to fight a losing battle. With the single exception of the public indignation aroused by the conduct of the French Directory, which has been recited, the drift had been steadily against them. The country was every year becoming more democratic. The Republican party was a unit, controlled by a masterly politician, who was now to be for the second time its candidate for the presidency ; while in the cardinal State of New York,* on which the coming national election was to turn, Mr.

The fourth presidential election.

Jefferson had as his political manager an able, brilliant, and unscrupulous man, the soon-to-be-forever infamous Aaron Burr, in whom strong ambition joined with intense hatred of Hamilton to induce him to strain every nerve to detach that now wavering State from its traditional allegiance to Federalist principles. As the leading Federalists had too well

* The Republicans had carried the city in 1798, and early in 1800 carried the State in the Gubernatorial election. The political organization of that party in the city was then almost as complete and effective as in these later days.

foreseen, their party was doomed to defeat. New York, which before had voted for Adams, transferred its votes to Jefferson and Burr, who received, in all, seventy-three votes each, against sixty-five for Adams and sixty-four for C. C. Pinckney.

The Republicans triumph —Adams defeated.

It had been thought that South Carolina might possibly change the result by casting her electoral votes for her own son, Pinckney, while rejecting Adams, just as, four years before, she had voted for the other Pinckney, then the Federalist candidate for Vice-President, while voting also for Jefferson. Indeed, it was charged that precisely this had been Mr. Hamilton's expectation and the purpose of his efforts. He had strongly urged the northern Federalists to vote for Pinckney and not to throw away a single ballot. In fact they had done so, with the exception of one vote given to John Jay by Rhode Island. But if Mr. Hamilton really expected South Carolina to vote for Pinckney, while voting also for Jefferson, he was disappointed, as that State gave an equal vote to the Republican candidates. General Pinckney throughout refused to be a party to the plot to bring himself in, instead of Mr. Adams. There had been but one other opportunity to avert the impending result. Hamilton had written to Jay, then Governor of New York, urging that, inasmuch as the State had gone Republican, the legislature, which, though adjourned for the year, had still some weeks of its legal term unexpired, should be called together, in special session, to anticipate the action of its successors and provide for the choice of Electors by congressional districts. This letter the high-minded Governor filed away, with the endorsement, "Proposing a measure for party purposes, which I think it would not become me to adopt."

But, while the Republicans had defeated their opponents they had not themselves elected anyone either President or Vice-President, owing to the absurd provision of the Constitution already mentioned. The election had resulted in a tie. The contest was, therefore, according to the Constitution, thrown into the House of Representatives, where each State was to have one vote. The number of States being now sixteen, nine were necessary for a choice. Here was a situation which gave room for those great talents for intrigue which afterward made Burr so evilly famous. He believed that the Federalists would rather have him President than Jefferson ; and he determined to betray his party and his own chief and secure the glittering prize for himself. Such a contest was an immorality. Burr's action was simply rascally. The course of the Federalists in Congress, who were willing to vote for him in order to defeat Jefferson, was bad enough, though it did not involve personal or party infidelity. For a while it seemed as though Burr would succeed in his design. The balloting continued about a week without choice, Jefferson receiving the votes of New York, New Jersey, Pennsylvania, Virginia, North Carolina, Georgia, Kentucky, and Tennessee ; Burr receiving those of New Hampshire, Massachusetts, Rhode Island, Connecticut, Delaware, and South Carolina. Vermont and Maryland were divided. The Federalists, with but two or three exceptions, voted steadily for Burr. At last, a growing sense of the impropriety of the Federalist course, and an increasing savor from Burr's bad fame, combined with the fear that March 4th might come without an election, put an end to this disgraceful contest. On the thirty-sixth ballot the Federalist member from Vermont purposely stayed away, while the Maryland Federalists cast blank ballots in their State delegation. As a re-

The election thrown into the House— Burr's intrigue.

sult, Jefferson was elected by the votes of ten States,
Burr becoming Vice-President.

Such was the outcome of the fourth presidential election, which effected a most important change of direction in the politics of the United States.   Causes of
The downfall of the Federalist party had the Federalist
been due, first, to mistaken legislation, as in downfall.
the case of the Alien and Sedition Laws, to divided councils, and to jealousies and animosities among its leaders ;
secondly, to the remarkable political astuteness and sagacity of Mr. Jefferson, and to the unrelenting persist-
ency with which for twelve years he followed out his ideas
and purposes ; thirdly, to the organized power of the
first New York Democratic " machine," under Aaron
Burr ; and lastly to a steady change which had been
going on in the body of the American people in the
direction of democracy.   That change had in it much
that was good.   The distrust of " the plain people," to
use the phrase of President Lincoln, the unwillingness
to believe in the essential patriotism, justice, and honesty
of the masses, which had been so freely avowed in the
Constitutional Convention of 1787, and which throughout had profoundly affected the Federalist policy ; the
reliance upon estates and powers within the commonwealth, which was of the very essence of Hamilton's
philosophy of government, and in which even Washington and John Adams shared ; the disposition to resort, on one side, to the influence of wealth, and on
the other, to intimidation and repression for checking
the violence of political discussion : these things were
to disappear, and disappear forever, from American public life.   For good or for evil, but altogether, as we may
well believe, for good, in the large, the long result, the
American people had taken the direction of more pure
and intense democracy ; and the nation was hereafter

to be governed by men who professed to believe and in general did believe, in the integrity, honesty, and patriotism of the masses. From the time of the defeat of the Federalists onward, no man, of whatsoever party, could long hold a conspicuous place in American public life while avowing sentiments such as had been in a high degree characteristic of those to whom the destinies of the nation were at first entrusted. All this we may well believe to have been of good. On the other hand, the incoming party, alike through reaction and through lowness of aims and ideas on the part of many leaders, was long to manifest a jealousy of wealth and culture, a preference for mean motives and unworthy arts, and even a disposition to truckle to the dishonest elements of society, especially in matters of financial legislation, which cannot be too severely condemned.

For the defeat of the Federalist party Mr. Adams long had to bear the chief blame. Mr. Hamilton and the late President's Secretaries did not cease to declare that it was Mr. Adams's vanity, wilfulness and obstinacy, and especially his disregard of their advice and influence, which had brought about the disaster. And this view has, thinkingly or unthinkingly, been adopted by most writers on the history of that time. But at this distance we may well inquire who made Mr. Hamilton a ruler and a judge over Mr. Adams? Both through his official position and through the wider confidence reposed in Mr. Adams than in Mr. Hamilton by the mass of the Federalist party, the President was far better entitled to decide upon the policy of the administration than was his great rival or his small critics. Certainly in the greatest matter of all, impending war with France, Mr. Adams took the more sagacious and the more patriotic part. With respect to the Alien and Sedition Laws he had no responsibility, except for not vetoing bills which had been passed without any initiative or impulse from him.   Mr. Adams had undoubtedly faults of bearing, of manner, and in some *The degree of Mr. Adams's responsibility.* degree, also, of character.   But his name will go down to the later generations of his countrymen as that of one of the most brave, loyal, and pure-minded among the statesmen of the early republic. In one quality he surpassed them all, except only Washington, in that he had neither Gallican nor Anglican sympathies.   An unfriendly critic might indeed say that he hated both England and France equally ; but at any rate, and this was a virtue in those times, he was neither for one nor for the other, but for America, first, last, and all the time, holding every other nation friend or foe according as its power was exerted for the welfare or the injury of his own country.

But while the Republicans thus triumphed, Mr. Adams was yet, in the closing hours of his administration, to perform an act which should have a great influence upon the destinies of the United States through a long future.   On January 31st, Judge Ellsworth having resigned his office, John Marshall became Chief-Justice, an event second to but few in our history.   Marshall had nothing to do with *John Marshall, Chief-Justice.* making the written Constitution.   Perhaps no man has had so much to do with making the Constitution as it really is.   For thirty-four years Chief-Justice, it is to him, more than to all other judges, we owe that splendid series of judicial decisions—masterly, comprehensive, and overwhelming—which have established American nationality upon an impregnable basis.

CHAPTER IX

JEFFERSON'S FIRST TERM

Twelfth Amendment to the Constitution—Alleged Corrupt Bargain
—Removal of Officeholders—Repeal of the Circuit Courts Bill
—War on the Judiciary—Impeachment of Judges Addison,
Chase and others—Admission of Ohio—Reapportionment of
Representation—Military Academy Founded—Repeal of Excise
Duties—Naturalization—Repeal of Bankruptcy Act—Florida
and Louisiana—Spain Cedes Louisiana to France—Napoleon
Sells it to the United States—Political Consequences of this
Measure—Republican Party Surrenders Principle of Strict
Construction—Difficulty with Spain—Abortive Treaty with
England—Changes in the Cabinet—Re-election of Jefferson—
Burr Kills Hamilton.

THE country had borne long enough with the stupid
provision regarding the choice of President and Vice-
President. Such a source of mischief and annoyance
could no longer be tolerated. Accordingly, Congress
The Twelfth proposed the Twelfth Amendment to the Con-
Amendment stitution, which provided that, in the electoral
to the Consti-
tution. ballots, persons voted for as President should
be distinctly named, and likewise the persons voted for
as Vice-President ; and that separate lists of all persons
voted for as President and of all persons voted for as
Vice-President, with the number of votes for each, should
be sent to the President of the Senate. In case no person had received the votes for President of a majority of
the whole number of electors appointed, then from the
persons having the highest numbers, not exceeding
three, on the list of those voted for, the House of Representatives should elect the President. But in choosing

the President the votes should be taken by States, the representation from each State having one vote. The quorum for this purpose should consist of a member or members from two-thirds of the States ; and a majority of all the States should be necessary to a choice. Should the House fail thus to choose a President before the fourth day of March, then the Vice-President should act as President. In like manner should no person receive the votes of a majority of the whole number of electors appointed, for Vice-President, then, from the two highest on the list, the Senate should choose the Vice-President ; a quorum for the purpose to consist of two-thirds of the whole number of Senators, and a majority of the whole number to be necessary to a choice. The amendment thus proposed was ratified and became a part of the Constitution.

Let us now consider the civil service under Mr. Jefferson. Congress having, just before the close of Mr. Adams's administration, provided for additional officers —judges, attorneys, and marshals, in connection with a large extension of the United States courts * —Mr. Adams proceeded, during the last three weeks of his term, to make appointments for these offices, mainly out of his own immediate supporters. These appointments were continued up to the last day. One dramatic story, with perhaps more of poetry than of truth, represents Mr. Adams as engaged in signing commissions until the clock struck twelve on the night of the third of March. Hence the term "midnight," as applied to this whole batch of appointments. Even the Federalists could hardly blame Mr. Jefferson for refusing to consider himself bound by commissions issued thus in the last hours of a dying administration.

> Mr. Adams's "midnight" appointments.

* It was by this act that the Circuit Courts of the United States were established.

Mr. Jefferson, however, in not a few cases, issued new commissions to the persons selected by Mr. Adams.

But the President was subjected to censure for his dealings with public offices, at this time, in two other respects. It was charged, and deposition to that effect was formally made, by James A. Bayard, of Delaware, afterward Senator from that State, and one of the Commissioners who negotiated the treaty of peace with Great Britain, in 1814, to the effect that, while the presidential election was pending in the House of Representatives, he sought and obtained, through General Smith, assurances from Mr. Jefferson that, if elected, he would not, on political grounds, disturb "subordinate public officers employed only in the execution of details established by law." Among those specifically mentioned by Mr. Bayard, in conversation with General Smith, were the collectors of customs at Philadelphia and Wilmington. That assurance proving sufficient, according to Mr. Bayard's deposition, "the opposition of Vermont, Maryland, and Delaware was immediately withdrawn, and Mr. Jefferson was made President by the votes of ten States." This charge produced a great sensation at the time ; but, looking back upon the situation, we may see how the circumstances could have arisen without any thought of a corrupt bargain on Mr. Jefferson's part. General Smith might naturally enough have asked Mr. Jefferson if it was in accordance with his views that subordinate officers charged by law with precise duties should be removed on political grounds. If General Smith had asked the question of Mr. Jefferson, that gentleman would assuredly have given but one answer, a decided "No." This, being communicated to Mr. Bayard, might easily have satisfied that gentleman and his friends, and have led to the result stated. The whole tenor of Mr. Jefferson's

The alleged corrupt bargain.

life is so strongly adverse to anything like a corrupt bargain that no shadow of imputation from this source should rest upon his name.

Mr. Jefferson did, however, shortly after his inauguration, give cause for some complaints by his removal of civil officers fairly belonging to the class characterized by Mr. Bayard. The case which caused the greatest scandal was the displacement of Elizur Goodrich, as collector at New Haven, and the appointment of an aged and infirm man to the position. Upon this the merchants of that city addressed a remonstrance to the President. In his reply, Mr. Jefferson insisted upon the propriety of his action ; and, in closing his letter, made use of the expression which afterward became so famous, "that state of things when the only questions concerning a candidate shall be, is he honest ? is he capable ? is he faithful to the Constitution ?" However virtuously Mr. Jefferson might write, he in fact made not a few removals upon partisan grounds. Yet that number was ludicrously small in comparison with what we have become accustomed to in the later days of the republic. A good, smart assistant-postmaster-general, of these times, would not think he had earned his luncheon if he had not taken off more heads in one morning than Mr. Jefferson did in eight years.

Partisan removals from office.

The natural antagonism of the Republican party to any extension of the jurisdiction or any magnifying of the authority of the national judiciary, combined with the indignation aroused by the judicial appointments made by President Adams in the last hours of his administration, secured an early repeal of the law establishing the Circuit Courts of the United States and creating a new body of judges and law officers therefor. The repeal was the more easily effected because it was shown that the business of the national courts was not increasing in a degree to require this addition to the judicial system. But the wrath of the Republicans was not satisfied by this measure ; and the representatives of that party proceeded to something like war upon the judiciary, under cover of the constitutional power of impeachment.

The war upon the judiciary.

Pennsylvania led off in this direction by impeaching and removing one of her own Federalist judges, Addison, a man of the highest character and ability. In 1804 the House of Representatives, at Washington, impeached and secured the conviction and removal, for good and sufficient cause, it must be confessed, of a District Judge of the United States, Pickering ; and then proceeded, under the instigation of the President, to the impeachment of Judge Chase, of the Supreme Court, whose bearing in the cases under the Sedition Law had been deeply resented. That Judge Chase had done much which was properly the subject of animadversion was undeniable ; but there is reason to believe that the impeachment was really for the purpose of intimidating the national judiciary in general, and diminishing the influence which this new force was exerting in moulding the Constitution and shaping the development of the nation. The trial,* poorly conducted by John Randolph on behalf of the impeaching House, resulted in the acquittal of Judge Chase on most of the eight articles, while on none did the vote for conviction reach the required two-thirds. This most fortunate result terminated a movement which, had it been carried as far as its promoters desired, might have broken the spirit of the national judiciary and seriously impaired its great and beneficent function in the develop-

* It seems strange to read that at this trial Aaron Burr, then under indictment for the murder of Hamilton, presided over the Senate, by virtue of his office as Vice-President.

ment of the nation.   The Legislature of Pennsylvania, indeed, sought to pursue this war upon Federalist judges, and impeached three judges of the Supreme Court of that State ; but here again the requisite two-thirds vote for conviction could not be obtained.   Probably these rude assaults upon the judiciary, both State and national, were not altogether without an effect for good, in teaching our judges to be careful regarding the display of partisanship upon the bench ; but, while we may not wonder at the vindictiveness of the triumphant Republicans toward those who had been engaged in the odious prosecutions under the now extinct Federalist *régime*, we may rejoice that the issue was so far nugatory as to leave the judiciary independent and in unimpaired efficiency.   Even in the height of this crusade no responsible Republican had dared to attempt to reconstitute the Supreme Court or to take away any part of its jurisdiction, though there were many men prominent in that party who would have delighted to do so, had they not been restrained by the fear of weakening the hold of their party upon the northern States.   These men saw " the writing on the wall," although even then, perhaps, they did not fully realize the extent of the influence which the Supreme Court, under the Chief-Justiceship of Marshall, was to exert in moulding the Constitution and building up a real nation.

It was in this administration that the great and splendid State of Ohio was added to the Union.   No citizen of the republic can glance over the history of the nation, and not be thrilled as he con- Ohio a State. templates the part which this State has played in that mighty drama, both in war and in peace ; and as he reads the roll of its great men, its judges, its generals,*

---

* To speak of generals only, Ohio produced Grant, Sherman, Sheridan, Buell, McPherson, McDowell, Rosecrans, D. S. Stanley, and A. D. McCook.

its statesmen. The population of Ohio at the date of its admission was only 45,365. It is now nearly one hundred times as much.

In the reapportionment of representation in Congress which followed the second census, the total number of Reapportion- members of the House was increased from ment. 105 to 141, the ratio taken being one representative to 33,000 people. The number assigned to each State was as follows: New Hampshire, 5; Massachusetts, 17; Vermont, 4; Rhode Island, 2; Connecticut, 7; New York, 17; New Jersey, 6; Pennsylvania, 18; Delaware, 1; Maryland, 9; Virginia, 22; North Carolina, 12; South Carolina, 8; Georgia, 4; Kentucky, 6; Tennessee, 3. From the foregoing it will appear that there were now four distinctly large States which, together, sent 72 representatives to Congress, or more than one-half the total number. We have also to note that there was no proper group of States of the second rank, North Carolina, with twelve, being the only State which had more than nine and fewer than seventeen representatives.

It was in this administration that the Military Academy, destined to such a glorious career, was established The Military at West Point. It may with confidence be Academy. asserted that no equally successful school is known to history. When the war of 1861–65 broke out, there were probably fewer living graduates of West Point than of Williams, Dartmouth, or Amherst; yet out of this small number arose a Grant, a Lee, a Sherman, a Meade, a Jackson, a Thomas, the two Johnstons, a Hancock, a Longstreet, a Reno, a Reynolds, and a Sheridan, not to mention scores of others who commanded divisions and corps with a skill, courage, and address which have excited the admiration of the professional soldiers of Europe.

We now come to a series of legislative measures which, while they do not seem, on the face of them, of a partisan character, were all essentially involved in the downfall of the Federalists and in the accession to power of the more democratic party.   The first of these was the repeal of the internal duties imposed in the   The repeal administrations of Washington and Adams.   of internal duties. This was done, not as a matter of expediency, but as a matter of preference and definite policy.   It was not alone because the whiskey tax and the stamp duties had aroused public opposition, even to the point of armed rebellion ; it was in a far higher degree because Mr. Jefferson's party, and particularly Mr. Jefferson himself, hated internal duties and eschewed them as any proper part of the revenue system of the United States, that it was perfectly safe, on March 4, 1801, to predict that these laws would not long remain on the statute-book.   The repeal was effected by an act approved April 6, 1802 ; and the United States were thus thrown back upon customs and the sale of public lands as their principal sources of revenue.   The loss of revenue Mr. Jefferson hoped to see partly compensated by an increase in the customs duties, and partly provided for by a reduction of expenses all along the line, but especially at the cost of the army, the navy, and the judiciary.   All these services were subjected to a searching retrenchment, which was bitterly resented by the victims and by the now helpless Federalists.   The anticipated increase of receipts from customs did not take place within the time allowed, so that the readjustment of expenditures and income was mainly effected by reductions in the military and civil list.   In the retrenchments proposed at the outset of Mr. Jefferson's administration, because of the loss of revenue from internal duties and for the sake of diminishing the patronage of the general government, it was even proposed to abolish the mint. It was disagreeable to the extreme opponents of national power, headed by John Randolph, to see the emblems and insignia of sovereignty circulating among the people, even though it were in no more impressive form than copper cents, then practically our sole coinage. These statesmen desired to have foreign coins used in our currency, that the people might not be daily reminded that there was a nation.

Another measure of Mr. Jefferson's first Congress was not less expressive of the sentiments and purposes of the Republican party. On the inauguration of government it had become necessary to define the terms on which foreigners should be admitted to citizenship. By an act of 1790 an alien might become a citizen after two years' residence, upon application to the proper courts of any State in which he had resided one year. By an act of 1795, in Washington's second term, five years' residence was required, application to be made three years before admission. In Mr. Adams's administration distrust and dislike of foreigners had become almost a characteristic virtue of the Federalists ; and, in 1798, the year of the Alien and Sedition Laws, an act was passed requiring not less than fourteen years' residence, application to be made five years previous to admission. Moreover, this act, in the very spirit of the obnoxious Alien Law, placed under surveillance all white aliens who resided or who should arrive in the United States, requiring such persons to be reported and registered. It is not to be wondered at that the accession to power of the Republican party, which had always been exceedingly favorable to foreigners, led to the early repeal of a rule of naturalization so severe, inhospitable, and almost proscriptive, as that which the Federalists had set up. Eight days after the repeal of the

internal duties, Congress restored the term of residence
to what it had been by the act of 1795.

But even more expressive still of the affiliations, sentiments, and purposes of the party newly come to power,
was the act of December 19, 1803, by which The repeal
Congress repealed the general bankruptcy of the bankruptcy law.
law of 1800. Although no power of the
general government was more explicitly and unreservedly granted in the Constitution, the Republican, or
Democratic, party has always been unfavorable, both in
the early and in the latter days of the republic, to the
exercise of this power. Mr. Jefferson himself had a
peculiar animosity to bankruptcy laws, growing out
of his dislike of commerce, to which allusion has been
made. " Is commerce so much the basis of the existence of the United States as to call for a bankruptcy
law?" he writes. "On the contrary, are we not almost merely agricultural? Should not all laws be
made with a view, essentially, to the poor husbandmen?" Those same "poor husbandmen" have been
made the excuse for a good deal of rascality in the
United States. The bankruptcy system was doomed
when Mr. Jefferson was elected President; and by act
of December 9, 1803, Congress repealed the law of 1800,
throwing the credit and commerce of the country back
upon the widely varying, inconsistent, and often dishonest legislation of the several States.

Such were some of the measures of internal policy
which signalized the accession of the Republican [Democratic] party to power for the first time, in 1801. Let
us now consider the course of foreign affairs in the earlier part of Jefferson's administration. Al- The Spanish
though by the heroic enterprises of Ponce de power.
Leon and Fernando de Soto, the Spaniards were the
discoverers of both the Floridas (East and West) and of

12

Louisiana ; and although the organization of our government found that power in possession of these vast territories, the Spanish occupation had not been continuous. France had, prior to the close of the Seven Years' War, 1756–63, asserted and maintained her claim to Louisiana; and when France and Spain, the conquered in that struggle of giants, came to make terms with victorious England, Spain was obliged to relinquish the Floridas to England, while France indemnified her ally and companion in misfortune by the cession of Louisiana. England was not, however, long to be left in possession of her conquests at the South. The close of the Revolutionary War, 1783, found her glad to accept peace on less favorable terms than in 1763, and Florida returned to Spain. The same treaty bounded the possessions of the United States upon the west by the Mississippi River. We have already referred to the difficulties which the new government encountered in dealing with Spain respecting the navigation of the Mississippi and the right to land and store goods at New Orleans. Undoubtedly one great reason for the value which Spain, and afterward France, was disposed to put upon the lower Mississippi, was found in the expectation, not extravagant at the time, that a confederation would yet be formed in the great valley, the patron and protector of which would naturally be that power which could give or withhold access to the sea. To European diplomatists and statesmen the Alleghenies appeared a barrier to sovereignty not easily to be passed. By Louisiana is here to be understood not merely the present State of that name, but the vast region west of the Mississippi, extending from the Gulf of Mexico northward to the British possessions, westward at least as far as the Rocky Mountains.

In 1800, by a secret treaty, Spain ceded back to

France the Louisiana which she had received from her by the treaty of 1763. Rumors of this negotiation having reached Washington, our ministers at Madrid and Paris were instructed to oppose the cession by every argument in their power. The French government, however, persistently denied the fact of such a cession for more than a year. It then became known that an expedition, under General Victor, was fitting out to take possession of the province. At this juncture President Jefferson appointed Mr. Monroe to be an associate of Mr. Livingston, our minister at Paris, and also, if necessary, of Mr. Pinckney at Madrid. The instructions were to prevent the cession of the Floridas and of New Orleans. But before Mr. Monroe's arrival negotiations of a surprising character were begun, which were destined to end these difficulties in a manner altogether unexpected and with consequences the most tremendous. The French Minister of the Treasury, Marbois, proposed nothing less than the cession of Louisiana. Mr. Livingston was not prepared for such a stroke of business; but, on the arrival of Mr. Monroe, the vast importance of the set- *The purchase of Louisiana.* tlement so pressed upon the ministers of the United States that they assumed the responsibility of transcending their instructions, and on April 30, 1803, concluded a treaty by which France ceded to the United States the whole vast territory of Louisiana, "forever and in full sovereignty." The consideration for the cession was 60,000,000 francs and the relinquishment of debts due by France to citizens of the United States, amounting to about fifteen millions more. Napoleon's reasons for thus alienating an empire can only be conjectured. Most probably the dominating consideration was an apprehension that, in the then impending war, an English fleet would seize New Orleans and thus practically control the Mississippi Valley.   Moreover, it is to be said that the First Consul's thoughts were at this period almost wholly engrossed by his plans of conquest and glory in the Orient.   Egypt, Constantinople, and India had become the immediate objects of his high-soaring ambition.   On the other hand was the possibility that, should he cede Louisiana to the United States, it might become the means of embroiling us with England, which would give him a new ally.   Then there was the fact of a large money payment to be made at once, a welcome addition to his finances.   Finally, we are not to forget the levity, petulance, and fickleness which mingled so strangely with the greatness and daring of Napoleon's mind.

Although the treaty was contrary to the instructions of our ministers, and also, as the dominant party in the government was bound to believe, contrary to the Constitution, yet, in view of the supreme importance of the transaction, it was promptly ratified by the Senate ; and the necessary steps taken for the temporary government of the territory, and for the payment of the consideration.   An act of 1804 organized the Territory of Orleans (the present State of Louisiana) and the District of Louisiana, the latter having its principal settlement at St. Louis.   It has been said that the dominant political party in the government, viz., the Republican party, was bound to hold this acquisition of territory unconstitutional.   Not only can no authority be found in the Constitution, through any exercise of a strict construction, for such an acquisition of territory without the consent of the States parties to the original compact; but the palpable, necessary consequences of this acquisition, through its effect upon the membership of the Union and upon the "balance of power" within the government, were so overwhelming as to amount to almost a revolution.

Political significance of the Louisiana purchase.

We have seen that, in the Convention of 1787, grave apprehensions were expressed lest the States to be formed from the territory west of the Alleghenies should, in time, weigh down the Atlantic States ; and it was even proposed to set a limit to the total number of members who should ever be admitted to Congress from that region. Yet here was a new territory, of a million square miles, which did not belong to us and never had belonged to us ; which, so far as occupied at all, was settled by other races than our own ; and Mr. Jefferson had undertaken, upon his own motion and notion, to say that this vast territory should become a part of the United States forever ; and that its inhabitants should be " incorporated in the Union of the United States and admitted as soon as possible, according to the principles of the Federal Constitution, to the enjoyment of all the rights, advantages, and immunities of citizens of the United States." If we look at the usurpation of authority involved in framing such a treaty, it may fairly be said that all the encroachments which had been in contemplation by any member of the Constitutional Convention, as to be apprehended from the executive, were child's play in comparison. On the other hand, if we look at the practical consequences of this treaty, as affecting the future membership of the Union, as threatening the rights and powers of the original parties * to the " federal compact," and as bearing upon the balance of power within the government, we shall not the less admit this measure to have been of an absolutely revolutionary character. The original thirteen States comprised about half a million square miles ; and we have seen that they felt grave apprehensions lest their rights

* John Randolph had refused to vote even for the admission of Ohio on the ground that the admission of a new party without the consent of the original members constituted an infraction of the compact between the States.

and proper influence should, in time, be overborne in Congress by votes from the trans-Appalachian territory, which was of nearly equal extent. Yet here we have a new territory, equal to both halves of the original country, brought into the Union by act of the executive, with the assent of a Senate not especially authorized thereto, without any participation in the matter by the House of Representatives, and without any reference of the question either to the States or to the people. With no opportunity to assent or to object, the original States were at once made to become only one-quarter part of the Union, if we take territory as the measure. And, indeed, we have already, in 1895, come to the point where the original thirteen States form but a little more than a quarter of the actual number of constituent members. If the Union was, indeed, as according to the States-rights' doctrine, merely a federal compact, then we must say that the cession and acceptance of Louisiana constituted not less than a revolution. This, too, was a revolution in the direction of centralization and the impairment of the powers of the original States, brought about by the very party which had undertaken to maintain the principle of strict construction and to provide the needed opposition to inevitable tendencies toward encroachment on the part of the general government.

The Louisiana purchase revolutionary.

In the last clause is found the chief significance of that momentous transaction. It was the States' rights party which had done this imperial act. It was the very founder of that party who had put his hand to what he admitted was an extra-constitutional, if not unconstitutional, measure,* for the purpose of aggrandizing the na-

---

* Mr. Jefferson said, "The Executive has done an act beyond the Constitution. The Legislature must ratify it and throw themselves upon the country for an act of indemnity." In further urging this view upon

tion beyond what had been conceived by the most sanguine. There had been two parties to the interpretation of the Constitution. One consistently declared that that instrument created a nation from which its members could not secede ; a nation which was competent to determine all matters of common concern through its own judiciary, executive, and legislature ; which was sovereign in its sphere. This party had uniformly asserted that the revenues should be ample ; that there should be an adequate army to enforce the laws ; that the dignity and authority of the general government should be magnified and extended just so far and just so fast as the common good might require. The other party had uniformly maintained the idea of a federal compact ; of a strict construction of the powers given to the general government ; of holding the revenues and the agencies of that government down to its absolutely necessary uses. This latter party, under the immense temptation offered by Bonaparte, had surrendered its principles ; had committed an imperial act *The Republican party* of far-reaching and permanent consequences ; *surrender the* had overwhelmed the original States by the *doctrine of strict construction.* certain future access of an indefinite number of new members, all of them possible rivals and competitors, perhaps unfriendly, perhaps hostile ; had magnified the Union vastly beyond what had been in contemplation only sixteen years before. The influence of this surrender of the federal, as distinguished from the national principle, by the only party which had undertaken to maintain it, upon the subsequent course of our constitutional history, cannot be estimated. The Re-

his supporters he said : " Our peculiar security is in the possession of a written Constitution. Let us not make it a blank paper by construction." Yet, after saying so much, Mr. Jefferson finally acquiesced in allowing the Louisiana purchase to pass as done solely by himself and a score, or so, of senators.

publican party never did and never could get back to its
original position as the advocate of a strict construction.
However its statesmen might declaim about the original
compact, whatever Republican conventions might declare, the great empire beyond the Mississippi was to
stand forever as a contradiction of their theories. Thereafter no man could, in the country-store, around the
post-office stove, on the court-house steps, at the county
fair, or upon the road, advance the "compact" theory
of the government, without being liable to have the
Louisiana purchase thrown in his face. No human ingenuity could twist this act so as to make it fit into the
States' rights doctrine. Looking at it in its relations
to the development of American nationality, we do not
hesitate to say that the purchase of Louisiana was an
act second in our history only to the adoption by the
Constitutional Convention of Randolph's resolution :
" That the government of the United States ought to
consist of a supreme legislative, judiciary, and executive."

There was one ultimate consequence of the purchase
of Louisiana which requires to be noted at this point,
though the full effect of it was not for some
time to be made manifest, and the consideration of its influence upon the politics of the
United States falls within the province of
my successor in this series. That was the enormous impulse thereby given to the domestic trade in slaves.
The opening of the vast region beyond the Mississippi,
to be settled under the laws and the protection of the
Union, was destined to create a demand for negro labor,
to cultivate the cotton-fields of Louisiana, Arkansas, and
southeastern Missouri, which should long make slave-
holding profitable in Virginia and Kentucky.

The French cession of Louisiana did not, however,

conclude our difficulties respecting the navigation of the Mississippi. Spain was equally surprised and disappointed at the use made by France of her cession *Difficulties* of 1800. To cede the territory to France, *with Spain.* her ally, was one thing ; to have it ceded to the United States, a power already so great as to threaten the security of the Floridas and the West Indies, was quite a different thing. Only reluctantly did Spain withdraw her objections to the cession; * while the transaction was undoubtedly the cause of her long delaying the ratification of a treaty which she had concluded with the United States in 1802, providing for the adjustment of claims for spoliations upon our commerce. Nor did the assent of Spain to the acquisition of Louisiana determine the vexed question of boundary. By a diplomatic complication which we need not take time to narrate, the line between the Louisiana ceded to France and by France to the United States, and the Florida retained by Spain, was in dispute. Spain claimed that her territory extended to the Mississippi and Lakes Pontchartrain and Borgue, while the United States claimed eastward to the river Perdido. This question was left to be settled later, partly by force of arms, partly by negotiation ; but meanwhile the United States had to complain of the conduct of Spanish cruisers, which infested our southern coasts and harassed our trade with the West Indies. In 1806, at the dictation of Napoleon, reinforced by the eager demands of the slave-holding States, which feared the influence of a successful slave-insurrec-

* Spain having ceded the territory to France on the express stipulation that that power should not transfer it to any other, some were at first disposed to hold that the cession to us was not valid without the consent of Spain. But our government very properly took the position that the matter of such a stipulation was wholly a question between Spain and France, and could not affect our rights. This was sound reasoning enough, but did not dispose of the possibility that Spain might attempt to prevent our acquiring the territory.

tion, Congress passed an act prohibiting trade with the revolted blacks of San Domingo. This measure was really a part of the negotiation with France and Spain regarding the interests of the latter power.

In 1803, Rufus King, our minister at London, concluded a treaty which adjusted the boundary line be-

Boundary between the United States and Great Britain. tween the two countries. The Senate, however, in its ratification, excepted one article ; and the amended treaty was sent back to London for concurrence. Great Britain failed to give her assent to the amendment, and the treaty failed, the question being left to long and angry negotiations to take place one and two generations later, when the United States should be grown stronger and better able to enforce its claims.

We have already alluded to the tribute exacted by the Barbary powers, as the condition upon which they con-

Contest with the Barbary powers. sented to permit the navigation of the Mediterranean by American vessels. The insolence of these licensed pirates only grew by indulgence. When Captain Bainbridge, of our navy, in 1800, bore to Algiers the stipulated tribute for that year, the Dey actually compelled him to carry despatches to the Sultan of Constantinople. Tripoli and Tunis also made outrageous demands, accompanied by threats. But the growing sense of American nationality would not allow this humiliating state of things to continue. Mr. Jefferson was not much of a fighting man ; but on this occasion he acted with decision. Commodore Dale was sent to the Mediterranean with a small fleet ; and by his energetic demonstrations, which included the capture of one Tripolitan cruiser, for a time overawed the piratical governments. Tripoli, however, renewing her acts of outrage, Congress recognized a state of war as existing, and the Mediterranean fleet was reinforced.

In the summer of 1803 several of the enemy's cruisers were captured or destroyed. This display of energy, followed by the arrival of additional vessels, under Commodore Preble, sufficed to keep the other Barbary states out of the contest, for which they had been hankering, and left Tripoli to be dealt with alone. Unfortunately, the frigate Philadelphia, under Bainbridge, while pursuing a ship of the enemy, ran upon a rock and was captured. The vessel was set on fire in the most gallant manner by Lieutenant, afterward Commodore, Decatur ; but her crew were still held as slaves. The war now having become a serious affair, the Mediterranean fleet was further reinforced, and Commodore Barron was sent out to take command. The town of Tripoli was invested and bombarded, and the hostile cruisers were driven in or destroyed ; but the enemy kept Bainbridge and his men prisoners. At last, in June, 1805, a treaty of peace was framed, which provided for the restoration of the captives and for the recognition of our rights in the Mediterranean. The spirited action of the United States in respect to Tripoli not only served to deter the other Barbary powers, but became an example to the European states, which did not much longer submit to blackmail from that source.

Let us now consider the cabinet, the movement of parties, and the fifth presidential election. Mr. Jefferson had originally selected his cabinet as follows : James Madison, of Virginia, Secretary of State ; Henry Dearborn, of Massachusetts, Secretary of War ; Levi Lincoln, of Massachusetts, Attorney-General. Dexter and Stoddert were for a short time continued in office, after which Albert Gallatin became Secretary of the Treasury, and Robert Smith, Secretary of the Navy. Joseph Habersham, of

Georgia, who had been appointed Postmaster-General in 1795, was for a few months continued in office. He was then succeeded by Gideon Granger, of Connecticut. The head of the Post-office Department, however, was not called into the cabinet until the administration of General Jackson. The *National Intelligencer*, so long famous in the history of our politics, was started in Mr. Jefferson's administration, as the official organ of the government. The popular revulsion from the Federalist principles of the late administration continued in full force, reducing the party which had represented them to a state of extreme weakness. That this was in a degree due to the increasing insolence of England, and not wholly to the acts and principles of the Federalists themselves, is most probable. England, with her gigantic naval power, was again looming up on the national horizon as our great "natural enemy." The steady gains of the Republicans were, also, in no small measure, due to the popularity of Mr. Jefferson, whose easy manners, whose philosophical habit of mind, whose optimistic way of looking at public affairs, and whose unquestioning confidence in the integrity, honesty, and patriotism of the masses, "just suited" the American people. State after State, traditionally Federalist, came over to the support of the administration in its first year. In 1804 the usual party nominations were made

Jefferson's re-election. for the approaching presidential election. Burr, having entirely fallen out of the confidence and sympathy of his party, was dropped; and George Clinton, of New York, was substituted as the candidate for Vice-President. Charles C. Pinckney and Rufus King were nominated by the Federalists. They received, however, only 14 votes—9 from Connecticut, 3 from Delaware, and 2 (out of 11) from Maryland. Jefferson and Clinton received 164 votes each, and were

overwhelmingly elected.   Even Massachusetts cast her
votes for Jefferson.

But we cannot close this account of Jefferson's first
term without alluding to a tragedy of which only a faint
shadow has been thrown over the generation in which
we live ; but which to our fathers was scarcely less impressive and terrible than many of us remember the
murder of Lincoln to have been in our day.   Aaron
Burr, cast off by his party, took his broken fortunes
and his bad name to the Federalists of New York, who
nominated him for Governor in 1804.   Defeated by the
bitter opposition of many of the party which had
adopted him, chief among them Hamilton, who had returned to the practice of law in New York City, and
goaded to fury by attacks upon his life and character,
he challenged Hamilton to mortal combat.   The antagonists met at Weehawken, on July 11th, Hamilton's
and Hamilton received a wound of which he tragic death.
died the next day.   Thus perished, at the age of forty-
seven, in the prime of his powers, a statesman whose
name has been held second to none, in point of ability,
among those who framed the Constitution and inaugurated the Union.   His rival and murderer dragged out
his dishonored life, " by reason of strength," to four-
score years.

CHAPTER X

JEFFERSON'S SECOND TERM

Foreign Affairs—English and French Outrages—The Right of Search—Insolently Exercised by British Cruisers—Impressment of American Seamen—The Affair of the Chesapeake—"Contraband of War"—Right of Blockade—England and France Compete in Injuries to our Commerce—England Sets up the "Rule of 1756"—The British Blockades—Napoleon Retaliates upon the "Orders in Council" with His Berlin and Milan Decrees—The Bayonne Decree—The Monroe Treaty with England—Jefferson Refuses to send it to the Senate—Jefferson's Proclamation Ordering British Men-of-War out of American Waters—The Non-Importation Act—The Embargo—Resentment of the Commercial States—Mr. Jefferson Hostile to the Carrying Trade and to General Commerce—The Embargo Breaks Down—Troubles with Spain—Proposed Purchase of Florida—Measures of National Defence—Jefferson's "Mosquito Fleet"—The Cumberland Road—The Policy of Internal Improvements—Fulton's Steamboat—Trial of Aaron Burr for Treason—Burr's Designs—The Finances under President Jefferson—Abolition of the Slave Trade in 1808—Anti-Slavery Agitation—Lewis and Clarke's Expedition—Cabinet Changes—Mr. Jefferson Refuses a Re-nomination—The Sixth Presidential Election—No longer the Vice-President Succeeds; It is Now the Secretary of State—James Madison of Virginia Nominated—His Services to his Party and to the Country.

FOREIGN affairs demand our first attention. The re-inauguration of Jefferson, March 4, 1805, found the sky black with coming war. Great Britain and France were engaged in their deadly grapple. Napoleon was sweeping all before him on the continent of Europe; England dominated the seas with a resistless sway. Neither, in such a contest, could be expected to show much consideration for the young republic. Contempt for the rights of the United States and for the laws of neutral trade characterized the acts of both combatants. England, however, as the great naval power, was in the position to do us the deeper wrong.

It was stated in connection with the notice of the Jay treaty that England reserved the question of the right of search and impressment, and maintained the rigor of its commercial system. The time had come when these questions were of supreme importance. The necessities of England's naval warfare would not allow the right of impressment to remain a right unexercised ; while, with the steady progress of the arms of Napoleon on the continent, the occasion for starving France and choking her off from the trade of the world became imperative. It is scarcely possible to say which of the two forms of injury adopted by England more roused and exasperated the United States. The "right of search," with wanton impressment of American seamen, was not only exercised on the largest scale against our merchant marine, and that, too, with the greatest insolence and brutality ; but the arrogance of England went to the astonishing extent of stopping armed vessels upon the seas, searching them against the protests of their officers, and taking from them all persons whom the British commander, in greater or less straits for men to work his vessel, might choose to regard as British subjects.

Of the right of search, a few words : The right of search exists. This is not questioned. What are its limits and conditions ? No right of search exists as against the national vessels of recognized powers. Toward merchant vessels, of whatever name and nationality, the right of search exists, but for

English and French outrages.

The right of search.

two purposes only. For determining whether the vessel searched is a pirate, *i.e.*, is making war upon all nations ; and secondly, for determining whether that vessel is engaged unlawfully in assisting the enemies of the power to which the vessel conducting the search belongs, by carrying "contraband of war." The right of search does not exist for the purpose of recovering escaped seamen. Much less could it be said to exist for the purpose of exercising impressment upon persons who had never entered the service of the power exercising the search. But while the right of search for such objects exists, yet, being a right to be exercised only in exception to the general exercise of a contrary right in all vessels to pursue their course unmolested, search much be *bona fide*, that is, upon reasonable ground of suspicion ; must be carefully conducted within the limits of the necessity which alone justifies it at all ; and must be free from discourtesy or unnecessary violence. As a matter of fact, the British men-of-war exercised this right unnecessarily, insolently, and violently. That they did so was partly due to the traditions of the British naval service, which had erected arrogance and brutality into a virtue. It was perhaps in greater part due to the special exigencies of that service at this time, which were so great as to lead naval officers to break all bounds of law and justice, even in dealing with their own countrymen at home. Press-gangs swept at night through the streets of English seaports, carrying away their helpless victims ; and naval officers dared to say in Parliament that no British ship-of-war should put to sea undermanned, whatever had to be done to secure her proper complement. Under such circumstances it can hardly be wondered at that, as against foreigners whom they still continued to regard as rebels, the bullies of the quarterdeck hesitated not to resort to any measure of violence to fill up their depleted

crews. Outrageous as was the quality of the wrong inflicted by England through the exercise of impressment
upon our helpless merchant marine, the quantity of that
wrong was something monstrous. Six thousand of our
seamen were alleged to have been, first or last, seized by
British cruisers, while the number certainly exceeded
four thousand. British frigates were kept permanently
" on station" off the port of New York, for the purpose
of recruiting their fleets by these captures.

Allusion has been made to search and impressment as
conducted against our national vessels. Incredible as
this may seem, it was actually done. In 1798, the commander of an American ship, the Baltimore, was compelled to send a large number of his crew on to the deck
of a British cruiser, that they might there be inspected
as to their nationality. Of these the British commander
picked out five as subjects of the king, and returned
the others. This outrage was vehemently resented by
President Adams, and the British government disavowed
the act. In 1805, however, Admiral Collingwood took
three men from an American gunboat, off Cadiz ; and
this time the act was not disavowed. But the climax of
insolent aggression was reached on June 22, 1807, when
the British frigate Leopard overhauled the frigate Chesapeake, putting out to sea from Hampton Roads, under
command of Commodore Barron ; and, after receiving a
refusal to surrender three seamen, alleged to be deserters
from the British navy, opened fire. The American ship
was of inferior strength, and was, moreover, utterly and
culpably unprepared for action, unable to discharge a
single one of its guns. Barron was, therefore, after sustaining considerable loss, compelled to strike his flag and
surrender the seamen. The last outrage which has been
recited aroused the country to fury ; and for a time an
outbreak seemed inevitable. Men wore crape for the

13

dead of the Chesapeake, as for personal friends, and a
cry for war came from every quarter. "This country,"
wrote Mr. Jefferson, "has never been in
such a state of excitement since the battle of
Lexington." Preparations for the contest
were at once begun ; but years were to pass before the
dastardly act of Hampton Roads should be avenged.

The affair of the Chesa-peake.

While the insult to our national dignity through the
exercise of impressment was so great, the practical wrong
done us by the measures relating to neutral trade which
were adopted in swift succession by England and France,
was not less difficult to be endured. Let us here state
briefly and simply two principles of international law
relating to neutral trade, avoiding all discussion of the
difficult question what shall be done with the goods of
a neutral found in an enemy's ship, or with the goods
of an enemy found in a neutral's ship : First, a certain
line of articles, not to be defined without dispute (the
definition, indeed, depending in a degree upon subsist-
ing treaties ; depending, also, in a degree, upon existing
circumstances), yet having certain generally recognized
bounds, are "contraband of war ; " and, if
destined to an enemy's ports, may be captured in vessels to whomsoever belonging.
Secondly, a nation at war may lay under "blockade"
the ports of its enemy, just so far as it has the power
substantially to close such ports against ingress and
egress, and to render it clearly and highly dangerous
for vessels to try to enter. Doing this, it may give
public notice of blockade ; and all vessels thereafter
tending to such ports, or found in suspicious proximity
thereto, are liable to seizure. If convicted of attempting to "run the blockade," vessel and cargo are forfeit,
and passengers and crew are subject to detention and
annoyance without just cause of complaint. A notice

"Contra-band of war," and the right of blockade.

of blockade, unaccompanied by an actual naval force
off the blockaded port, competent to support it, constitutes of itself an imposition and a wrong.

The things which have been recited are all, absolutely
all, which a nation at war may do to hinder undoubted
and unmixed neutral trade. Subject to these restrictions the nations which choose to remain at peace may
continue their industry and commerce unharmed, un-
hindered. But in the time we are considering, England
was held by our statesmen to encroach grievously upon
the rights of neutral trade in two important respects.
First, she had attempted to establish a rule, most prejudicial to neutral rights and American interests, known
as the Rule of 1756, namely, that a trade from a colony
to its parent country, not permitted to other nations in
time of peace, cannot be made lawful in time of war.
This rule was contrary, not only to the law of nations,
but to England's own practice. Secondly, England
was charged with abusing the privilege of blockade.
By Orders in Council, August, 1804, she The British
declared all ports, from Ostend to the Seine, blockades.
in a state of rigorous blockade ; and in May, 1806, our
government was notified that measures had been directed to be taken for the blockade of the coasts, rivers,
and ports, from the river Elbe to Brest. The latter
blockade our government insisted as regarding "a
paper blockade," that is, one not supported by a sufficient force to preserve continuously the state of things
described above as the proper condition of a blockade.

But we were not to suffer wrong from England alone.
In November, 1806, Napoleon retorted upon England
with the Berlin decree, which declared the British Islands in a state of blockade and prohibited all commerce
and correspondence with them. This was so outrageous
as to be positively funny. At the time, a French man-

of-war could not have been insured, for ninety per cent. of its value, to go over-night within ten miles of the British coast. The Berlin decree was answered by Orders in Council, of January 7, 1807, known as Lord Howick's Orders, subsequently superseded or merged in Orders of November 11th, known as Percival's Orders, by which all ports and places belonging to France and her allies from which the British flag was excluded, and all colonies of his Britannic majesty's enemies, were declared in a state of blockade. All trade in the produce or manufactures of those countries or colonies was prohibited ; and all vessels trading to or from them, and all merchandise on board, were made subject to capture and condemnation ; with an exception only in favor of direct trade between neutral countries and the colonies of his majesty's enemies. To this France replied with the Milan decree, December, 1807, which declared every ship, whatever its nationality and whatever its cargo, sailing from the ports of England or of her colonies, or of countries occupied by British troops, and proceeding to England or to her colonies, or to countries occupied by the English, to be good prize. And every ship, of whatever nation, which had submitted to search by an English ship, or had made a voyage to England, or had paid any tax to that government, was declared denationalized and lawful prize. It has by some been alleged that the French people, while exceedingly witty, are destitute of humor ; and certainly the Berlin and Milan decrees afford a striking corroboration of this view. The claim of England that such extensive blockade as was expressed in her Orders of Council was or could be made effectual, was never admitted by our government or by other neutral powers ; but the declaration by France of blockade, not only of the British Islands, but of British

France and England compete in wrongs to the United States.

colonies and of all countries occupied by British troops, exceeds anything seen upon the stage in opera bouffe. In April, 1808, Napoleon issued the decree of Bayonne, which directed all American vessels entering the ports of France, Italy, or the Hanse towns, to be seized and condemned. The recital of the successive decrees, issued in retaliation by the French and English governments, shows those two powerful nations eagerly competing with each other in outrages upon neutral commerce. The struggle between them had become one of life and death ; and no consideration of neutral rights was for a moment allowed by either to give the slightest additional chance of success to the other. Between these two giants, in their death-grapple, the young republic was in great danger of being crushed ; and was certain, at the best, to be sorely crowded and hustled, to the great impairment of its dignity and with much loss of its legitimate trade.

Through all this course of outrage what did the United States do ? In May, 1806, James Monroe, of Virginia, and William Pinkney, of Maryland, The Monroe were associated as envoys to Great Britain ; treaty. and on December 31st concluded a treaty. By this treaty England did not relinquish the right of search and impressment ; but the treaty was accompanied by assurances to our ministers that, while Great Britain did not feel able to relinquish this right in the existing situation of Europe, yet the practice would be essentially if not completely abandoned, so much so that the United States would be in fact as secure against impressment as if these had been formally given up. This treaty Mr. Jefferson did not even submit to the Senate, regarding it as unworthy of the United States. His course in this respect caused great public dissatisfaction on grounds both of constitutionality and expediency.

Of the policy of ratifying this treaty different opinions might reasonably be held. On the one side it might be said that we had had treaties enough with England which reserved the great questions at issue between that power and ourselves, leaving her still at liberty to pursue her course of outrage and insult. On the other side it was said that the United States sacrificed none of its claims by the treaty ; that those claims could only be enforced by war ; and that the United States was not in a condition to go to war. But, if the United States did not propose to make its claims good by arms, wisdom required that the state of peace should be made as tolerable as possible. Moreover, it was urged with some reason that the wrongs done by Great Britain were to be looked at in a different light from what they would have been had Great Britain taken its course gratuitously and under ordinary circumstances. Great Britain had no wish to distress or insult us. The acts we complained of were primarily intended to harass and injure France. While this did not make Great Britain right, it put the question of national honor in a very different relation. The hostile animus was against France and France alone. We suffered wrong incidentally to the great contest for life or death between the European powers. So the British treaty of 1806 was not ratified. Mr. Monroe was much displeased at the rejection of the treaty, which he deemed honorable and advantageous. It is only fair to say that the assurances given our commissioners had been explicit, direct, and emphatic. On the other hand, in view of England's subsequent wrongful and violent acts, it is not unreasonable to doubt whether those assurances would have been made good had the treaty been ratified.

The outrage upon the Chesapeake was resented by Mr. Jefferson in a proclamation which ordered all British men-of-war out of American waters. This the British government made an excuse for refusing to enter into negotiations for the reparation admittedly Jefferson's due for that outrage. They demanded that proclamation. the proclamation be withdrawn before they would proceed to treat. To this our government replied, first, that the proclamation was not issued solely on account of the affair of the Chesapeake, but by reason of a long train of injurious acts of which this was the latest and most flagrant; secondly, that, as the British government still held the seamen taken from the Chesapeake, the aggression of England still continued. Negotiations being thus broken off, the reparation of England was delayed for four years.

We now come to the positive acts of our government to redress or retaliate the wrongs to our trade. Early in 1806 Congress passed an act, which, however, The Non-importation Act. was not to go into effect until November,* prohibiting the importation, from any of the ports of Great Britain or of her colonies, of a long list of manufactured articles. The idea of bringing England, as a great industrial and trading nation, to terms by means of commercial war, instead of by force of arms, had a strong hold upon the popular mind at this time and in succeeding years. It had come down from the period of the contest of the colonies with the mother country before the outbreak of the Revolution, when there was no other course which we could take. To touch the pockets of the wrong-doer was believed to be a more potent means of securing redress than to appeal either to his conscience or his fears. Great Britain had need to obtain food and cotton and "naval stores" from the United States; and, on the other hand, had been accustomed to

---

* "A dose of chicken-broth to be taken nine months hence," as Mr. John Randolph called it.

look to this country as its best customer in respect to its fabrics and its hardware.   By non-intercourse it was hoped so to distress the trading and industrial classes as to bring a pressure upon the offending government strong enough to secure the repeal of the Orders in Council and the discontinuance of the lawless practice of impressment.   This notion was peculiarly suited to the mind and temper of the President, and scarcely less to that of Mr. Madison.   The Non-importation Act did, indeed, cause great suffering in the industrial and commercial counties of England ; and month after month petitions and addresses poured in upon Parliament and the government, urging a friendly settlement of the difculties with America.   But it was to require a long and humiliating experience to show the inefficiency of this resort, as against a nation engaged, as England was, in a struggle for life and death with a powerful continental antagonist.

In view of the wrongs done us in the Orders in Council and by the Berlin decree, Mr. Jefferson recommended, The Embar- and Congress, on the 22d of December, 1807, go. enacted, a law, without limit of time, famous as the Embargo Act, by which all vessels in the jurisdiction of the United States, bound to a foreign port, were prohibited from sailing, excepting foreign armed vessels and foreign merchantmen which were either in ballast or with goods on board when notified of the act.   Coasting vessels were required before departure to give bonds to land their cargo at some port of the United States.   John Quincy Adams, the son of the second President, formerly minister to the Hague and to Berlin, and then a member of Congress, at this point broke with the Federalists and gave in his adhesion to the embargo as a measure necessary to vindicate the rights, the interests, and the dignity of the United States. The embargo to all appearances passed through Congress solely on the strength of the President's recommendation, so powerful was Mr. Jefferson with his party in and out of Congress. No adequate discussion was had; even the usual parliamentary delays were waived. So hurriedly had the bill been pressed to a conclusion that it became necessary to enact two supplementary measures, and a little later, to pass an Enforcing Act, which gave the executive the most despotic powers in dealing with both foreign and domestic trade.

The embargo was hailed by one party as the height of wisdom; by the other denounced as the depth of folly. Sectional feeling was aroused to an incredible extent. The commercial States deemed the measure a blow maliciously dealt at them; and with every day their sufferings were protracted their hatred and exasperation increased. Mr. Jefferson was charged with suppressing correspondence which went to show that the embargo was not answering its sole, avowed purpose of distressing the two nations which were competing in injuries to our commerce; and also to show that England had, through Mr. Canning, expressed a willingness to mitigate the severity of the Orders in Council so far as they affected American trade. If we concede the President's entire honesty in the business of the embargo, we must at the least admit that he had a very unfortunate record in such matters. Mr. Jefferson had been much given to denouncing international commerce as a curse; he had expressed his unwillingness to see great commercial cities built up within the United States. His hostility to the banking and financial interests was notorious. It was, therefore, easy for those who suffered by the embargo to assert that he was rather pleased, than otherwise, to have this opportunity of striking a blow at trade and navigation. Had the embargo been the work of a statesman friendly to commerce, it might have been accepted by the sufferers as a necessary act of national defence ; but Mr. Jefferson, however conscious he might be of his own integrity in the matter, had no right to complain if New York and Boston believed the measure to have been gratuitous, and even a wilful blow at their interests.

During the latter part of 1808 the exasperation in New England over the embargo had reached the point of threatening the secession of that section from the Union. The Republicans in power had now to learn how ill this talk sounded, by hearing it from the lips of their opponents. There is no such mode of teaching as through the objective study of a subject, especially across the barriers of party. To Virginia statesmen, doctrines of nullification and secession seemed only wicked when advanced by hot-headed Federalists in Massachusetts. Mr. Jefferson was alarmed at the prospect and began to be doubtful of the virtue of his panacea. The connection between making grass grow in the streets of Boston, Salem, Newport, and New Haven, and overthrowing the British government, appeared to him somewhat less plain than at the beginning. The customs of oriental nations were not so well known at that time as at present ; and Mr. Jefferson was not able to strengthen his own convictions by a reference to the usage in certain provinces of India, by which a person who has been wronged sits down before the door of the evil-doer and there rips open his abdomen, in order to bring a curse down upon his enemy. Had Mr. Jefferson known this, it might have been a great comfort to him. As it was, unfortified by such a classical example, his courage gave way ; and in February, 1809, the last month of his term of office, the embargo was repealed, and the policy of non-intercourse with England and France was substituted, the change to take effect in March. We thus see Mr. Jefferson's administration close with our foreign difficulties unadjusted, while the questions of search and impressment were handed on to his successor. There can be no doubt that the last part of Mr. Jefferson's otherwise remarkably successful administration had been to him a very painful one, and embittered his cup for many years. Long after, when the war which he sought so carefully to avoid had come and gone, and his country had taken its proper place among the nations of the earth, he could review this period of his life and satisfy himself that what he did was best to be done. But at the time, the foreign difficulties of his administration must often have caused him to wish he had remained the serene philosopher of Monticello, instead of venturing upon the stormy ocean of practical politics.

The embargo breaks down.

During the session of 1805–06 an appropriation of two million dollars was made for extraordinary expenses of foreign intercourse, the real object being to secure Florida, or at least the western part of it, by purchase, from Spain, thereby solving our difficulties with that power. A resolution was adopted, however, declaring that "an exchange of territory between the United States and Spain would be the most advantageous mode of settling the existing differences about their respective boundaries." At this time our relations with Spain were very much strained, owing to the dispute regarding Florida and to the action of the Spanish cruisers which infested the Gulf of Mexico. There was a large, active party among the supporters of the administration who desired to see the Spanish possessions on our border invaded and the questions at issue

Florida.

settled by the expulsion of the Spaniards. The two million appropriation was a sop to this faction.

With such a condition of our foreign relations it scarcely needs to be stated that preparations for war were made by Congress. It is, perhaps, of sufficient curious interest to be mentioned, that Mr. Jefferson's fixed aversion to large armaments, combined with his inveterate propensity to dabble in every art, science, or device, gave rise to a very peculiar system of coast defence. Although Mr. Jefferson knew absolutely nothing about naval warfare, or any kind of warfare, he was yet serenely confident that his opinions on the subject of a navy were wiser than those of all the men who had learned their profession under Nelson and Collingwood. His scheme was, and he urged it so strongly upon Congress as to secure its partial and temporary adoption, that the government should build gunboats, of diminutive size, each manned by five to seven men, and carrying one gun, instead of the powerful ships of war then sanctioned by the naval science of the world. In 1803 Congress appropriated $50,000, for fifteen boats ; and later, in 1806, $250,000 for fifty more. The "mosquito fleet" was brought into existence ; but its utter inefficiency was soon demonstrated to the entire satisfaction of everybody but Mr. Jefferson.

After so much space devoted to foreign affairs, let us now pass to the consideration of domestic affairs in this administration. In 1806 an act was passed authorizing the construction of a road from Cumberland, Md., into the State of Ohio. Although the construction of this road was urged upon the ground that it would open up the public lands to settlement, and though the cost of construction was defrayed, or supposed to be defrayed, out of the proceeds of sales,

Measures of national defence.

The Cumberland road.

this act is yet of considerable historical interest with respect to the question of internal improvements, the question which became of so much impor- Internal im- tance immediately after the peace of 1815. provements. The propriety of opening rivers for the purposes of navigation, of improving and protecting the ports of commerce, of building lighthouses and breakwaters, never came into question. It was by all parties admitted that the United States had ample authority under the Constitution to do just as much of these things, pertaining to commerce, as its means allowed and as the public good seemed to require. The right of the United States, again, to construct forts, arsenals, and navy-yards, as well as appropriate buildings for all branches of the civil government, could not be questioned, although the influence of the Democratic-Republican party was always thrown in favor of diminished appropriations for such purposes, whether from opposition to a large establishment or from a preference for primitive simplicity in carrying on the public service. But in regard to another class of constructive works, namely, main roads and canals, the party of Jefferson and Madison from the first took high ground, declaring that appropriations for this purpose were in violation of the Constitution. If the members of this party were not always consistent in the matter, it was because of the seductions of local interest and the additional charm which an appropriation acquires to the mind of any citizen when it is to be expended in his own immediate locality. The contest over this question went on for about one human generation. Then, in the development of science and the arts, the railroad came into being, and relegated both the " national road " and the canal to insignificance and obscurity. Inasmuch as no one, not even the most ardent Whig, was ready to propose that railroads should be built by the national government, the issue died out of our politics, affording a rather curious instance how far laws and policies and constitutions may be affected by social and industrial developments.

But while the steam-railway was yet far in the distance, the steamboat was just coming into use on the great rivers of the United States. Repeated efforts had been made to apply the new motive-power to the propulsion of vessels ; but it was not until 1807 that Robert Fulton, upon the Hudson, solved the problem by sending his paddle-wheel steamer, of twenty horse-power, with berths for one hundred passengers, from New York to Albany, "sail-less, against the tide," in two-and-thirty hours. By an act of the State Legislature, Fulton and his patron, Chancellor Livingston, were given a monopoly for thirty years of steam navigation in New York. This monopoly was, in 1824, declared by the Supreme Court of the United States [Gibbons *vs.* Ogden] to be in collision with acts of Congress regulating the coasting-trade, and therefore void. Long before this our rivers and lakes had become covered with steamboats, of ever-increasing capacity and speed. The enormous extension thus given to intercommunication between States and communities not only served to promote the rapid settlement of the great West, but became a powerful factor in the development of American nationality.

Aaron Burr, a hounded outcast, was arrested by the authorities of Mississippi Territory, and tried before Chief-Justice Marshall and the District Judge of Virginia, for treason. It was charged that he had, in Virginia and elsewhere, organized an expedition to take possession of portions of Mexico and of our own southwestern territory, for the purpose of setting up an independent government. The question of Burr's guilt was largely made a party question, as was nearly everything in those days. Greatly to Mr. Jefferson's wrath and disgust, Burr was acquitted, in September, 1807, on technical points, not reaching the merits of the case. The President persisted in regarding himself as very much abused by the result of the trial, charging the fault upon the Federalists generally, and especially upon the Chief-Justice. The fact appears to be that Mr. Jefferson had himself to thank, having, in his own peculiar *laissez-faire* fashion, failed to take any adequate means to secure competent legal evidence regarding Burr's operations, either at the time or before the trial. The President might, and doubtless would, have been willing to hang Burr upon his character or on general fame ; but judges and juries cannot be blamed if they insist upon something more concrete, objective, and substantial. It is to be remembered that the definition of treason by our Constitution is a very strict one ; and that the requirement as to the evidence necessary to convict of this crime is exceptionally severe.

Just what it was Burr had in view will never be known. Possibly he did not exactly know, himself ; probably he had several things in contemplation, as to be done in succession, if the earlier enterprises went off well, or as alternatives, if these failed. Almost certain it is that, to different persons whom he sought to enlist, he made different representations and held forth inducements adapted to the needs or the weaknesses of the individuals addressed. To seize Florida from Spain ; to annex Texas and Mexico to the United States ; to detach the Mississippi Territory from the United States ; to pillage New Orleans ; to undertake a harmless but gigantic scheme of settlement and land speculation : each one of these things

seems to have been in the mind of some one of Burr's
dupes or tools. It is needless further to inquire into the
matter. One thing is certain : General Wilkinson, the
commander of the United States forces, and the Governor
of the Mississippi Territory, was improperly, if not crimi-
nally, enlisted in the conspiracy. It is certain, also, that
Burr would never have undertaken his scheme, whatever
that scheme in fact was, but for the long-smouldering
discontent of the trans-Appalachian communities at the
failure of the government at Washington to see to it
that "the Mississippi ran unvexed to the sea." The
disaffection of the Creole population of Louisiana, who,
without their own consent, had been transferred first
by Spain to France, and then by France to the United
States, was in all probability an important element in
Burr's schemes and plans.

The finances of the United States had been singularly
prosperous throughout Mr. Jefferson's entire administration, partly through the parsimony which
The finances. refused the means requisite for putting the
nation on a footing to resent and repel the injuries suffered at the hands of England and France ; but more
through the growth of the customs revenue, in consequence of the marvellous extension of our carrying trade
during the wars which convulsed Europe. The receipts
of the government rose continually, until the annual
surplus amounted to many millions, which were system-
atically devoted to the still further reduction of the
Revolutionary debt, now almost extinguished.

The Constitution had provided that the migration or
importation of such persons as any of the States then
existing might think it proper to admit, should not be
prohibited by Congress prior to the year 1808. It is to
the honor of our government that not one day's grace
was allowed this infamous traffic, after Congress ac-

quired the constitutional competence to deal with it. By an act of the session of 1806–7, it was declared a high misdemeanor to take on board, in any foreign country, any colored person, with intent to sell him in the United States. Severe penalties were imposed upon the violation of the act, and the purchase of any person who had been so imported was punishable by fine. The fitting out of vessels for this trade involved forfeiture and heavy fines. The president was authorized to man and equip cruisers to enforce the law and bring its violators to punishment. On the question what should be done with slaves when unlawfully brought into the country, there was naturally much controversy. It was finally disposed of by referring the subject to the States.

The abolition of the slave-trade.

But while, in the immediate matter of the slave-trade, the year 1808 witnessed a great victory on the behalf of human rights, that period marks "the parting of the ways" in the still more important issue of domestic slavery. At the close of the War of Independence every State, except possibly Massachusetts, had slaves within its borders ; although throughout New England and the Middle States these were so few, and the profits of their labor so slight, that it was not to be doubted that "the domestic institution" must there soon cease to exist. By the time the Constitution was adopted, all the New England States, with Pennsylvania, had abolished slavery outright, or had provided for its gradual extinction. New York passed her act of emancipation in 1799, New Jersey in 1804. Throughout the border Slave States of 1789, viz.—Delaware, Maryland, and Virginia—slaves were found in considerable numbers ; but here, again, the profits of their labor, mainly employed in raising tobacco and the cereal crops, were not so great but that the sentiments and scruples of large numbers

14

of citizens, embracing perhaps a majority of the men of influence and of social importance, favored the project of ultimate emancipation. In the Constitutional Con-
Anti-slavery vention some of the strongest declarations
agitation. against slavery had come from Virginians; and it long remained within the bounds of possibility that this State would lead its immediate neighbors in some act of gradual abolition. But by 1808 the course of events, both economic and political, had put a stop to all movements for emancipation throughout that section, and had committed the border States definitively to the side of slavery. Among the forces thus operating were, on the one hand, the increasing profitableness of cotton-culture at the South and the Southwest, which created an active market for slave labor; and, on the other hand, the irritation felt by the slave-holding populations, generally, at the agitation for abolition which had been so actively prosecuted at the North, and particularly, during this period, in Pennsylvania, where the powerful Quaker element arrayed itself solidly upon that side. This agitation had naturally involved the most passionate denunciations; and, while it had created a deep aversion to slavery throughout the North, it had, by a necessary reaction, solidified and strengthened the slave-holding sentiment of the South.

It was during the administration of Mr. Jefferson that the northern portions of the newly acquired territory were explored by two gallant adventurers, whose names are now familiar as household words, Lewis and Clarke.
Lewis and The expedition was honorable to the United
Clarke's expe- States, and has connected the names of the
dition. explorers, and of their political patrons, Gallatin and Jefferson, with some of the grandest features of the great northwestern empire.

The cabinet changes in Jefferson's second term really

affected only the Attorney-Generalship. In 1805 Robert Smith, of Maryland, up to this time Secretary of the Navy, became Attorney-General. Jacob Crowninshield, of Massachusetts, who had *Cabinet changes.* been appointed to the Navy Department, preferred to retain his seat in Congress, and Smith returned at the close of the year to his former office, being succeeded in the Attorney-Generalship by John Breckinridge, of Kentucky. Upon Breckinridge's death, Cæsar A. Rodney, of Delaware, became Attorney-General, in January, 1807. The remaining officers of the cabinet in the first term were continued through the second.

As the sixth presidential election approached, it was manifest to all that there would be very little politics in it. The Federalist party was so completely broken up as to offer but slight resistance. Mr. Jefferson firmly and consistently refused to be considered a *Mr. Jefferson retires.* candidate for re-election. In addition to a sense of increasing infirmities, he had long entertained a sincere conviction that the period of the presidential office should not be extended beyond that of Washington, namely, two terms of four years each. "If some period," he had once written, "be not fixed, either by the Constitution or by practice, the office will, though nominally elective, become for life, and then hereditary."

In deciding upon the candidate of the dominant party we note a change regarding the natural succession to the presidency. At first it had seemed appropriate that the vice-president *The sixth presidential election.* should succeed. John Adams had been Washington's vice-president, and followed him in office. Indeed, during his vice-presidency Adams humorously, and yet not altogether without serious intention, referred to himself as the "heir-apparent." Jefferson, again, had been vice-president with Adams, and in turn succeeded him, though, it must be admitted, for other reasons than those which brought Adams to the executive chair. But now, at the close of Jefferson's administration, we find that it is Madison, the Secretary of State, who is nominated for the succession. And if we look forward eight years, to the close of Madison's administration, we shall see that it is his Secretary of State, Monroe, who is nominated. And, going still further forward, to the close of Monroe's administration, we find that it is his Secretary of State, John Quincy Adams, who takes the succession. The change upon which we have thus dwelt was not accidental. It was due to the overwhelming predominance which our foreign relations had acquired in the politics of the country.

It is not, however, improbable that, but for the strong hold which the Virginians had upon the politics of the nation at this time, the claims of Governor George Clinton, of New York, who, as vice-president with Jefferson, during his second term, felt himself to have acquired a certain prescriptive right, according to previous usage, and who had, moreover, a very remarkable record of public and party services, might have been recognized by a nomination for the presidency. But the grip of the "Virginia Dynasty" upon that office was, as yet, too strong to give a northern republican anything like an equal chance. If it had not been Madison, it would not have been Clinton; it would have been Monroe. Indeed, as it was, the president had much difficulty in holding Monroe's partisans back and in appeasing Monroe's own sense of injustice. That it was, after all, for Mr. Jefferson to select his successor, seems to have been generally conceded, even by the Monroe faction. Was he not the party's founder, leader, and owner?

Personally Mr. Madison had earned the promotion he was to receive. Mr. Jefferson owed him support, for no political chieftain ever had a more faithful and efficient lieutenant. For twenty years he had thought Mr. Jefferson's thoughts and fought his battles. He had carried out Mr. Jefferson's political plans with more of steadiness, more of discretion, and more of capacity for detail, than the chief himself possessed. The Republican party, too, was under profound obligations to give its support to Mr. Madison before any other man. With clear convictions, with untiring industry, and with high partisan fidelity, he had, next to Jefferson, contributed to its success. Finally, the nation did well to raise Mr. Madison to this exalted station. He had been one of the leading spirits of the Convention of 1787, and one of the chief defenders of the Constitution before the people. In setting the government fairly on foot, in organizing the departments which should carry on the public service, and in shaping the legislation of the first critical years, his influence had been great, and, on the whole, highly useful. If we may rejoice that the United States have not become altogether what Mr. Madison planned and desired, the bitterest partisan cannot regret that his labors were so rewarded. The result of the election was a foregone conclusion. Mr. Madison received 122 votes, against 47 for General C. C. Pinckney and 6 for George Clinton. The last named also received 113 votes for vice-president and was elected. Rufus King, formerly of Massachusetts and then of New York, received, as the federalist candidate for the vice-presidency, an equal vote with General Pinckney.

Madison's nomination and election.

CHAPTER XI

THE CONTROVERSY WITH ENGLAND

Madison's Cabinet—His Policy of Conciliation toward the Federalists—*Rapprochement* of the two Parties—Randolph's Faction of "Old Republicans" and the Irreconcilable Federalists of New England Hold Aloof—The Trouble with England—Napoleon Retaliates with the Rambouillet Decree—Alleged Repeal of the French Decrees—Non-Intercourse Act Withdrawn as Against France—Controversy over this Action—Secretary Smith Resigns—His Protest—James Monroe becomes Secretary of State and Heir-Apparent—Of the two Nations Doing us Wrong, the Administration Selects England as an Antagonist—The War Party—The New Men—Congress Meets—Warlike Preparations—The Henry Episode—Madison's Renomination—War Declared against England—The Federalist Protest—Failure of Further Negotiations—The Hanson Riot in Baltimore.

MR. MADISON constituted his cabinet as follows : Robert Smith, of Maryland, Secretary of State ; William

Madison's cabinet. Eustis, of Massachusetts, Secretary of War ; Paul Hamilton, of South Carolina, Secretary of the Navy. Gallatin and Rodney continued in office as Secretary of the Treasury and Attorney-General, respectively. The cabinet thus formed was not a strong one as a whole, although it contained some good men. Smith was by far the weakest of the lot. The worst feature of its organization was in the failure to promote Mr. Gallatin to the then all-important post of Secretary of State, as he, and as the country, had reason to expect. Gallatin was, far away, the ablest man of the group— the only truly great man of the Cabinet, ranking next to Hamilton among all the men who have held the office of Secretary of the Treasury. Had he been left in the Treasury simply because he was a masterly financier, it might have been considered in the interest of good government. But he had shown himself as great in state-craft as in finance ; and every one knew that the reason why he was not made Secretary of State was to be found in the jealousy and envy which existed among many leaders of the administration party in Congress, and es-pecially in the intrigues of the Smith brothers—one a Senator from Maryland ; the other, the man chosen to take the place destined for his better. The arrange-ment, therefore, became one which, from the start, weakened Gallatin's influence, and exposed him to the insults and assaults of venomous enemies and impaired the harmony of the Cabinet within, and its prestige before Congress and the country.

From the first Mr. Madison, partly by force of temper-ament, partly by intention, adopted a conciliatory pol-icy toward the moderate federalists, whom Madison's the aggressions of England were driving policy. into something like an approach to the administra-tion. It suited Mr. Madison's interests, as well as his disposition, to strengthen his party from this quarter. On the opposite side, there was some disaffection, owing to Mr. Madison's comparative moderation. A section,* under the half-famous "Randolph of Roanoke," had long done all in its power to embarrass the administra-tion in Congress ; had disputed Mr. Madison's nomina-tion, presenting Mr. Monroe instead, even going so far as to attempt to set that gentleman up as an indepen-dent candidate, and were now not unprepared to make it hot for Mr. Madison.

* Known as the "Quids." This faction, attempting to pose as a third party, had been at first called a *tertium quid* (a third something). The epithet was finally abridged, as stated.

The foregoing statements rather represent the form which the politics of that day took, than express their real significance. The essential fact was that while old federalists were rapidly giving up their party organization, individually, yet still in vast numbers, owing to the defeats and humiliations which they had sustained at the polls, to the disgust and anger which they felt at the recent conduct of England, once the object of their admiration and attachment, and to the lack of anything like bold, strong, and able leadership on their side, the republican party, on the other hand, had, during the past few years, been going over bodily to meet the federalists, and that, even more than half-way. In truth, the republican party of the last days of Jefferson's administration had come to occupy no small portion of the ground on which the federalists of Washington's and Adams's administrations had stood. This was due partly to an increasing sense of American nationality, the natural product of twenty years living together under the Constitution, but even more to the inevitable effect upon the republican party of coming into power and taking up the duties and responsibilities of office. No body of men in the world's history ever did this without becoming self-assertive, and without magnifying the authority of the government they administered.

Changed positions of the two parties.

Against this *rapprochement* of the large majority of the former federalists, and of almost the whole mass of former republicans, at the outset of Madison's administration, and that, too, chiefly upon traditional federalist ground, there were two bodies of remonstrants and protestants, the one consisting of John Randolph's "Quids," now a mere handful, who denounced Madison, and even Jefferson, for their aggrandizing tendency, bewailed the spirit of consolidation, and clamored for a re-

turn to the "old Republicanism" of 1798-99 ; the other
consisting of the remnant, now "a feeble folk," of the
once omnipotent federalist party, represented in the
Senate from only three or four States, and in the House
by a small but courageous, aggressive, and Two irre-
vindictive band, hardly numerous enough to concilable fac-
enforce the briefest parliamentary delays tions.
upon the strictly party measures of the administration,
as was strikingly shown in the case of the embargo
law, which passed the House in three days and the
Senate in about the same number of hours. Just as
the triumphant republicans had largely passed over to
the ground once occupied by their political opponents,
so the unreconciled federalists, now found mainly in
New England, and there chiefly in Massachusetts and
Connecticut, had, in the vehemence and bitterness of
their antagonism to the measures of the government,
completely apostatized from the doctrines of Hamilton
and Adams, and had taken up positions scarcely less
hostile to the authority of the government than those
represented in the nullification resolutions of 1798-99.

The new administration took up the questions pending between the United States and England where they
had been left, without any progress toward The troubles
adjustment, but after much meddling and with England.
muddling, by Mr. Jefferson. In April (1809) Mr. Erskine, the British minister at Washington, represented
that if the United States would rescind the Non-intercourse Act in favor of Great Britain, that power would
recall its Orders in Council. In accordance with this
suggestion Mr. Madison issued a proclamation reopen-
ing trade with Great Britain. That government, however, disavowed Mr. Erskine's act and promptly recalled
him ; so that the President was obliged, on August 3d,
with no great addition to the dignity of our position, to

issue another proclamation declaring the Non-intercourse Act still in force. The new British minister, "Copenhagen Jackson," a man with an evil reputation in the matter of neutral rights, immediately gave cause of offence by declaring that the United States had all along known that Mr. Erskine was exceeding his instructions. Our government, stirred by this imputation of ill faith, declined to hold any further communication with him, and he accordingly returned home. No successor was appointed by his government until 1811.

Now, on his part, Napoleon issued what is known as the Rambouillet decree, March 23, 1810, by which every American vessel and cargo which, since May 20th previous, had entered, or which should thereafter enter, any port of France, or her colonies, or of any country occupied by the French, was liable to be seized and sold. The scope of the order extended to Spain, Holland, and Naples. This measure can only be characterized as an outrageous and monstrous aggression upon our rights, dictated by the insolence of Napoleon, now grown to a masterful and self-destroying passion. The practical consequences of the Rambouillet decree were most disastrous to our interests, vessels numbered by the hundreds being seized thereunder.

Napoleon retaliates.

The Non-intercourse Act, having been limited in its duration, expired early in 1810 ; and on May 1st Congress passed a new act,* providing that, if either Great Britain or France should, before March 3, 1811, revoke or so modify her edicts that they should cease to violate our neutral commerce, and if the other nation should not, within three months thereafter, do the same, then the act interdicting intercourse should be revived against the nation refusing to revoke. On August 5th the Duc de Cadore, French Minister of Foreign Affairs,

* Known as "Macon Bill, No. 2."

informed General Armstrong, our minister at Paris, that "the Berlin and Milan decrees were revoked and would cease to have effect after November 1st following." The reason stated was that "the Congress of the United States had retraced its steps and had engaged to oppose the belligerent (Great Britain) which refused to acknowledge the rights of neutrals." The condition of the revocation was "that the English shall revoke their Orders in Council and renounce the new principle of blockade (*i.e.*, that blockade might lawfully be extended to unfortified ports and to the mouths of rivers), which they have wished to establish, or that the United States shall cause their rights to be respected by the English." Now, inasmuch as the reason stated was false, the United States never having announced any such determination as was assumed, and inasmuch as the condition proposed was one the United States never accepted, it is difficult to see how this amounted to a repeal of the French decrees, in the sense of the act of May 1, 1810. Yet Mr. Madison jumped over these difficulties, and, receiving the report of General Armstrong as conclusive of the action of the French government, issued a proclamation, November 2, 1810, declaring the restrictions removed as respected France and her dependencies. Three months later, namely, March 2, 1811, Congress passed an act declaring these restrictions in force against Great Britain.

The alleged repeal of the French decrees.

This measure was followed by the retirement from office of Mr. Robert Smith, the Secretary of State, who appealed to the country in a review of the whole subject. Mr. Smith declared that the decrees of France had not been actually repealed ; and that, therefore, the proclamation restoring intercourse with France and the act prohibiting intercourse with England were unwarranted. Mr. Smith

Secretary Smith's protest.

adduced the following facts in support of his opposition :
First, that France had notified us, before the passage of
the act of March 2d, that she would not restore the
property seized under the recent decree, although the
State Department had informed France that this would
be a condition, *sine qua non,* of our favorable action.
Secondly, that he (Secretary Smith) had by Mr. Madison's indifference been checked in his intentions to
obtain from the French minister definite and positive
statements regarding the position of his government ;
that Mr. Madison modified in an important degree Mr.
Smith's despatches seeking to place the United States
right in the matter of the outrages perpetrated under
the Rambouillet decree, and that Mr. Madison had finally
refused to allow a letter to be despatched which contained specific inquiries deemed by the Secretary essential to the proper determination of the question whether
France had, in truth and fully, repealed the obnoxious
decrees.   Mr. Smith was succeeded, as Secretary of
State, by Mr. Monroe, who, in assuming the office be-

Monroe be-   came recognized as the "heir-apparent" to
comes heir-ap- the presidency.   Down to this time Mr.
parent.
          Monroe had been put forward by Randolph's
faction, and by Mr. Madison's opponents generally, as
the champion of the "old Republicanism," and had
been incited by them, on every occasion, to exert his influence against the administration.   His public "adoption" by Mr. Madison brought all this to an end, and
removed the most important of the President's enemies
or rivals within his own party.

Of course, England was not satisfied with the action
of the United States regarding the French decrees, and
in a lengthy correspondence asserted the bad faith of
the French government ; the insufficiency of the so-
called revocation ; and the partiality of the United

States, at the expense of Great Britain. Our government, through Mr. Pinkney, at London, and through Mr. Monroe, at Washington, maintained the justice and impartiality of its acts. It was easy to show that Great Britain was in the wrong toward us, and had little cause of complaint whatever measures of self-defence we might adopt. It was not easy to show that France was not equally to blame ; and this part of our case must be esteemed much less satisfactory than the other. But the true explanation of the situation is not found to be in the diplomatic expressions of the State department and of our minister in London. The dominant party had made up their minds that war with England must come ; and that, therefore, war with France must be avoided. To this latter end we would accept from France, not what we wanted, not what we ought to have, but what we could get. Our people had long been, through the powerful attraction of an unsettled question, producing an ever wider and deeper irritation, drifting into war with England, just as England, forty years later, in the phrase of Lord Aberdeen, drifted into the Crimean War. The measures of non-intercourse could scarcely be considered as rational means of preparation. They left the country no better off for the great struggle. They were rather the acts of annoyance and offence by which those who know they must come to blows work themselves up to the fighting point. Meanwhile the angry feelings of the two nations received further exasperation by an accidental collision between the American frigate President and the British sloop-of-war Little Belt, in May, 1811.

We do not say that war with England was inevitable ; that it was even likely to relieve the hardships which the United States had indisputably suffered through the arrogance of England ; but the ill-suppressed hostility

As between France and England.

of twenty years was now culminating. Of all the prominent republican politicians, the president probably was the one least disposed to conflict. Indeed, Mr. Madison had of late been writing and talking much more about the outrages of France than those of England ; he had even sent very threatening letters to Mr. Barlow, our minister at Paris, denouncing the course of that country and not vaguely intimating hostile intentions toward her ; but the tide now running strongly against England carried him steadily forward to the end which was in view of the most ardent fire-eaters of his party. And here we have to note that the impetus to war was not being supplied by the older statesmen of the country, the men who had opposed the British treaty of John Jay, and who had long been known as the anti-Anglican leaders, but by young men of mark who belonged to a new generation—foremost among them, Henry Clay, of Kentucky, and John C. Calhoun, of South Carolina. But for these, it is probable the result of war would not have been reached. The United States had borne with the injurious acts of France and England for six years. Two years more would have seen all the issues—search, impressment, blockade, and infringements of neutral trade—disappear in the downfall of Napoleon and the restoration of peace in Europe.

The regular meeting of Congress was anticipated in consequence of the political situation ; and that body met on November 4, 1811, when the President communicated the diplomatic proceedings of the government during the year. He declared that " the period had arrived which claimed from the legislative guardians of the national rights a system of more ample provision for maintaining them." On the 29th of the month the Committee on Foreign Relations, under the chairmanship of Mr. Peter B. Porter, of New York, made a very warlike report, which concluded with the recommendation that the army be increased, that the navy be put into condition for service ; and that merchant vessels be allowed to arm in self-defence.

On March 9, 1812, the President communicated an alleged attempt of the British government to disaffect and detach from the Union the northern and northeastern States. The fact disclosed The Henry episode. was that Sir James Craig, Governor-General of Canada, had employed one John Henry to proceed to Boston and to keep him informed as to the state of public opinion with regard to general politics and to the probability of war with England ; as to the comparative strength of the parties ; and the views and designs of that which might ultimately prevail. Henry passed through Vermont and New Hampshire to Boston, whence he wrote a number of letters to the Governor-General and his secretary. It does not appear that he communicated directly on the subject of separation with any person of importance, or that his mission amounted to anything in fact. He was recalled ; and upon the Governor-General failing to confer upon him the office he had promised, Henry sold information of his mission to our State Department, which is exactly what the man who would volunteer for such a service would be likely to do. Considerable excitement was caused by the discovery, both here and in England, where the opposition assailed the course of the Governor-General as treacherous and of a hostile tendency. It cannot be said that the mission of Henry was in violation of international usage, though it certainly was not a friendly act. The matter would hardly be worth mentioning, but for the notoriety which the whole affair assumed to exist as to the disaffection of the New England States, and the intimation it conveyed of a possible antagonism between the two sections of the country in the event of war.

On April 1st the President sent to Congress a confidential message, recommending an embargo for sixty days. This, as preliminary to a declaration of war, was a sound and sensible measure, differing widely from Mr. Jefferson's embargo, as a policy of negotiation. On May 18th, the Republican caucus was held for the nomination of candidates for the seventh presidential election. Mr. Madison was unanimously renominated, Elbridge Gerry, of Massachusetts, being named as vice-president with him. Here we have to note the familiar charge that Mr. Madison, who had been known to be strongly disposed to peace, accepted war as the condition of his renomination. This is one of those charges which are certain under such circumstances to be made ; but which can neither be proved nor disproved. Probably Mr. Madison could not have told how far he was influenced by the fact that his supporters were resolutely bent on resenting the aggressions of Great Britain. At the same time it is to be said that Mr. Madison's own previous declarations gave a high degree of probability to the charge of being thus influenced. Mr. Madison was, in due course, elected.

A fortnight later, *i.e.*, on June 1st, the President sent in another confidential message, recommending war. Foremost among the causes mentioned was the impressment of our seamen. Next came the blockades, in violation of the accepted rules and definitions of international law, persisted in after the French had withdrawn the decrees by which the English government had sought to justify its own acts. Finally, the President expressed the belief that the recent renewal of hostilities by the northwestern Indians was due to British instigation. Meanwhile a fresh correspondence was going on between Mr. Monroe and the British minister at Washington, covering the whole ground at issue between the two countries. No result, however, could be reached so long as the United States insisted upon regarding the announcement to General Armstrong as sufficient evidence of the repeal of the offensive decrees ; while the English government looked upon this as "a deceitful declaration." Just in this crisis of affairs information was received of the full and unconditional revocation of the Berlin and Milan decrees by Napoleon. The order making the revocation was dated nearly a year previous. It was naturally charged that this was a trick, the order having been called out by the exigency which had arisen in the United States, and having been dated back to make good the assertions of our government in respect to the action of France. It would seem, now, as if a little time should have been given to ascertain what England would do ; whether she would revoke her Orders in Council since France had recalled her decrees. It did not, however, suit party purposes to await the action of England, and June 18, 1812, war was declared. The vote on the final passage was 19 to 13 in the Senate, and 79 to 49 in the House of Representatives. The division was largely on sectional lines. Fourteen of the nineteen senators voting for the declaration lived south of the Delaware River ; sixty-two of the seventy-nine representatives who constituted the majority came from the same region.

Before adjournment the federalist members published an address to the people, which strongly arrayed the reasons against war and vindicated their course in opposing the declaration. It was **The Federalist protest.** charged that the war had been urged on by party considerations ; that the conquest of Canada, and not redress

15

for alleged injuries, was the real object in view. It was asserted that the acts of the British government in respect to impressment were accordant with the usages of all the governments of Europe, including France ; and that England had shown an earnest disposition to effect an amicable adjustment of this vexed subject, having, in 1802, made an offer to renounce the right of impressing American seamen, whether native or naturalized Englishmen, upon the high seas, only retaining the right upon the narrow seas ; the ministry, on another occasion, having offered to pass laws making it penal for British commanders to impress American citizens upon the high seas, provided the United States would pass laws making it penal for its officers to grant certificates of citizenship to British subjects. The address undertook to show that the blockade of 1806 was at first accepted by our government as favorable to the United States. In proof it was alleged that when Mr. Jefferson's administration, in 1808, offered to repeal the embargo upon certain conditions, the withdrawal of the blockade was not one of them ; nor was this made a part of the negotiations with Mr. Erskine in 1809. The address further dwelt on the matter already adduced, to show that the Berlin and Milan decrees had not been in good faith and fully revoked. This address was signed by thirty-four members of the House of Representatives, all federalists—nineteen from New England ; six from New York, Pennsylvania, and Delaware ; nine from Maryland, Virginia, and North Carolina. Fifteen republicans had voted against the declaration, eleven of them being from New York and New Jersey ; one, each, from Massachusetts, Pennsylvania, Virginia, and North Carolina.

But though war was declared, negotiations were not yet concluded. Soon after the declaration the British minister left for London, bearing a letter from Mr. Monroe to our chargé at the court of St. James, instructing him to propose an armistice upon certain conditions, which were made more liberal by a second letter. Meanwhile the news was travelling across the Atlantic that England had, on June 23d, only five days after the declaration, revoked her Orders in Council. To detail the miserable contretemps and misunderstandings by which the two nations, which had thus reduced their causes of quarrel from two to one, about which both parties professed to be anxious to reach a satisfactory adjustment, allowed themselves to go on to actual hostilities, would occupy more time than we can spare. The Atlantic cable would in all probability have made war impossible. As it was, with the tedious communications of that day, our government professed to fear that awaiting negotiations would enable England to fortify Canada and give time for the Indians, who had taken the British side, to commit wholesale ravages on our settlements. And so, after one or two abortive attempts of the two governments to get together, hostilities commenced. The history of the war of 1812 is not an entertaining one for Americans ; yet it will not be from an excess of patriotic sensibility that we shall make our account of it very short, but because there is little in it which belongs to the story of American political development.

Failure of negotiations for peace.

The war opened with an evil omen, for the first blood shed was that of Americans, spilled in miserable civil strife. One Hanson had set up in Baltimore a paper opposed to the administration and to the war policy. This so exasperated some of the "lewd fellows of the baser sort" that they destroyed Hanson's printing-office and presses, and for a time put a stop to his enterprise. A few weeks later, however, he resumed publication, this time under the protection

The Hanson riot in Baltimore.

of some prominent federalists, among them two distinguished revolutionary officers, General Lingan and General Harry Lee, the latter famous for the eulogy on Washington, pronounced before Congress, in which occurred the words, " first in war, first in peace, and first in the hearts of his countrymen." A mob having attacked Hanson's office by night, these gentlemen with a small party conducted a desperate defence, which was only relinquished upon the assurance of the Mayor that they should be given a legal trial for the deaths which had occurred, with full protection meanwhile. Having surrendered upon this promise, the defenders were subjected to the most cowardly indignities while on their way to prison. The night following, the prison was broken open by armed men ; General Lingan was beaten to death ; General Lee was crippled for life ; and their comrades were subjected to abuse and torture of the most monstrous character. The very spirit of hell was manifested by the ruffians, who worked their mischief under the eye of the Mayor and the commander of the city militia. At last, upon the mob threatening to break open the United States post-office, in order to seize the copies of the offending publications which had been deposited in the mails, the authorities actively intervened ; and the riot was quelled. But the prosecutions instituted against the perpetrators of these crimes completely failed through the culpable delinquency of the Attorney-General, who openly expressed his regret that every person concerned in the defence of Hanson's house had not been killed, and refused to demand a change of venue ; while the city council, after a professed investigation of the affair, laid the whole blame upon Hanson, who had presumed to publish a paper not agreeable to the rioters, and upon his friends who had defended him from murder and arson. There is little doubt that the

Baltimore riot was welcomed by many hot-headed partisans of the war in other sections of the country, as likely
to exert a wholesome effect in deterring federalists from
the public expression of their views.   To the honor of
the people of Maryland, it should be mentioned that
this dastardly outrage worked a complete political revolution in the State, which at the next election went
federalist by a large majority, Hanson himself being
sent to Congress, where, it may be added, he did not
distinguish himself by patriotism or good sense.   "Mar-
tyrs" of that sort rarely do.

CHAPTER XII

THE WAR OF 1812-15

IF those are in the right who charge that the administration of Mr. Madison provoked war, not to redress our wrongs upon the ocean, but to gain glory and territory by the conquest of Canada,* then the general results of the war would seem to show the most remarkable discrimination upon the part of Providence in apportioning honor and shame, success and failure, according to the direction in which our efforts were put forth. Upon

---

* " The cession of Canada, the fulcrum for these Machiavellian levers, must be a *sine qua non* at a treaty of peace " (Jeff., vi., 70, cf. 78).

the ocean, our little navy of eight or ten frigates and as
many sloops and brigs, was, in anything like equal combat, almost uniformly victorious. The nation which
had learned to think itself invincible on the ocean,
"mistress of the seas," was astonished to find its vessels
of war beaten and captured by hastily built and rudely
equipped ships, manned by sailors taken from the fishing fleets of New Bedford, Marblehead, and Gloucester.
Again and again the flag of England went down before
the fire of our extemporized gunners, commanded by
such heroes as Hull, Jones, Porter, Bainbridge, and Decatur. It is true these brilliant successes did not give
us the command even of our own waters ; Our remark-
and that, when the British squadrons finally able success
closed in, our few frigates were driven under on the water.
cover of the guns of the forts, or fell into the hands
of the enemy through an overwhelming superiority of
force, while our coast was ravaged from Maine to Virginia. Not the less did these gallant exploits raise the
fame of the American nation all over the world, and go
far to redeem the failures and disgraces of the war.
Twice, upon the Lakes, hastily built squadrons, under
Perry and McDonough, defeated superior forces of the
enemy, and compelled the retreat of formidable armies.
Remarkable as were the achievements of our national
vessels, these were equalled, if not surpassed, by the
enterprise, audacity, and resourcefulness of the private
armed vessels which, under cover of "letters of marque,"
poured forth from all the seaports of the Atlantic, from
Machias to Baltimore, and swiftly and terribly avenged
the wrongs to which the merchantmen of the United
States had been helplessly subjected during The priva-
twenty years. American "privateers," free teers.
lances on the ocean, commanded by men of the utmost daring, manned by powerful crews of expert and

hardy seamen, largely fishermen from Newfoundland and the banks of St. George, worked havoc with the commerce of England, and did not hesitate upon occasion to match themselves against the royal cruisers. It is stated that during the three years of the war seventeen hundred British ships were captured. The culmination of the achievements of the privateers was when the brig General Armstrong, lying at Fayal, beat off, with terrible slaughter, the boats of three British war-vessels.

On the other hand, our ambitious enterprises against Canada were in the main characterized by blundering incompetence on the part of our generals, and too often by misconduct and seeming cowardice on the part of the troops engaged. Altogether our efforts in that direction were not only futile, but humiliated us at home and disgraced us abroad. So it came about that many persons who doubted the good faith of the administration in going to war, were much disposed to see, in the distribution of success and failure, as between the sea, where we had undoubtedly suffered wrong, and the land, where these persons deemed us the aggressors, something in the nature of divine retribution.

Ignominious failure on land.

More strictly natural causes may, however, be assigned for our differing fortunes by land and by sea. If there is any work or knowledge or device under the sun in which the single quality of " gumption " tells, it is in working and fighting a ship ; and if there ever was a people who pre-eminently possessed that quality, it was the northern half of the American people, in the time of which we are speaking. Our ships were worked by volunteers, all good seamen, hot for fight and eager for prizes ; all of them natural mechanics, quick to spread or take in sail, quick to cut

Our naval victories accounted for.

away the wreckage of battle and to rig masts or put out
spars to draw their vessels out of fire. Our ships, too,
were more liberally manned than the English. It ought
not to be a matter of surprise, therefore, that the steady
discipline, unflinching courage, and bulldog tenacity of
the English sailors did not carry the day against the
adroitness, adaptability, suppleness, and fertility of resource which characterize the Yankee, and pre-eminently the Yankee sailor. On the other hand, our land
forces were composed largely of fresh levies, through
the traditional policy of the Republican party, which
had discouraged the increase of the regular army. The
rank and file were men of generous strain enough, but
they were new to the business ; they were not well disciplined ; they had little confidence in themselves, and
in the majority of cases, and with better reason, less
confidence in their officers. Then, again (which has a
great deal to do with this question of courage or cowardice), being inland and with land behind, they could
run away, which sailors cannot do.

The census of 1810 had shown the population of the
United States to be about seven and a quarter millions,
while the population of the United King-
dom was eighteen and a half millions. But
this difference in numbers does not fully express the difference in strength and resources. England
was a rich and powerful nation, packed with the accu-
mulations of successful industry. By the side of every
Englishman employed in her mills or mines or on her
fields worked one, two, three laborers, asking no wages,
costing nothing for their support, representing the
power of past production—capital. To this people were
tributary scores of millions of human beings, in all quarters of the globe, whose industry and trade were despot-
ically controlled so as to yield the largest possible tax to

*Compara-
tive strength
of the belliger-
ents.*

the public and private revenues of Great Britain.   This
nation, moreover, with such power and resources, was
organized for war.   Her army was large, compact, and
highly disciplined.   Her fleets, though no longer commanded by Nelson, were the terror of the seas.   There
is no doubt that, comparing the two nations with each
other, as to their offensive power upon neutral, intermediate ground, had such existed, Great Britain would
have been as five to one.   It is true that, on our chosen
battlefield, Canada, we had the advantage of proximity.
On the other hand, Great Britain enjoyed there the possession of many strongholds.   What, then, made it less
than madness for us to enter upon the War of 1812 ?
We answer, the fact that England was still engaged with
her great enemy, Napoleon, upon the continent of Europe.   Although the disasters of successive Spanish
campaigns had already befallen that aspiring conqueror,
Russia and Moscow were still to come.   Had it been
1813 instead of 1812, we should scarcely have declared
war.   Had it been 1814, we should have had no occasion
to declare war, for the questions at issue would then
have disappeared of themselves.

We had refused to delay hostilities lest we should lose
the advantage we assumed we had in invading Canada *
before she was fully prepared.   We were now to find out
how contemptible were the dispositions of the government for the conquest of this territory, how destitute
of all administrative efficiency was Mr. Madison, and
how great was the incompetence of our commanders.
In July, less than a month after the declaration, General Hull, Governor of Michigan Territory, crossed from
Detroit into Canada.   In August, without striking a

* In the debate on the Non-intercourse Act of 1806, Mr. Crowninshield, of Massachusetts, confidently asserted the ability of the militia of
Vermont and Massachusetts, alone, to capture Canada and Nova Scotia.

blow, he surrendered to General Brock. This invasion of Canada was over. At once we were put on the defensive. The British occupied the whole of Michigan, and pressed our troops, now commanded by General William Henry Harrison, afterward President, in their efforts to capture Ohio. In January, 1813, a detachment of Kentucky troops under Winchester surrendered at Frenchtown, on the river Raisin ; and during April and May, and again in July, our forces stood siege at Fort Meigs, on the Maumee.

The invasion of Canada collapses.

Nothing, seemingly, saved Ohio but our quickly raised fleet on Lake Erie. On the 10th of September, 1813, Lieutenant Oliver Hazard Perry, of the United States Navy, then twenty-seven years of age, leading a motley crowd of vessels, all but two of which had been hastily converted from peaceful to warlike purposes, engaged the British squadron, of slightly superior force as respected men and guns, led by an officer who had served under Nelson at Trafalgar, and, by pure force of pluck and brains, won a complete victory, capturing the entire force of the enemy. This action saved Ohio and recovered the greater part of Michigan. General Harrison, in command of the lake, was able to throw troops upon the enemy's lines of communication, compelling the evacuation of Detroit. In his pursuit, General Harrison brought on a battle, upon the banks of the Thames, in which the famous Indian ally of the British, Tecumseh, was slain.

Perry's victory on Lake Erie.

So much for the operations on the Michigan end of the line. On the New York frontier General Van Rensselaer was in command of the American forces. In October, 1812, he crossed and attacked Queenstown, but was driven back and a portion of his force captured. The British commander, Brock, was killed. General Van Rensselaer

Further disasters on the Canada line.

resigned immediately after. In the spring of 1813 General Henry Dearborn, who had been Secretary of War under Jefferson, took Toronto, then York, burning the Parliament House and captured the forts on the Niagara River. Dearborn having been relieved, Generals Wilkinson and Hampton undertook a campaign against Montreal, which resulted in shameful failure. Meanwhile we were driven out of Fort George; and our commander retired to the American side, burning the village of Newark. During the winter the British crossed in turn, captured Fort Niagara, which they held to the close of the war, and swept the country with fire and sword as far as Buffalo. In the spring of 1814 General Wilkinson again left his quarters, only to make another exhibition of helpless imbecility. And thus we come to the third year of the war in which Canada was to be conquered and glory gained to the administration : nothing done but what the navy had done ; much suffered, both of loss and of disgrace. Hereafter the operations on the Canada line were destined to be less discreditable to the American arms, though still wholly fruitless.

The British forces were now greatly strengthened by arrivals from Europe, the fall of Napoleon having enabled the government to send hither a large body of veterans, under eminent officers. On the American side our troops were settling down more and more to the real business of war ; while they were rid of the generation of incompetents who had thrown away the royal opportunity afforded them when England was engaged in its deadly struggle on the Continent. Younger commanders of merit were coming to the front, as has to be the case in nearly every war before success becomes possible. Major-General Jacob Brown, afterward Commander-in-Chief of the United States Army, who had distinguished himself in the defence of Sackett's Harbor, in 1813, had succeeded to the command of our forces on the frontier. With him was Colonel Winfield Scott, also destined to become in time General-in-Chief. On the 2d of July, *Creditable actions under Brown and Scott.* having crossed to the Canada side, Brown took Fort Erie ; and three days later, at Chippewa defeated the enemy under General Riall. The latter, having been reinforced by Drummond, pushed back our column ; and on the 25th of July was fought the fiercely contested action of Lundy's Lane, within the roar of Niagara. The American forces were successful upon the field ; but were obliged to fall back to Fort Erie, where they stood siege (under General Gaines, Brown having been wounded) until September, when Fort Erie was blown up and abandoned.

Meanwhile an action had been fought on Lake Champlain which added much to the credit of the American name. The British General Prevost, with 12,000 regular troops, supported by a squadron, attacked Plattsburg ; but before the *McDonough's victory on Lake Champlain.* land forces could fairly engage each other (our infantry being much inferior in numbers), Captain McDonough, commanding the American squadron upon the lake, brought to utter defeat the superior naval force of the enemy, involving the precipitate retreat of Prevost and putting a stop to all projects for invading the territory of the United States from that quarter. And this was how we took Canada in the War of 1812.

Turn we now to other quarters, where the British forces were pushing strongly against us, with full and fell determination to punish the insolence of the young republic. By the close of 1813 we had scarcely a vessel on the water. Our gallant cruisers had been driven under cover of the forts or captured by the powerful squadrons closing in upon our coasts. From Machias to Alexandria our harbors were blockaded and our towns and villages burned. The barbarities of the English fleet, under distinct orders to " destroy and lay waste all towns and districts of the United States, found accessive to the attack of the British armaments," were doubtless an unwarrantable extension of the ravages of war ; but we must not fail to remember the burning of Newark and of the Parliament House at Toronto.

Burning of Washington— Defence of Baltimore. In August, 1814, two powerful fleets, under Admirals Cockburn and Cochrane, occupied the Chesapeake and the Potomac, and landed a detachment of troops, under General Ross, which marched on Washington. At Bladensburg, five or six miles from the capital, the British put to disgraceful rout the militia which had been assembled to oppose them. The day following, the public buildings, including the Capitol and the President's mansion, were plundered and burned, whereupon the British troops retired. There was worse fortune for the invaders when they appeared, two weeks later, before Baltimore. At the battle of North Point the American forces, though ultimately obliged to retire, gallantly held their ground, General Ross, the British commander, being killed ; and upon the fleet moving up to attack Fort McHenry, the defence was so spirited that the British withdrew with loss. It is to the bombardment of Fort McHenry, upon this occasion, that the " Star-Spangled Banner " has reference.

Let us once more shift our place, this time to the scene of operations in the Southwest, where we may see the last of the War of 1812. It has been noted that the Northwest Indians, under Tecumseh, had made themselves the allies of the British. In 1813 the Creeks at the South rose in arms, and, after inflicting severe

loss upon our volunteers, were brought to extremity
and routed with terrible slaughter at Tohopeka, March
27, 1814, by General Andrew Jackson, of   Jackson's
Tennessee, a man new to fame but possessing victories at
extraordinary qualities as a leader of men, the South.
whether in war or in peace. This victory led to the
submission of the Creeks and the cession of the larger
part of their lands. In the fall of the same year we
find General Jackson operating against the British
forces in the direction of Pensacola and Mobile. A
little later, the British, in heavy force of veteran troops,
advanced to the attack upon New Orleans. On the
23d of December, Jackson, with a far inferior force of
raw troops, made a successful night-attack upon the
British camp, inflicting considerable loss. On the
8th of January, 1815, General Pakenham, commanding
the invading forces, attacked Jackson's position covering New Orleans, but was repelled with great slaughter,
Pakenham and his second in command being killed.

The battle of New Orleans was in all respects a very
remarkable action. When it was fought, England and
the United States were at peace, a treaty The treaty of
having been signed at Ghent, in the Decem-   peace.
ber previous, by the commissioners of the two powers.
The objects of the war on the part of the United States
were not even mentioned. The rights of neutral trade
were not defined in the treaty. England did not withdraw her claims to the right of impressment; and the
status quo was stipulated as to territory. A week later
the President recommended the navigation of American vessels exclusively by American seamen, either natives or such as had been naturalized. But while thus,
so far as appears by the treaty of peace, the United
States obtained nothing for which it had fought, the
issues as to neutral rights and impressment had, of

themselves, sunk out of all practical importance, in the course of events. As war had ceased in Europe, there was no longer any question of neutral rights; while the wholesale reduction of the English navy, upon the conclusion of peace, made it no longer necessary to resort to impressment to man its ships.

We have thus far confined our account of the War of 1812 to its purely military features, in order that we might get a connected view of the whole, without the intrusion of the civil and political embarrassments of the administration. In point of fact, the conduct of the war was greatly interfered with by the persistent opposition of the federalist party, which still controlled the commercial States. These States had opposed the embargo, and still hated its memory and execrated its author. They believed that Mr. Jefferson's policy was dictated by a desire to establish, in his own words, " an equilibrium between the occupations of agriculture, manufactures, and commerce, which shall simplify our foreign concerns to the exchange of that surplus which we cannot consume for those articles of reasonable comfort or convenience which we cannot produce." If these persons misunderstood Mr. Jefferson in this respect, it was his fault, not theirs. His writings abound in expressions of reluctance to see the United States become a commercial nation ; and upon retiring from the presidency we find him congratulating his countrymen (as represented by the Democratic-Republican delegates from the townships of Washington County, Penn.) upon the fact that, if the embargo laws " had not had all the effect in bringing the powers of Europe to a sense of justice

Opposition to the war.

which a more faithful observance of them might have produced," they had at least tended to establish the equilibrium described above in his own words ; that is, they had served the interests of the country by distressing, and in a degree destroying, that commerce which other statesmen valued and sought to cherish, but which he regarded as baleful and dangerous.

Mr. Jefferson may have been right in his estimation of general commerce, *i.e.*, trade carried beyond the mere exchange of the national surplus for articles destined to consumption by the nation itself ; but it can scarcely be a matter of surprise that the commercial communities of the North and Northeast, whose enterprise had developed an enormous " carrying trade," in which their capital was invested and upon which their people depended for subsistence, failed to take the same view, or that deep and bitter hatred was engendered by what they deemed the wanton and unconstitutional destruction of the navigation interests of the country. The fact is, Mr. Jefferson was the most extravagant protectionist ever placed in a position importantly to influence the trade and industry of a civilized nation. Other protectionists have sought to build up manufactures or commerce. Mr. Jefferson is the only one in the range of our reading who could congratulate himself and the country upon the success of measures for the destruction of trade, as promoting the harmonious development of national life. His writings at about the time to which we refer contain easy-gliding descriptions of how the surplus commercial capital of the Northeast could be diverted to other uses.

Mr. Jefferson's political economy.

The embargo, so bitterly opposed in New England, was repealed, as we have seen, in 1809 ; and three years later came the war, brought on, as the same States persisted in believing, for the purpose of strengthening the

16

administration with the agricultural and planting sections, through the enhancement of the prices of their products,* and for the glory of conquering and annexing Canada. To this end, their principal means of subsistence, trade and the fisheries, must again be cut up by the roots ; their coast be ravaged from one end to the other ; their vessels rot at the wharves. It is no matter for wonder that the idea of war was exceedingly obnoxious to these communities ; that their representatives opposed the declaration bitterly to the last ; and that the continuance of hostilities was felt to be a grievous and almost intolerable affliction. But it is charged that these States, particularly Massachusetts and Connecticut, carried their rightful political opposition to the war, as a measure proposed, over into the war itself, Alleged treasonable opposition to the war. as a fact existing and for the present inevitable ; and that, by their public acts and by the language and behavior of the great body of their citizens, they embarrassed the government in the conduct of the war, and gave aid and comfort to the enemy. If the federalist party was not guilty of this, it was at least the appearance of this which destroyed the federalist party. Those who will not be careful to avoid the appearance of evil may not complain if they suffer the blame of it. The language used by the opponents of the war was extremely violent. We have seen how the knowledge of disaffection led Governor-General Craig to send his emissary into New England, to observe

---

* " To keep the war popular, we must keep open the markets. So long as good prices can be had, the people will support the war cheerfully." —Jefferson, vi., 93.

" That grain (wheat) has got to $2 at Richmond, this is the true barometer of the popularity of the war."—Jefferson, vi., 102.

Exactly what was to make the war popular with the people who lived by other means than by raising wheat and tobacco, Mr. Jefferson does not state.

how far these States might be ripe for separation from
the rest of the Union.   There is reason to believe that
the possibility of a rising in this quarter mingled with
the strictly military plans of the British commanders,
however much or however little ground there may have
been for such an expectation.   But in addition to much
wild and ferocious talk, two distinct things * are alleged
against the federalist party in New England.

The first of these was the refusal of the governors of
Connecticut and Massachusetts to allow the militia of
their States to march upon the president's
requisitions.   These refusals were based on The militia.
the assumption that no invasion was in progress ; and
that no danger thereof existed in any such degree as to
raise a constitutional obligation to comply with the
requisitions.   It will be seen that the governors of these
States made themselves judges of the exigency.   It is
not altogether certain that, however unpatriotic their
action may be considered, they were yet outside their
authority in so doing.   The Constitution had authorized Congress "to provide for the calling forth of the
militia to execute the laws of the Union, suppress insurrections, and repel invasions."   Congress had, by the act
of February 28, 1795, prescribed the limits within which
the executive might make requisitions for this purpose.
It is fairly a question whether such a requisition from
the president does anything more than create an occasion which justifies a State executive in calling out the
militia ; whether it imposes upon him any legal duty, as
distinguished from a patriotic obligation.   It is still
more a question whether the governors of Connecticut
and Massachusetts may not have been technically, as

---

* We take no account of the charge that false signals were put up on
the shore to mislead our vessels or betray them to the enemy.   Those
tales, which gave rise to the expression "Blue-light Federalists," are
too monstrous to be believed.

distinguished from morally, right in asserting that, if they officially knew that the exigency assumed in the requisition did, in fact, not exist, it was competent to them to withhold compliance : in a word, that they were rightful judges of the situation.

The second measure on the part of the New England federalists, alleged to be of a disloyal if not treasonable nature, was the Hartford Convention. This famous gathering of the disaffected took place in December, 1814. The idea of a convention of the States opposing the war was started in Massachusetts. It was later modified to the form of a " Conference " between the New England States, action upon subjects of a national nature to be left to a future convention of all the States. The Massachusetts legislature appointed twelve delegates, and invited other New England States to send representatives. Connecticut appointed seven ; and designated Hartford as the place of meeting. Rhode Island appointed four. Two counties in New Hampshire and one in Vermont appointed one delegate each. The *personnel* of the gathering was of the most distinguished character, as to ability and social position. The list of the Massachusetts members will suffice : George Cabot, Nathan Dane, William Prescott, Harrison Gray Otis, Timothy Bigelow, Joshua Thomas, Stephen Longfellow, Jr., Daniel Waldo. Mr. Cabot was chosen president.

At the time, and for many years after, the Convention was spoken of by the republicans, and their successors, the democrats, as a treasonable gathering. On the 6th of January, 1817, General Jackson, writing to the president-elect (Monroe), says, " Had I commanded the military department where the Hartford Convention met, if it had been the last act of my life, I should have punished the three principal leaders of the party."

Punishing, with General Jackson, meant hanging or shooting. He was very apt to say such things ; and what is more to the point, he was, as Arbuthnot and Ambrister found, very apt to do them. It will be remembered that he promised the leaders of the nullification movement of 1832–33, that he would hang them from the walls of the Capitol. The publication of the journal of the Convention and of a history of its inception and proceedings by the secretary, Theodore Dwight, has completely controverted the charges of treasonable deliberations and conspiracy. And, indeed, to all but the bitterest partisans, the slightest knowledge of the men composing the Convention would have been a guaranty that nothing of such a nature was possible. Yet for many a long year the term " Hartford Conventionist " was, in the ears of a great majority of the American people, synonymous with traitor. Not only did the Convention destroy the federalist party beyond all possibility of a resurrection ; but it proved to be the blighting of many a fair and promising career. Every man who took part in it was a marked man ; and, so far as the utmost rage of the republican party and press could go, he was outcast and outlawed politically.

The actual work of the Convention issued in a lengthy report, containing four resolutions, the last of which presented to the States seven proposed amendments to the Constitution, some good, some bad, which were as follows :

1. Excluding slaves from the basis on which representation and direct taxes are apportioned.

2. Requiring for the admission of new States the concurrence of two-thirds of both houses.

3. Prohibiting Congress from laying an embargo for more than sixty days.

4. Prohibiting Congress from interdicting commercial intercourse with foreign nations without a two-thirds vote of both houses.

5. Requiring a two-thirds vote to declare war or authorize acts of hostility against a foreign nation, except in defence and in cases of actual invasion.

6. Making ineligible to any civil office under the general government any person thereafter naturalized.

7. The president to be eligible only for a single term and not to be chosen two terms in succession from the same State.

The latter clause was aimed at Virginia, which had already furnished three out of the four presidents; while Mr. Monroe was closely in line of succession as a fourth Virginian.

The most seriously objectionable portions of the report, however, were those which recommended to the States the adoption of measures to prevent the execution of certain provisions of the enlistment laws of the United States, deemed unconstitutional, and which contemplated independent provision for defence on the part of States, or groups of States, in case of invasion. All military and political considerations oppose the latter recommendation. The former is in the true spirit of the nullification resolutions of 1798; and indeed it must be said that, since 1808, the extreme federalists of New England had not refrained from expressing opinions which, if made good by action, would have destroyed the authority and even the existence of the government under the Union. But, after all, the great objection to be made to the Hartford Convention lies against the mere fact of the Convention itself. For all purposes not of mere courtesy and ceremony the only place where the States ought to be found represented is in Congress. It is to be confessed, however, that such gatherings have been since held, some of them for very highly patriotic purposes, as in the case of conventions of the governors of the loyal States during the War of Secession.

One is tempted to say that the terms of peace were creditable neither to our diplomacy nor to our arms; yet, when it is considered that the negotia- The terms of tors, upon the part of the United States, in- peace. cluded John Quincy Adams, Henry Clay, and Albert Gallatin, it is doubtless only just to lay the blame for an unsatisfactory settlement wholly upon our lack of national prestige and upon the failure of our warlike enterprises. We had gone to war chiefly on the question of impressment, refusing to accept the compromises offered by England on that subject. In the treaty which closed three years of doubtful fighting, our commissioners were obliged to waive the question of impressment, reserving it for future settlement, as it had been reserved by the Jay treaty twenty years before. Two extravagant and wholly impossible demands were made by England during the negotiations which deserve to be noted. One was, that not only should the Indian allies of England be included in the pacification (which was well enough), but that a definite and permanent boundary should be established between them and the United States, our government to be precluded from any future purchase of their territory. The second demand was that the United States should relinquish the right of maintaining military posts on the northern lakes. Both these demands were decisively denied by our commissioners. The treaty as signed provided for the mutual restoration of conquered territory, and for the appointment of commissioners to settle the boundary on the northeast and to run the northern line as far as the Lake of the Woods.

As to fishing on the shores of British America, the English commissioners declined to renew the privileges formerly enjoyed by our citizens, which they deemed to have been terminated by the war. The loss of the right to fish on the shores of British America, thus occurring, continued, in spite of a partial adjustment in 1818, at intervals to threaten the peace of the two nations until, by the treaty of Washington, in 1870, this right was regained in the exchange of benefits and payments therein provided for.

In this connection let us note an act, passed before the close of Mr. Madison's administration, which has remained in force down to the present time, to regulate the relations of our people toward foreign powers, friendly to us but at war with each other. This was the general Neutrality law of 1817, which made provision against fitting out vessels within the jurisdiction of the United States, to aid or co-operate in warlike measures against nations with which we should be at peace. This act has been of great service, having frequently been invoked against "filibustering" enterprises, whether under the impulse of the slave power or due to misguided sympathy with communities struggling for independence.

The Neutrality law.

Fresh acts of hostility on the part of Algiers had followed the outbreak of our war with England; but of these the government at Washington wisely took little notice until the conclusion of the treaty of peace left our hands free, when a powerful fleet, under Commodore Decatur, was sent to the Mediterranean and speedily coerced the pirates, the Dey being compelled to sign terms, upon Decatur's quarter-deck, by which he renounced all claims to future tribute or presents from the United States, and agreed to surrender American captives held in slavery by his

Coercion of the Barbary powers.

people. Tripoli and Tunis were also brought to submission, and the "Barbary powers" ceased from that
time to vex our commerce.

Indian troubles had preceded the War of 1812. These
still continued, in some degree, after its close. We have
seen that Great Britain had sought, in the   The Indian
treaty of peace, to give special and extraor-   allies of Great
dinary protection to her late allies by secur-   Britain.
ing them their lands in perpetuity ; but that the commissioners on the part of the United States accorded to
that part of the British propositions little consideration.
In September, 1815, peace was made with the tribes
lately at war.

CHAPTER XIII

THE CIVIL EVENTS OF MADISON'S ADMINISTRATION

The Seventh Presidential Election—DeWitt Clinton Nominated by the Disaffected Republicans and Supported by the Federalists —Madison Re-elected—The Third Census—Redistribution of Representatives—The Strengthening of National Authority —The Olmstead Case—Chief Justice Marshall's Contributions to American Nationality—Expiry of the National Bank—Financial Measures Incident to the War—The Republican Party Driven to Direct Taxes and other Offensive Means of Obtaining Revenue — The Salary-Grab Bill — New States—Economic Measures—The New Age—President Madison Advocates a Protective Tariff—The Protectionist Argument of that time —Position of the South—The Tariff of 1816—The Second National Bank—The Navigation Act—Internal Improvements —Changes in the Cabinet—Mr. Monroe Chosen President—Retrospect.

HAVING briefly described the war with England, let us return to consider the chief civil events and measures of Madison's administration. The interest taken by the people in the controversy which resulted in the declaration of July 18, 1812, was so intense and absorbing that nearly all the political thought and feeling of Mr. Madison's first three years expended itself in discussing our national wrongs and in considering the political measures of retaliation or redress. Mr. Madison having, as

The seventh presidential election. stated, been nominated by the administration party, DeWitt Clinton, of New York, was put up by the disaffected republicans, with the understanding that he would receive the votes of the federalists. Mr. Clinton, the nephew of George Clin-

ton, had become early distinguished in the ranks of the
republicans ; but he now placed himself in opposition,
partly from ambition, partly from his dislike of the
"Virginia Dynasty." He received 89 electoral votes,
all the votes of New York, Massachusetts, New Jersey, New Hampshire, Connecticut, Rhode Island, and
Delaware, with 5 from Maryland. These were substantially federalist votes, reënforced by opposition to the
war and dislike of Virginian domination within the
government. One blank vote was thrown from Ohio.
Mr. Madison received 128 votes, all the votes of Vermont and Pennsylvania ; 7 from Ohio, 6 from Maryland, and the full vote of the southern and southwestern States except those already named. Elbridge Gerry,
of Massachusetts, received 131 votes as vice-president.
Ohio, as a State settled mainly from the northeast, exhibited its natural affiliations with New England and
New York. Kentucky and Tennessee went with Virginia and North Carolina, their parent States, respectively.

The third census, taken in 1810, showed a total population of 7,239,903, of whom 1,191,364 were slaves. The
four largest States were Virginia, with 977,622 ; New
York, with 959,049 ; Pennsylvania, with 810,091 ; Massachusetts (still including Maine), with 700,745. These
four States obtained 93 representatives out of a total of
182, or more than half. Though Virginia was the most
populous of all, yet the three-fifths rule, applied to her
slaves, brought her representation in Con- Representa-
gress below that of New York (27) and ex- tion.
actly on a level with that of Pennsylvania (23), while
Massachusetts obtained 20. The three smallest States
were Rhode Island, Delaware, and Louisiana, which, together, had only 5 representatives. North Carolina had
13 ; Kentucky, 10 ; South Carolina and Maryland, 9

each ; Connecticut 7 ; while, by a curious coincidence, the six remaining States had 6 each. Here again we note the absence of any considerable group of the second rank, North Carolina alone being about at the mean of such a group as might naturally have been expected to be formed among so many as eighteen States.

We have seen how, little by little, the Constitution set up in 1789 was being " tried on " in application to the life of the American people, to find how it would fit and whether it would work in practice. We have seen Kentucky and Virginia, by the nullification resolutions of 1798–99, declaring that there was " no common judge " The strength- between State and Nation, in cases of con- ening of na- flicting authority or of abuses of federal tional author- ity. power. We have noted the hostility of the republican party to all enlargements of the judicial function in our government ; we have witnessed the attempts, which followed the accession of that party to power, to break down the judiciary by the process of impeachment. We have seen President Adams, in the last days of his administration, place upon the supreme bench of the United States the great Chief-Justice, Marshall, who was to make history faster than it could be unmade by all the opponents of American nation- ality.

We are now to see the government of the United States and of one of its original constituent States in actual collision over a mandate of the Supreme Court. In the first weeks of Madison's administration a case of long standing—the Olmstead case—concerning the disposition of certain moneys, the proceeds of a Brit- ish prize, taken away back during the Revolutionary war, came to a final decision. The United States mar- shal, attempting to carry out the decree of the bench, was forcibly resisted, in Philadelphia, by militia acting under instructions from the legislature and Governor of Pennsylvania, to make good the decisions of the State courts regarding the same subject-matter. A bloody issue was for the moment postponed ; and, during the respite accorded, the authorities of Pennsylvania withdrew from their attitude of resistance, intimidated by the firm front of Mr. Madison, who without any faltering asserted the powers of the national judiciary. The precept of the court was in time duly executed. The officer commanding the militia and cer- *The Olmstead* tain of his men were tried by the United *case.* States Circuit Court and convicted of unlawfully resisting the service of judicial process ; but their sentences were wisely remitted by the President, on the ground that they had acted under a mistaken sense of duty. So ended, in favor of the national authority, a contest which had at one time threatened the gravest issues. The two great constitutional principles, the establishment of which, beyond all the power of men to subvert or uproot them, we owe chiefly to Marshall are these : First, that, while the general government is limited as to its objects, it is yet, as to those objects, supreme. Secondly, that in enforcing its constitutional authority, in doing its constitutional work, in reaching its constitutional ends, the United States government is not confined to narrow courses ; is not shut up to any single line of action ; is not limited in its agencies or methods. It has a full, fair, and free choice among all the means, not expressly forbidden in the Constitution, which are reasonable, expedient, and politic means to those ends ; a choice as full, fair, and free as if the objects of the government were not limited.

As has been stated, the charter of the first National Bank ran twenty years from 1791. Application for a renewal of the charter was made in ample season to

allow a full discussion as to the merits of that measure.
The bank had been highly successful, from a stock-
holder's point of view ; and there was little
reason for questioning its usefulness alike to
people and to government. The management
had, in general, been conservative and sound ; and the
bank had been a capable and honest agent in the custody
and transmission of public funds, as well as a convenient
source of occasional loans and supplies to the Treasury.
But, rapidly as the republican party of that day had
progressed toward occupying the federalist position of
1789–91, it had not yet got so far that "the rank and
file" were prepared, without strong opposition, to accept
Hamilton's bank as one of the permanent institutions of
the country. Moreover, an interested competition had
sprung up, through the establishment of State banks,
generally of a low order, deeply infected with political
animus, with little capital actually paid in, and often
managed speculatively, if not dishonestly. The unfortunate result was that, although the recharter was urged
by Gallatin, our strongest as well as safest financier
since the day of Hamilton, and was supported by many
leading republicans, it just failed of success. In the
House of Representatives indefinite postponement was
carried, 65 to 64. In the Senate a separate bill was
defeated by the casting vote of Vice-President Clinton.
The bank, therefore, went out of existence through the
expiry of its charter.

Expiry of the National Bank.

Notwithstanding the tremendous drain on the Treasury involved in the military and naval enterprises which
have been recited, no serious proposition was
made to resort to legal-tender paper-money.
This fact is creditable to President Madison,
to Mr. Gallatin, Secretary of the Treasury, and to the
Congress of that time. It is to be said, however, that

Financial measures in-cident to the war.

this result was due more to a belief that such a power did not inhere in Congress than to any enlightened convictions as to the economic folly of such a resort. "Treasury notes," without the legal-tender quality, were issued according to the exigencies of the government; and as those exigencies were always of the most trying character, the notes became greatly depreciated. As they were receivable for taxes, the Treasury was continually taking in notes which it found difficult to put out again. In November, 1814, the Secretary of the Treasury was compelled to give notice that he would be unable to meet the interest due on the public debt. The general suspension of banks throughout the country added to the financial disorder. The normal industry of the nation was crippled; and the profitable trade of the north and the northeast was practically destroyed, not only by the proper effects of war, but by the Embargo Act of 1813–14, which was so stringent that even the coasting-trade was almost annihilated. Everywhere, except in the agricultural regions, deep distress prevailed. Notwithstanding these adverse conditions Congress made a manful effort to increase the revenue from taxation. At the outset the duties on imports were increased. In the second year of the war a direct tax of $3,000,000 was laid upon real estate and slaves. A duty of four cents a pound was levied on all sugars refined in the United States; stills were taxed upon their capacity; licenses for retailing spirits and wine were also taxed; stamp duties were imposed on bank-notes, on bonds or promissory notes discounted by banks, and on bills of exchange; pleasure-carriages were taxed heavily, and all other carriages in smaller amounts.

It seems very strange to read of whiskey taxes, stamp duties, and direct taxes levied by a Congress controlled by a republican majority. But that party had met the inevitable fate of all parties coming into power. It had taken the government upon its own hands ; it had be-

The repub- gun war upon its own declaration ; and it
lican party
imposes di- had to get the means to carry on the war
rect taxes. and sustain the government as best it could.
The financial measures it had denounced in opposition it was now obliged to defend. In spite of the utmost efforts to collect revenue, the public debt rose, in great waves, until it reached the enormous sum, as it seemed in those days, of $127,000,000. Mr. Gallatin remained in the Treasury until 1814, when he was succeeded by George W. Campbell, of Tennessee, who, after a brief service, gave way to Alexander J. Dallas, of Pennsylvania. The year following the close of the war, Congress passed a joint resolution requiring the Secretary of the Treasury to cause, as soon as might be, all public dues to be collected and paid in specie or Treasury notes or notes of specie-paying banks. By the efforts of the Treasury and the improved industrial conditions of the country, specie payments were restored at the beginning of 1817. Before the close of Mr. Madison's administration Congress passed an act appropriating $10,000,000 annually, out of current revenues, as a sinking fund to provide for the public debt at its maturity. The embargo of 1813–14, which we spoke of as causing dire distress, had been soon repealed, whether in consequence of the outcry raised against it or of the complete destruction of Napoleon's continental system, following the fatal battle of Leipsic.

In speaking of the first ten amendments of the Constitution we referred to an amendment proposed at the
The Salary same time to the States, but not by them
Grab Bill. adopted, according to which it would have been impossible for Congress to change the compensation of its own members until an election should

have intervened. By an act of the session of 1815–16, the compensation of members, which had been at the rate of $6 per day of actual attendance, was placed at $1,500 per year, with the usual mileage. Writing to Mr. Gallatin, June 16, 1817, Mr. Jefferson says : " According to the opinion I hazarded to you a little before your departure, we have had an almost entire change in the body of Congress. . . . In some States, it is said, every member of Congress is changed ; in all, many. . . . I have never known so unanimous a sentiment of disapprobation ; and what is remarkable is that it was spontaneous. The newspapers were almost entirely silent ; and the people, not only unled by their leaders, but in opposition to them."

In 1812 Louisiana was admitted as a State, with its present boundaries. The resistance to this act from the unreconciled federalists was of the most in- New States. tense and furious nature. In his speech against the bill, Mr. Quincy said, " If this bill passes, it is my deliberate opinion that it is virtually a dissolution of the Union ; that it will free the States from their moral obligation ; and, as it will be the right of all, so it will be the duty of some, definitely to prepare for a separation, amicably if they can, forcibly if they must." Here was the " old Republicanism " of 1798–99 with a vengeance ; and this time from a Massachusetts federalist ! In 1816, without any such antagonism, Indiana was admitted. In 1810 its population had been 24,820 ; in 1820 it had risen to 147,178. At the session following, Mississippi, with a population estimated at 64,000, was authorized to form a constitution and State government. The remainder of what had been the Mississippi territory was constituted the territory of Alabama.

We now come to a group of economic measures, passed by Congress in the brief interval between the conclu-

17

sion of the war with England and the close of Mr. Madison's administration, which were not only of great importance in themselves, but which have an even higher interest, historically, in that they marked a vast change in the ideas, feelings, and purposes of the American people. The group of measures to which we refer not only presaged but introduced a new era in the life of the United States. Down to this time the political thought of our people had been almost entirely absorbed by foreign affairs. We have now reached the period when economic concerns became supreme. It was by no accidental coincidence that the years immediately following the peace of 1815 witnessed the enactment of a large body of important commercial and financial legislation.

Economic measures— The New Age.

Mr. Madison had been the leader of the opposition to protection in Washington's administration. He was now, under the pressure of the financial difficulties created by the war, and under the impulse of his supporters from the extreme South, where the cotton-planting interest had become dominant, to appear in the *rôle* of an advocate of incidental protection. In his message of December, 1815, he said to Congress, " In adjusting the duties on imports to the object of revenue, the influence of the tariff on manufactures will necessarily present itself for consideration. However wise the theory may be which leaves to the sagacity and interest of individuals the application of their industry and resources, there are, in this as in other cases, exceptions to the general rule. Besides the condition, which the theory itself implies, of a reciprocal adoption by other nations, experience teaches that so many circumstances must occur in introducing and maturing manufacturing establishments, especially of the more complicated kinds, that a country may re-

President Madison advocates a protective tariff.

main long without them, although sufficiently advanced, and in some respects even peculiarly fitted, for carrying them on with success. Under circumstances giving a powerful impulse to manufacturing industry, it has made among us a progress and exhibited an efficiency which justify the belief that, with a protection not more than is due to the enterprising citizens whose interests are now at stake, it will become at an early day not only safe against occasional competition from abroad but a source of domestic wealth and even of external commerce. In selecting the branches more especially entitled to the public patronage, a preference is obviously claimed by such as will relieve the United States from a dependence on foreign supplies, ever subject to casual failures, for articles necessary for the public defence or connected with the primary wants of individuals. It will be an additional recommendation of particular manufactures when the materials for them are extensively drawn from our agriculture, and consequently impart and insure to that great fund of national prosperity and independence an encouragement which cannot fail to be rewarded."

Three features of the protectionist argument of 1816 require to be clearly indicated. The first claim for protection was not then for the defence of American wages and the American standard of living, but for securing to government and people an indefeasible supply of articles necessary to life, and especially to national defence. The second claim was made in the interest of agriculture, not as furnishing the food for large operative classes (so favored an argument in later days) but as furnishing the materials for manufacture. We shall, further on, see the special significance of this argument. The third claim was on the ground that manufactures had been brought into existence by the embargo and by the war, as a means of supplying our people with the necessaries of life ; and that, in all fairness, those enterprises, in which so much capital had been invested, should not be allowed to collapse under foreign competition, now that peace was restored.

What was it that made the South, always the advocate of a strict construction of the powers of government, and also naturally, as composed of planting communities, opposed to duties on manufactured goods—what was it that made this section now support a protective tariff ? In the answer to this question we find the significance of Mr. Madison's argument. The profits of cotton culture had become enormous, thanks to the ingenuity of a Yankee schoolmaster. We saw that, at the inauguration of the government, the export of cotton amounted to but a few thousand pounds a year. The difficulty was not, then, in raising the plant, but in treating it for the market. Any amount of cotton could be produced upon the rich, moist lands of the South, under its warm sun ; but only a very small amount could be cleaned. At the time of which we speak, Eli Whitney's cotton-gin had done its great work, effecting a revolution, industrially, socially, commercially, and politically, hardly equalled in the history of invention. Any amount of cotton could be cheaply and effectively cleaned ; the only limit to its use was found in the amount which could be produced ; and, as the merits of this wonderful fibre were every year becoming more fully recognized, the profits of the culture had become, as we have said, enormous. In consequence, the cotton States were at this time in favor of protective duties on cotton goods, as a means of building up American manufactures which should take off their entire supply. Of the gigantic possibilities attending the export of that staple to Europe, they had

The position of the South toward the tariff.

no conception; or they would not have taken this side in 1816. Subsequent history shows that, as the export rose, their interest in domestic manufactures fell. Within twelve years after Mr. Madison's tariff, the planting States became the bitterest enemies of protection.

The bill of 1816, prepared by Mr. Dallas upon the principle of Mr. Madison's recommendations, had the urgent advocacy of Messrs. Calhoun and Lowndes, of South Carolina; but the strong- The tariff of 1816. est support of the tariff came from a less interested source. Henry Clay, of Kentucky, who was to come to be known as the father of the American (*i.e.*, the Protective) System, made this the occasion of assuming that leadership in the advocacy of measures for building up American manufactures which characterized his whole subsequent career. Whatever may be said of Messrs. Calhoun and Lowndes in 1816, or of Pennsylvania statesmen in all periods of our history, Mr. Clay was undoubtedly influenced, in his championship of protection, by large, unselfish, and patriotic motives. On the other hand, the New England States, being still mainly commercial, notwithstanding the destructive effects of the embargo and the war, opposed the bill. Daniel Webster, then a young member of the House of Representatives, made a powerful speech against it. John Randolph lent the aid of his restless genius to the opposition. The act passed, imposing duties ranging from twenty to thirty-five per cent.

The second of the great financial measures of this administration was the creation of a new national bank. We have seen how the bank of 1791 failed to secure a recharter in 1811. In 1814 Mr. Dallas, Secretary of the Treasury, prepared a huge banking scheme which, in its essential features, passed the Senate, but was defeated in the House by the casting vote of the Speaker.

Subsequently a compromise between this proposition and one offered by Mr. Calhoun was passed by both Houses, but was vetoed by Mr. Madison. In 1816 the scheme

The second of a national bank was stronger than in 1811 National Bank. or in 1814. Mr. Clay, then Speaker of the House, led in its advocacy ; and a bill was passed which received Mr. Madison's approval, April 10th. The capital was to be $35,000,000, of which one-fifth was to be owned by the United States. Of all subscriptions one-fifth was to be paid in specie. The bank was to pay the government $1,500,000 as a bonus. One-fifth of the directors were to be appointed by the president and confirmed by the Senate. The deposits of the United States were to be removable by the Secretary of the Treasury, for sufficient reasons, to be laid before Congress.

The third of the important economic measures of this administration was the Navigation Act, which restricted

The Naviga- the coasting trade to vessels wholly owned tion Act. by our citizens ; encouraged the employment of American seamen therein, through discriminating duties ; and restricted importations to vessels of the United States or of the country of production. The latter regulation, however, was to apply only to vessels of those nations which had similar regulations.

Finally, in the same period, an act was passed by Congress (86 to 84 in the House ; 20 to 15 in the Senate), but vetoed by the President upon the ground of unconstitutionality, which provided for a fund, out of the bonus to be paid by the bank and out of the dividends of the government stock therein : that fund to be applied, from time to time as Congress should direct,

Internal im- to measures of internal improvement. Mr. provements. Calhoun, of South Carolina, afterward the recognized leader of the States'-rights party, had been foremost in pressing this measure through Congress. It is not improbable that the smallness of the majorities by which the bill had passed the two houses had something to do with Mr. Madison's constitutional scruples.

We now turn to consider the changes in the cabinet and the eighth presidential election. We have already referred to certain changes in the office of Secretary of the Treasury, after Mr. Gallatin's withdrawal. Late in 1816 Mr. William H. Crawford, of Georgia, who was to be one of the conspicuous figures in the politics of the next ten years, became Secretary of the Treasury, being transferred to that office from the War Department. Other changes in Mr. Madison's cabinet were too numerous to be mentioned in full. It has already been stated that Mr. Smith was succeeded as Secretary of State, by Mr. Monroe, who in September, 1814, also assumed the duties of Secretary of War. Mr. Rodney was succeeded as Attorney-General, in 1811, by William Pinkney, of Maryland, whom tradition declares to have been the most eloquent advocate of the American bar in his time. Pinkney was in turn succeeded, early in 1814, by Richard Rush, of Pennsylvania, a man of great ability and one of the finer characters of our political history. In all, fourteen persons occupied seats in Mr. Madison's cabinet during the eight years of his administration.

Changes in the cabinet.

On the 16th of March, the usual congressional caucus was held for the nomination of Mr. Madison's successor. We have already spoken of practical objections to this procedure. In 1816 Mr. Clay and others strongly opposed the practice, but were overruled by their colleagues. Upon the first ballot Mr. Monroe was nominated by a large majority, Mr. Crawford being his competitor. Daniel D. Tompkins, of New York, was nominated for vice-president. Mr. Monroe had been urged by a section of the repub-

Mr. Monroe chosen President.

lican party, in place of Mr. Madison, eight years before ;
but various causes, especially the intervention of Mr.
Jefferson, had prevented a serious contest at that time.
Mr. Monroe was now to have his turn.   He was elected
by 183 votes, against 34 given to Rufus King, the federalist candidate.

RETROSPECT.

During the period of thirty-four years covered by this
narrative, a movement had been in continuous progress
for the westward extension of population, which far
transcended the limits of any of the great migrations of
mankind upon the older continents.   The story of the
geographical process of our national growth is among
the marvels of the human race.   Over the natural
water-way of the great Northern Lakes ; along the road
to Pittsburg, and thence down the Ohio ; up the road
which skirts the Potomac, and then down the Ohio ;
over the passes of Southwestern Virginia, into Kentucky ; and far to the south, around the end of the Alleghanies, into the Gulf States, the hardy pioneers
poured in an unceasing stream, carrying with them little but axe, spade, and rifle, some scanty household
effects, a small store of provisions, a liberal supply of
ammunition, and boundless faith, enterprise, and courage.   From 1790 to 1800, the mean population of the
period being about four and a half millions, sixty-five
thousand square miles were brought within the limits
of settlement ; crossed with rude roads and bridges ;
built up with rude houses and barns ; much of it, also,
cleared of primeval forests.

In the next ten years, the mean population of the decade being about six and a half millions, the people of
the United States extended settlement over one hun-

dred and two thousand square miles of absolutely new territory; annexed this from the wilderness; conquered, subdued, improved, cultivated, civilized it, all, of course, in rough pioneer fashion. During this time population was deepening upon the older fields; cities and towns were everywhere springing up and growing into industrial and commercial importance. Philosophic historians have been wont to attribute the long and hopeless decay of Spain to the drain upon its physical and intellectual powers involved in the conquest and occupation of Mexico and South America. Did the prodigious efforts of its first twenty years exhaust the vital force of the new nation of the West? Did a period of long sterility, with decay here and there of great branches, show that too much life had been allowed to flow into these new limbs of the great Northern Republic? The answer is found in this, that between 1810 and 1817, besides increasing the density of population upon almost every league of the older territory, and in spite of a three years' war waged against the powerful fleets and armies of England, the people of the United States advanced their frontier to occupy seventy thousand additional square miles, nearly equal to the combined areas of Belgium, Holland, Switzerland, Denmark, and Greece.

In 1790 the population of the United States had been 3,929,214; in 1817 it was, as nearly as can be computed, 8,866,000. In 1790 the area, more or less sparsely populated, had been two hundred and forty thousand square miles; in 1817 it was about four hundred and seventy-eight thousand. When Washington was inaugurated in 1789, the centre of population for the whole country was thirty miles east of Baltimore! At the close of Madison's administration, it had moved westward, past Washington, across the Potomac, across the Shenandoah, one hundred and twenty miles in all, but keeping ever close to the 39th degree of north latitude, as it was destined to do for a hundred years.* No other race that ever dwelt upon the globe could have extended settlement in so short a time over so vast a field ; have fenced and ditched it ; have covered the land with roads and the streams with bridges, have dotted the plains and hills over with houses, barns, schools, and churches of such an order of comfort and decency, and, from the soil thus enclosed, after maintaining the population in such an abundance and quality of food and clothing, have had left for export so many million tons of animal and vegetable produce in meat, in fibres, and in grain. No other people could have done this. No : nor the half of it. Any other of the great migratory races—Tartar, Slav, or German— would have broken hopelessly down in an effort to compass such a field in such a term of years. We have already indicated, when writing of the agriculture of the United States, the causes which made possible this astonishing increase of population and extension of the

---

* It is, indeed, one of the most remarkable facts in human history that during the first century of our national existence, while population increased sixteenfold, while settlement was extended over an area eight times as large as that occupied at the beginning, including vast territories not belonging to the United States in 1789—Florida, Louisiana, Texas, California, Oregon—the centre of population never moved away from the 39th parallel by more than nineteen " minutes " of latitude. This does not imply that population increased equally at the South and at the North. On the contrary, the increase in the latter section was, owing to immigration, always much the greater. But our territory extended northward from the 39th parallel only eight degrees, at the first, and only ten degrees, later, while toward the south it extended over nearly twice as many degrees. Consequently, inasmuch as the Southerner was, on the average, let us for brevity say, twice as far from the 39th parallel as the Northerner, he counted for twice as much in determining the " Centre of Population." He, so to speak, " bore down " twice as heavily upon the fulcrum.

settled area, namely, the popular tenure of the soil, the character of the agricultural class, and the mechanical and inventive genius of our people. The marvellous work that has just now been recited constitutes the main reason for the slow development of technical manufactures during the early stages of our history. The great manufacture of the United States, during its first fifty years, was the manufacture of farms.

While thus the new nation had been increasing with wonderful rapidity, both as to numbers and as to its occupied area, what had taken place to influence its character and to determine the direction of its ever-growing political forces ? We have traced the course of events from 1783 to the close of Mr. Madison's administration, in 1817. We have seen that the consciousness of American nationality and a common destiny, faint, feeble, and fluttering as it had been at the close of the war for Independence, was, through the great debate over the Constitution, alike in the Convention and before the People, so quickened and strengthened that the Thirteen States, resigning much of their independent power, renouncing many of their prerogatives of statehood, agreed together to form what promised to be a perpetual union. We have seen that, in the course of the twenty-eight years following, under the administrations of Washington, Adams, Jefferson, and Madison, the United States, which at the beginning was only what might under fortunate conditions, if everything, or at least the great weight of events, should tend that way, become a nation, had become a nation in fact, as fully as any of the powers known to the diplomacy of 1817. It might, indeed, be destroyed by insurrection and rebellion, as might any of its contemporaries ; but it was, to all intents and purposes, a single, sovereign people.

It has of late become the fashion among those who

renounce, as all real students of political history must do, the purely lawyer-like theory of the formation of the Constitution held by Story, Webster, and Curtis, to declare that the United States became a nation only by act of war, in the great struggle from 1861 to 1865. This is the view advanced by Mr. Randolph Tucker, in his able address before the American Social Science Association, at Saratoga, in 1877 ; and it has been more recently put forward by Dr. Albion W. Small, in his tract, "The Beginnings of American Nationality." Dr. Small says : "The people of the United States simply dodged the responsibility of formulating their will upon the distinct subject of national sovereignty, until the legislation of the sword began in 1861." We cannot accede to this view. Midway between those who hold that the adoption of the Constitution established an "indissoluble union of indestructible States," and those who hold that the question of nationality was decided seventy-five years later, by the arbitrament of arms, we assert that the United States became a true and virtual nation during the first three or four decades of its history.

It is perfectly true that the Convention of 1787 dodged the vital question of nationality. Had the Constitution contained an explicit declaration that, in any attempt of nullification or secession, the general government might raise the military force of the country, as was done in 1861, that instrument would not have had a chance of ratification by the States. On the other hand, it is also true that, even after the point reached in our story, the right of nullification was once practically asserted (1832–33) in a feeble manner ; while, thirty years later still, it required a tremendous exertion of the whole military and financial power of the government to put down a slave-holders' rebellion, which sought to shelter itself under a pretence of secession. But we are now talking, not of names, but of things; not of written instruments or public declarations, but of real social and political forces. And if, in this spirit, it is asked, when the United States became a nation, the most reasonable answer is, it became so during the period of which we have been writing.

Many causes contributed to that result in addition to the mere fact of the States living together for nearly thirty years, in more or less of harmony, accustoming themselves to the idea of common interests, common laws, and a common destiny, becoming familiar with the signs and emblems of sovereignty—a common flag, a common money, a national judiciary, a national army, and a Congress of the United States legislating for the general welfare and for the protection of the public honor. If, in spite of adverse conditions, the course of affairs be, on the whole, more favorable than unfavorable, there is, merely in such abiding together, virtue enough to create in time much of the sentiment of nationality. It is to be remembered that during the period covered by this narrative a vast majority of those who had helped to form the Constitution, with so much of doubt and reservation, passed away. At its close, a still larger proportion of the people were those who had been born under the government, or who had first come to understand the meaning of political terms since the Constitution was formed. To all of these the existence of the United States appeared a natural and necessary thing, as it could not possibly have appeared to any of the previous generation.

Moreover, great social and industrial changes had been at work. Population had more than doubled in the time, not only extending itself over new lands at the West, but growing ever deeper within its familiar seats

and filling up the vacant spaces upon the Atlantic seaboard of 1783. Transportation had been quickened, although the great changes in this respect were yet to
come, for the Erie Canal was not opened throughout its
entire extent until 1825. The beginnings of manufactures had appeared even before 1812 ; and the exigencies of the war with England caused a great upbuilding
of domestic industries for the supply of a market which
had become as broad as the whole extent of our settled
lands. How strong was the hold of these new interests
upon the American people, we have seen strikingly evi-
denced by the tariff of 1816.

Strictly political causes, too, had entered to made a
nation of that which at the beginning was only what
might become a nation. A hundred measures of legislation, whatever of opposition or animosity they might
have provoked, had asserted the authority of the United
States. The genius of Hamilton and his co-laborers
had built up a government which was real and vital,
and which made itself felt in all parts of the land.
Acts of executive power, whether against insurgents or
against public enemies, had taught the lesson of obe-
dience and respect. A noble judiciary, under a great
Chief-Justice, had taken righteous advantage of the ample provisions of the Constitution, to expand the frame
of the government to its proper proportions, and to
fill its veins with the life-blood of a real nationality.
War, too, had come, with its hopes and its fears, with
its triumphs and its reverses, with its pride and its
shame, to create the deep, instinctive feeling of common
interests and a common destiny.

Hardly less than any of these causes operating to
create nationality had been the influence, on which we
have before remarked, of the new States formed upon
the lands across the mountains. Few were the doubts

and small were the reservations with which these hardy pioneers rendered their allegiance, after the great question of the navigation of the Mississippi had been settled in their favor. Here no pride of Statehood diminished the affection and devotion of the citizen to the government under which he held the title of his land; to which he looked for protection from the savage foe; which opened up the navigation of the rivers to his clumsy flatboat; which endowed the school in which his children learned to read. Constitutional scruples were at a discount with these rude, strong, brave men; and lawyer-like distinctions over the divisions of sovereignty troubled them little. They wanted a government, and a strong government; and in the continually growing power of the Republic they found the competent object of their civic trust and pride and love.

But the greatest, by far, of the causes which, between 1789 and 1817, promoted the growth of nationality, was the change in the attitude and the relations of the republican party, the original trustee and guardian of the doctrine of States'-rights and "strict construction." That change itself was in part due to the social and economic causes we have here enumerated, ameliorating the original feelings of distrust and dislike with which the old leaders contemplated federal authority, and convincing them, more and more, of the absolute necessity of a real and efficient government, to provide for common defence and to promote the general welfare. In part, and in a large part, it was due to the coming-on of young leaders "who knew not Joseph," who had grown up under the Constitution, and were men of their age, ready to apprehend the needs of the time and prompt to act, with energy and decisiveness, upon questions affecting the country as they found it.

Chiefly, however, it was its own accession to power

and to responsibility which changed the attitude of the republican party upon all matters relating to the authority of the general government. The phenomenon is a perfectly familiar one ; and such changes are sometimes ludicrous in their precipitancy. The republican party had set out by striving to limit the exercise of power on the part of the United States ; it had denounced a national debt, as a sure means of political corruption ; it had complained of the multiplication of offices, as bribing and overawing the people ; it had opposed excises, stamp duties, and direct taxes, as forms of tyranny ; it had declared the National Bank to be grossly unconstitutional. When it obtained possession of the government we find it, after Mr. Jefferson's first virtuous impulse was exhausted, increasing expenses, making changes in the civil service for political reasons ; multiplying offices, and acting in every way as men do who have authority and like to exercise it. Then came the unexpected opportunity for the acquisition of Louisiana. Mr. Jefferson himself admitted it to be an act beyond the Constitution. It was, moreover, a measure of such tremendous scope, of such truly imperial character, one so profoundly changing the terms and conditions upon which the States originally entered the Union, as to be in the fullest sense revolutionary. Fortunately, the temptation was too great for Mr. Jefferson's constitutional scruples ; and the vast empire beyond the Mississippi became ours. After such a surrender of the principle of limited powers, by the only party which had undertaken to maintain it, what could stay the course of nationality ?

But this was not to be the end. Mr. Jefferson for eight years dodged, as well as he could, the stones flung at him alike by France and by England ; and Mr. Madison, with quite as little relish for fighting, hoped that the cup might pass from his own lips, and that he would be able to get through his term without resort to hostilities. But the young men of his party would not be denied ; war was forced upon him, and, by an inevitable consequence, his closing years of office witnessed every act and measure of federal usurpation against which he had been accustomed to protest. The republican party exercised the coercion it had denounced when attempted by a federalist administration ; it learned, by hearing it from the lips of federalist opponents, how hateful is the sound of threatened nullification and secession. The republican party, in its turn, created a great national debt and established a sinking fund ; it excised whiskey and stills ; it laid direct taxes ; it imposed stamp duties ; it passed a distinctly protective tariff. To crown all, the republican party chartered a National Bank, three and a half times as large as that of Hamilton. Who, then, was left to protest against the United States becoming a nation ?

18

DISTRIBUTION OF POPULAITON 1820

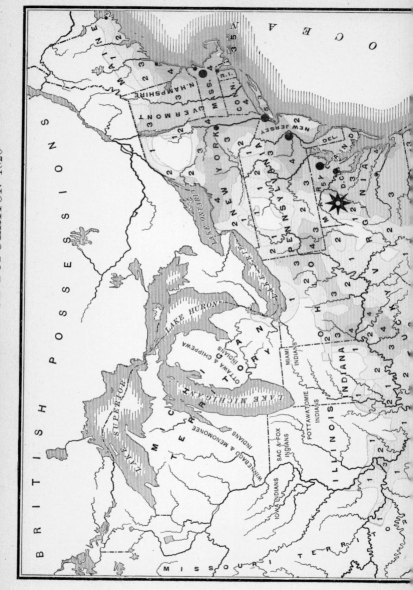

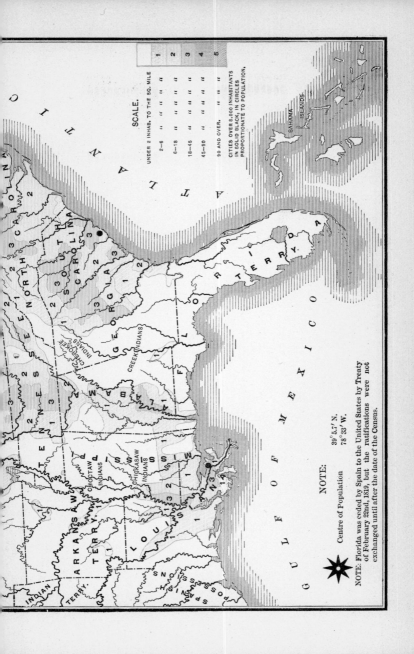

SCALE.

UNDER 2 INHAB. TO THE SQ. MILE 1
2—6 " " " " " 2
6—18 " " " " " 3
18—45 " " " " " 4
45—90 " " " " " 5
90 AND OVER, " " " "

CITIES OVER 8,000 INHABITANTS
IN SOLID BLACK, IN CIRCLES
PROPORTIONATE TO POPULATION.

NOTE:

Centre of Population   39° 5.7' N.
                        78° 33' W.

NOTE. Florida was ceded by Spain to the United States by Treaty
of February 22nd, 1819, but the ratifications were not
exchanged until after the date of the Census.

APPENDIX I

THE ELECTORAL VOTE IN DETAIL, 1789–1816

ELECTORAL VOTE OF 1789.

STATES.*	George Washington, of Virginia.	John Adams, of Massachusetts.	John Jay, of New York.	R. H. Harrison, of Maryland.	John Rutledge, of South Carolina.	John Hancock, of Massachusetts.	George Clinton, of New York.	Samuel Huntingdon, of Connecticut.	John Milton, of Georgia.	James Armstrong, of Georgia.	Benjamin Lincoln, of Massachusetts.	Edward Telfair, of Georgia.	Vacancies.
Connecticut	7	5	..	..	..	..	..	2	..	..	..	..	..
Delaware	3	..	3	..	..	..	..	..	..	..	..	..	..
Georgia	5	..	..	..	..	..	..	..	2	1	1	1	..
Maryland	6	..	..	6	..	..	..	..	..	..	..	..	2
Massachusetts	10	10	..	..	..	..	..	..	..	..	..	..	..
New Hampshire	5	5	..	..	..	..	..	..	..	..	..	..	..
New Jersey	6	1	5	..	..	..	..	..	..	..	..	..	..
Pennsylvania	10	8	..	..	..	2	..	..	..	..	..	..	..
South Carolina	7	..	..	..	6	1	..	..	..	..	..	..	2
Virginia	10	5	1	..	..	1	3	..	..	..	..	..	..
Total	69	34	9	6	6	4	3	2	2	1	1	1	4

* The New York Legislature failed to agree on the mode of choosing electors. North Carolina and Rhode Island did not ratify the Constitution in time to take part in the election. Each elector voted for two persons without designating which one he wished to make president.

ELECTORAL VOTE OF 1792.

STATES.	George Washington, of Virginia.	John Adams, of Massachusetts.	George Clinton, of New York.	Thomas Jefferson, of Virginia.	Aaron Burr, of New York.	Vacancies.
Connecticut	9	9	..	..	..	..
Delaware	3	3	..	..	..	..
Georgia	4	..	4	..	..	..
Kentucky	4	..	..	4	..	2
Maryland	8	8	..	..	..	..
Massachusetts	16	16	..	..	..	..
New Hampshire	6	6	..	..	..	..
New Jersey	7	7	..	..	..	..
New York	12	..	12	..	..	..
North Carolina	12	..	12	..	..	..
Pennsylvania	15	14	1	..	..	..
Rhode Island	4	4	..	..	..	..
South Carolina	8	7	..	..	1	..
Vermont	3	3	..	..	..	1
Virginia	21	..	21	..	..	..
Total	132	77	50	4	1	3

ELECTORAL VOTE OF 1796.

STATES.	John Adams, of Massachusetts.	Thomas Jefferson, of Virginia.	Thomas Pinckney, of South Carolina.	Aaron Burr, of New York.	Samuel Adams, of Massachusetts.	Oliver Ellsworth, of Connecticut.	George Clinton, of New York.	John Jay, of New York.	James Iredell, of N. Carolina.	George Washington, of Virginia.	John Henry, of Maryland.	S. Johnson, of N. Carolina.	C. C. Pinckney, of S. Carolina.
Connecticut	9	..	4	..	..	..	..	5	..	..	..	..	..
Delaware	3	..	3	..	..	..	..	..	..	..	..	..	..
Georgia	..	4	..	..	..	..	4	..	..	..	..	..	..
Kentucky	..	4	.	4	..	..	..	..	..	..	..	..	..
Maryland	7	4	4	3	..	..	..	..	..	..	2	..	..
Massachusetts	16	..	13	..	..	1	..	..	..	..	..	2	..
New Hampshire	6	..	..	..	..	6	..	..	..	..	..	..	..
New Jersey	7	..	7	..	..	..	..	..	..	..	..	..	..
New York	12	..	12	..	..	..	..	..	..	..	..	..	..
North Carolina	1	11	1	6	..	..	..	..	3	1	..	..	1
Pennsylvania	1	14	2	13	..	..	..	..	..	..	..	..	..
Rhode Island	4	..	..	..	..	4	..	..	..	..	..	..	..
South Carolina	..	8	8	..	..	..	..	..	..	..	..	..	..
Tennessee	..	3	.	3	..	..	..	..	..	..	..	..	..
Vermont	4	..	4	..	..	..	..	..	..	..	..	..	..
Virginia	1	20	1	1	15	..	3	..	..	1	..	..	..
Total	**71**	**68**	**59**	**30**	**15**	**11**	**7**	**5**	**3**	**2**	**2**	**2**	**1**

ELECTORAL VOTE OF 1800.

STATES.	Thomas Jefferson, of Virginia.	Aaron Burr, of New York.	John Adams, of Massachusetts.	C. C. Pinckney, of South Carolina.	John Jay, of New York.
Connecticut	..	..	9	9	..
Delaware	..	..	3	3	..
Georgia	4	4	..	..	..
Kentucky	4	4	..	..	..
Maryland	5	5	5	5	..
Massachusetts	..	..	16	16	..
New Hampshire	..	..	6	6	..
New Jersey	..	..	7	7	..
New York	12	12	..	..	..
North Carolina	8	8	4	4	..
Pennsylvania	8	8	7	7	..
Rhode Island	..	..	4	3	1
South Carolina	8	8	..	..	..
Tennessee	3	3	..	..	..
Vermont	..	..	4	4	..
Virginia	21	21	..	..	..
Total	**73**	**73**	**65**	**64**	**1**

ELECTORAL VOTE OF 1804.*

STATES.	PRESIDENT.		VICE-PRESIDENT.	
	Thomas Jefferson, of Virginia.	C. C. Pinckney, of South Carolina.	Geo. Clinton, of New York.	Rufus King, of New York.
Connecticut	..	9	..	9
Delaware	..	3	..	3
Georgia	6	..	6	..
Kentucky	8	..	8	..
Maryland	9	2	9	2
Massachusetts	19	..	19	..
New Hampshire.....	7	..	7	..
New Jersey	8	..	8	..
New York	19	..	19	..
North Carolina.....	14	..	14	..
Ohio	3	..	3	..
Pennsylvania	20	..	20	..
Rhode Island.......	4	..	4	..
South Carolina.....	10	..	10	..
Tennessee	5	..	5	..
Vermont	6	..	6	..
Virginia	24	..	24	..
Total... ...	162	14	162	14

*At the election of 1804, electors for the first time cast their votes separately for candidates for the presidency and for candidates for the vice-presidency. This was the effect of the twelfth constitutional amendment. See pp. 133, 163-5, 168-9.

ELECTORAL VOTE OF 1808.

STATES.	PRESIDENT.				VICE-PRESIDENT.					
	James Madison, of Virginia.	C. C. Pinckney, of S. Carolina.	George Clinton, of New York.	Vacancies.	George Clinton, of New York.	Rufus King, of New York.	John Langdon, of New Hampshire.	James Madison, of Virginia.	James Monroe, of Virginia.	Vacancies.
Connecticut	..	9	..	..	..	9	..	..	..	..
Delaware	..	3	..	..	..	3	..	..	..	..
Georgia	6	..	..	..	6	..	..	..	..	..
Kentucky	7	..	..	1	7	..	..	..	..	1
Maryland	9	2	..	..	9	2	..	..	..	..
Massachusetts	..	19	..	..	..	19	..	..	..	..
New Hampshire...	..	7	..	..	..	7	..	..	..	..
New Jersey	8	..	..	..	8	..	..	..	..	..
New York.........	13	..	6	..	13	..	..	3	3	..
North Carolina....	11	3	..	..	11	3	..	..	..	..
Ohio	3	..	..	..	3	..	3	..	..	..
Pennsylvania	20	..	..	..	20	..	..	..	..	..
Rhode Island.....	..	4	..	..	..	4	..	..	..	..
South Carolina....	10	..	..	..	10	..	..	..	..	..
Tennessee........	5	..	..	..	5	..	..	..	..	..
Vermont	6	..	..	..	6	..	6	..	..	..
Virginia	24	..	..	..	24	..	..	..	..	..
Total	122	47	6	1	113	47	9	3	3	1

ELECTORAL VOTE OF 1812.

STATES.	PRESIDENT.			VICE-PRESIDENT.		
	James Madison, of Virginia.	De Witt Clinton, of New York.	Vacancies.	Elbridge Gerry, of Massachusetts.	Jared Ingersoll, of Pennsylvania.	Vacancies.
Connecticut....	..	9	..	..	9	..
Delaware	..	4	..	..	4	..
Georgia........	8	..	..	8	..	..
Kentucky	12	..	..	12	..	..
Louisiana......	3	..	..	3	..	..
Maryland	6	5	..	6	5	..
Massachusetts..	..	22	..	2	20	..
N. Hampshire..	..	8	..	1	7	..
New Jersey.....	..	8	..	..	8	..
New York......	..	29	..	..	29	..
North Carolina.	15	..	..	15	..	..
Ohio	7	..	1	7	..	1
Pennsylvania ..	25	..	..	25	..	..
Rhode Island...	..	4	..	..	4	..
South Carolina.	11	..	..	11	..	..
Tennessee......	8	..	..	8	..	..
Vermont.	8	..	..	8	..	..
Virginia........	25	..	..	25	..	..
Total	128	89	1	131	86	1

ELECTORAL VOTE OF 1816.

STATES.	PRESIDENT.			VICE-PRESIDENT.					
	James Monroe, of Virginia.	Rufus King, of New York.	Vacancies.	D. D. Tompkins, of New York.	John E. Howard, of Maryland.	James Ross, of Pennsylvania.	John Marshall, of Virginia.	R. G. Harper, of Maryland.	Vacancies.
Connecticut	..	9	..	..	..	5	4	..	..
Delaware	..	3	1	..	..	..	..	3	1
Georgia	8	..	..	8	..	..	..	..	..
Indiana	3	..	..	3	..	..	..	..	..
Kentucky	12	..	..	12	..	..	..	..	..
Louisiana	3	..	..	3	..	..	..	..	..
Maryland.........	8	..	3	8	..	..	..	..	3
Massachusetts	..	22	..	..	22	..	..	..	..
New Hampshire ..	8	..	..	8	..	..	..	..	..
New Jersey.......	8	..	..	8	..	..	..	..	..
New York	29	..	..	29	..	..	..	..	..
North Carolina ...	15	..	..	15	..	..	..	..	..
Ohio	8	..	..	8	..	..	..	..	..
Pennsylvania... ..	25	..	..	25	..	..	..	..	..
Rhode Island.....	4	..	..	4	..	..	..	..	..
South Carolina ...	11	..	..	11	..	..	..	..	..
Tennessee	8	..	..	8	..	..	..	..	..
Vermont	8	..	..	8	..	..	..	..	..
Virginia...	25	..	..	25	..	..	..	..	..
Total	183	34	4	183	22	5	4	3	4

APPENDIX II

I.—POPULATION AT THE FIRST FOUR CENSUSES

II.—NET ORDINARY RECEIPTS AND EXPENDITURES, AND DISBURSEMENTS ON ACCOUNT OF THE PUBLIC DEBT, 1790–1817

POPULATION AT THE FIRST FOUR CENSUSES.

	1790	1800	1810	1820
United States.	3,929,214	5,308,483	7,239,881	9,633,822
Alabama	....	....	....	127,901
Arkansas	....	....	....	14,255
Connecticut	237,946	251,002	261,942	275,148
Delaware	59,096	64,273	72,674	72,749
District of Columbia	....	14,093	24,023	33,039
Georgia	82,548	162,686	252,433	340,985
Illinois	....	....	12,282	55,162
Indiana	....	5,641	24,520	147,178
Kentucky	73,677	220,955	406,511	564,135
Louisiana	....	....	76,556	152,923
Maine	96,540	151,719	228,705	298,269
Maryland	319,728	341,548	380,546	407,350
Massachusetts	378,787	422,845	472,040	523,159
Michigan	....	....	4,762	8,765
Mississippi	....	8,850	40,352	75,448
Missouri	....	....	20,845	66,557
New Hampshire	141,885	183,858	214,460	244,022
New Jersey	184,139	211,149	245,562	277,426
New York	340,120	589,051	959,049	1,372,111
North Carolina	393,751	478,103	555,500	638,829
Ohio	....	45,365	230,760	581,295
Pennsylvania	434,373	602,365	810,091	1,047,507
Rhode Island	68,825	69,122	76,931	83,015
South Carolina	249,073	345,591	515,115	502,741
Tennessee	35,691	105,602	261,727	422,771
Vermont	85,425	154,465	217,895	235,966
Virginia	747,610	880,200	974,600	1,065,116

Maine belonged to Massachusetts until 1820, and for all political purposes its population was included in that of the parent State. In order to show Maine in its continuous growth, we have here separated its population from that of Massachusetts.

To exhibit the further progress of this wonderful career, we give the figures of the total population at the censuses following :

1820............................. 9,633,822
1830............................. 12,866,020
1840............................. 17,069,453
1850............................. 23,191,876
1860............................. 31,443,321
1870............................. 38,558,371
1880............................. 50,155,783
1890............................. 62,622,250

TABLES SHOWING THE NET ORDINARY RECEIPTS AND EXPENDITURES, AND ALSO THE DISBURSEMENTS ON ACCOUNT OF THE PUBLIC DEBT, FROM 1790 TO 1817, INCLUSIVE.

A.—NET ORDINARY RECEIPTS, BY CALENDAR YEARS.

Year.	Customs.	Internal Revenue.	Direct Tax.	Public Lands.	Miscellaneous.	Dividends.	Total Net Ordinary Receipts.
1791	$4,399,473 09				$10,478 10		$4,409,951 19
1792	3,443,070 85	$208,942 81			9,918 65	$8,028 00	3,669,960 31
1793	4,255,306 56	337,705 70			21,410 88	38,500 00	4,652,923 14
1794	4,801,065 28	274,089 62			53,277 97	303,472 00	5,431,904 87
1795	5,588,461 26	337,755 36			28,317 97	160,000 00	6,114,534 59
1796	6,567,987 94	475,289 60		$4,836 13	1,169,415 98	160,000 00	8,377,529 65
1797	7,549,649 65	575,491 45		83,540 60	399,139 29	80,960 00	8,688,780 99
1798	7,106,061 93	644,357 95		11,963 11	58,192 81	79,920 00	7,900,495 80
1799	6,610,449 31	779,136 44			86,187 56	71,040 00	7,546,813 31
1800	9,080,932 73	809,396 55	$734,223 97	443 75	152,712 10	71,040 00	10,848,749 70
1801	10,750,778 93	1,048,033 43	534,343 38	167,726 06	345,649 15	88,800 00	12,935,330 95
1802	12,438,235 74	621,898 89	206,565 44	188,628 02	1,500,505 86	39,960 00	14,995,793 95
1803	10,479,417 61	215,179 69	71,879 20	165,675 69	131,945 44		11,064,097 63
1804	11,098,565 33	50,941 29	50,198 44	487,526 79	139,075 53		11,826,307 38
1805	12,936,487 04	21,747 15	21,882 91	540,193 80	40,382 30		13,560,698 20
1806	14,667,698 17	20,101 45	54,732 56	765,245 73	51,121 86		15,559,981 07
1807	15,845,521 61	13,051 40	34,732 56	466,163 27	88,550 42		16,398,019 26
1808	16,363,550 58	8,190 23	19,159 21	647,939 06	21,822 85		17,060,661 93
1809	7,257,506 62	4,084 29	7,517 31	442,252 33	62,162 57		7,773,473 12
1810	8,583,309 31	7,430 63	12,448 68	696,548 82	84,476 84		9,384,214 28
1811	13,313,222 73	2,295 95	7,666 66	1,040,237 53	59,211 22		14,422,634 09
1812	8,958,777 53	4,903 06	859 22	710,427 78	126,165 17		9,801,132 76
1813	13,224,623 25	4,755 04	3,805 52	835,655 14	271,571 00		14,340,409 95
1814	5,998,772 08	1,662,984 82	2,219,497 36	1,185,971 09	164,389 81		11,181,625 16
1815	7,282,942 22	4,678,059 07	2,162,673 41	1,287,959 28	285,282 84		15,696,916 82
1816	36,306,874 88	5,124,708 31	4,253,635 09	1,717,985 03	273,782 35	202,426 30	47,676,985 66
1817	26,283,348 49	2,678,100 77	1,834,187 04	1,991,226 06	103,761 08		33,099,049 74
1818	17,176,385 00	955,270 20	264,333 36	2,606,564 77	57,617 71	525,000 00	21,585,171 04

B.—Net Ordinary Expenditures, by Calendar Years.

Year.	War.	Navy.	Indians.	Pensions.	Miscellaneous.	Total Net Ordinary Expenditures.
1791	$632,804 03	....	$27,000 00	$175,813 88	$1,083,971 61	$1,919,589 52
1792	1,100,702 09	....	13,648 85	109,243 15	4,672,664 38	5,896,258 47
1793	1,130,249 08	....	27,282 83	80,087 81	511,451 01	1,749,070 73
1794	2,639,097 59	....	13,042 46	81,399 24	750,350 74	3,545,299 00
1795	2,480,910 13	$61,408 97	23,475 68	68,673 22	1,378,920 66	4,362,541 72
1796	1,260,263 84	410,562 03	113,563 98	100,843 71	801,847 58	2,551,303 15
1797	1,039,402 46	274,784 04	62,396 58	92,256 97	1,259,422 02	2,836,110 52
1798	2,009,522 30	382,631 89	16,470 09	104,845 33	1,139,524 94	4,651,710 42
1799	2,466,946 98	1,381,347 76	20,302 19	95,444 03	1,039,391 68	6,480,166 72
1800	2,560,878 77	2,858,081 84	31 22	64,130 73	1,337,613 22	7,411,369 97
1801	1,672,944 08	3,448,716 03	9,000 00	73,533 37	1,114,768 45	4,981,669 90
1802	1,179,148 25	2,111,424 00	94,000 00	85,440 39	1,462,929 40	3,737,079 91
1803	822,055 85	915,561 87	60,000 00	62,902 10	1,842,635 76	4,002,824 24
1804	875,423 93	1,215,230 53	116,500 00	80,092 80	2,191,009 43	4,452,858 91
1805	712,781 28	1,189,832 75	196,500 00	81,854 59	3,768,598 75	6,357,234 62
1806	1,224,355 38	1,597,500 00	234,200 00	81,875 53	2,890,137 01	6,080,219 36
1807	1,288,685 91	1,649,641 44	205,425 00	70,500 00	1,697,897 51	4,984,572 89
1808	2,900,834 40	1,722,064 47	213,575 00	82,576 04	1,423,285 61	6,504,338 85
1809	3,345,772 17	1,884,067 80	337,503 84	87,833 54	1,215,808 79	7,414,672 14
1810	2,294,323 94	2,427,758 80	117,625 00	83,744 16	1,101,144 98	5,311,082 28
1811	2,032,828 19	1,654,244 20	151,875 00	75,043 88	1,367,291 40	5,592,604 86
1812	11,817,798 24	1,965,566 39	277,845 00	91,402 10	1,683,088 21	17,829,498 70
1813	19,652,013 02	8,959,365 15	167,358 28	86,989 91	1,729,435 61	28,082,396 92
1814	20,350,806 86	6,446,600 10	167,394 86	90,164 36	2,208,029 70	20,127,686 88
1815	14,794,294 22	7,311,290 60	530,750 00	69,656 06	2,898,870 47	26,953,571 00
1816	16,012,096 80	8,660,000 25	274,512 16	188,804 15	2,989,741 17	23,373,432 58
1817	8,004,236 53	3,908,278 30	319,463 71	297,374 43	3,518,936 76	15,454,609 92
1818	5,622,715 10	2,953,695 00	505,704 27	890,719 90	3,585,839 51	13,808,673 78

C.—Disbursements on Account of Public Debt.

Year.	Interest.	Public Debt.	Year.	Interest.	Public Debt.
1791......	$1,177,863 03	$699,984 23	1805......	2,657,114 22	$4,583,960 63
1792......	2,373,611 28	693,050 25	1806......	3,368,968 26	5,572,018 64
1793......	2,097,859 17	2,633,048 07	1807......	3,369,578 48	2,938,141 62
1794......	2,752,523 04	2,743,771 13	1808......	2,557,074 23	7,701,288 96
1795......	2,947,059 06	2,841,639 37	1809	2,866,074 90	3,586,479 26
1796......	3,239,347 68	2,577,126 01	1810	3,163,671 09	4,835,241 12
1797......	3,172,516 73	2,617,250 12	1811......	2,585,435 57	5,414,564 43
1798......	2,955,875 90	976,032 09	1812......	2,451,272 57	1,998,349 88
1799	2,815,651 41	1,706,578 84	1813......	3,599,455 22	7,508,668 22
1800......	3,402,601 04	1,138,563 11	1814......	4,593,239 04	3,307,304 90
1801......	4,411,830 06	2,879,876 98	1815......	5,590,090 24	6,638,832 11
1802......	4,239,172 16	5,294,235 24	1816......	7,822,923 34	17,048,139 59
1803......	3,949,462 36	3,306,697 07	1817......	4,536,282 55	20,886,753 57
1804......	4,185,048 74	3,977,206 07	1818......	6,209,954 03	15,086,247 59

APPENDIX III

THE CABINETS OF WASHINGTON, JOHN ADAMS, JEFFERSON, AND MADISON

1789 TO MARCH 3, 1817

NOTE.—In preparing this table it has been an object in view to present to the eye, approximately, the length of service of each person named. Hence the repetition of names year after year. The statements, however, are only intended to be approximate. For example, if a cabinet officer were appointed on the 27th of December, he would not appear in these lists until the year following. The true and just effect is more nearly produced by this method than it would be by recording such very small fractions of the year. In several cases, where three persons in succession occupied the same office in one year, the exigencies of the types have caused one of the names to be mentioned in foot-note.

SECRETARIES OF STATE AND OF THE TREASURY

Year.	Secretaries of State.	Secretaries of the Treasury.
1789.....	Jefferson	Hamilton.
1790.....	Jefferson	Hamilton.
1791.....	Jefferson	Hamilton.
1792.....	Jefferson	Hamilton.
1793.....	Jefferson	Hamilton.
1794.....	Randolph................	Hamilton.
1795.....	Randolph. Pickering	Hamilton. Wolcott.
1796.....	Pickering.	Wolcott.
1797.....	Pickering................	Wolcott.
1798.....	Pickering................	Wolcott.
1799.....	Pickering...............	Wolcott.
1800.....	Pickering. Marshall	Wolcott.
1801.....	Marshall. Madison.......	Dexter. Gallatin.
1802.....	Madison	Gallatin.
1803.....	Madison	Gallatin.
1804.....	Madison	Gallatin.
1805.....	Madison	Gallatin.
1806.....	Madison	Gallatin.
1807.....	Madison	Gallatin.
1808.....	Madison	Gallatin.
1809.....	Madison. Smith	Gallatin.
1810	Smith	Gallatin.
1811.....	Smith. Monroe..........	Gallatin.
1812.....	Monroe..................	Gallatin.
1813.....	Monroe..................	Gallatin.
1814.....	Monroe	Gallatin. Campbell.
1815.....	Monroe..................	Dallas.*
1816.....	Monroe..................	Dallas. Crawford.
1817 † ...	Monroe..................	Crawford.

* Dallas became Secretary of the Treasury in October, 1814.   † March 3d.

SECRETARIES OF WAR AND OF THE NAVY

Year.	Secretaries of War.	Secretaries of the Navy.
1789 ...	Knox	
1790 ...	Knox	
1791 ...	Knox	
1792 ...	Knox	Department not created until
1793 ...	Knox	
1794 ...	Knox	Adams's administration.
1795 ...	Pickering	
1796 ...	Pickering. McHenry.	
1797 ...	McHenry............	
1798 ...	McHenry............	Stoddert.
1799 ...	McHenry............	Stoddert.
1800 ...	McHenry. Dexter...	Stoddert.
1801 ...	Dexter.* Dearborn..	Stoddert. Smith.
1802 ...	Dearborn............	Smith.
1803 ...	Dearborn............	Smith.
1804 ...	Dearborn............	Smith.
1805 ...	Dearborn............	Smith. J. Crowninshield.
1806 ...	Dearborn............	J. Crowninshield.
1807 ...	Dearborn............	J. Crowninshield.
1808 ...	Dearborn............	J. Crowninshield.
1809 ...	Dearborn. Eustis....	J. Crowninshield. P. Hamilton.
1810 ...	Eustis...............	P. Hamilton.
1811 ...	Eustis...............	P. Hamilton.
1812 ...	Eustis	P. Hamilton.
1813 ...	Eustis Armstrong ...	P. Hamilton. Jones.
1814 ...	Armstrong. Monroe †.	Jones. B. Crowninshield.
1815 ...	Monroe. Crawford...	B. Crowninshield.
1816 ...	Crawford............	B. Crowninshield.
1817‡..	Crawford............	B. Crowninshield.

* Roger Griswold was Secretary of War from February 3d to March 4th.
† In addition to his duties as Secretary of State.   ‡ March 3d.

ATTORNEYS-GENERAL

Year.	Attorneys-General.	Year.	Attorneys-General.
1789..	Randolph.	1804..	Lincoln.
1790..	Randolph.	1805..	Lincoln. Smith.*
1791..	Randolph.	1806..	Breckenridge.
1792..	Randolph.	1807..	Breckenridge. Rodney.
1793..	Randolph.	1808..	Rodney.
1794..	Randolph. Bradford.	1809..	Rodney.
1795..	Bradford. Lee.	1810..	Rodney.
1796..	Lee.	1811..	Rodney. Pinkney.
1797..	Lee.	1812..	Pinkney.
1798..	Lee.	1813..	Pinkney.
1799..	Lee.	1814..	Pinkney. Rush.
1800..	Lee.	1815..	Rush.
1801..	Lee. Lincoln.	1816..	Rush.
1802..	Lincoln.	1817..	Rush.
1803..	Lincoln.		

* Also Breckenridge.

APPENDIX IV

CONSTITUTION OF THE UNITED STATES

CONSTITUTION OF THE UNITED STATES.

WE, the people of the United States, in order to form a more perfect Union, establish justice, insure domestic tranquillity, provide for the common defence, promote the general welfare, and secure the blessings of liberty to ourselves and posterity, do ordain and establish this CONSTITUTION for the United States of America.

ARTICLE I.

SECTION I. All legislative powers herein granted shall be vested in a Congress of the United States, which shall consist of a Senate and House of Representatives.

SECTION II. 1. The House of Representatives shall be composed of members chosen every second year by the people of the several States, and the electors in each State shall have the qualifications requisite for electors of the most numerous branch of the State Legislature.

2. No person shall be a Representative who shall not have attained to the age of twenty-five years, and been seven years a citizen of the United States, and who shall not, when elected, be an inhabitant, of that State in which he shall be chosen.

3. Representatives and direct taxes shall be apportioned among the several States which may be included within this Union according to their respective numbers, which shall be determined by adding to the whole number of free persons, including those bound to service for a term of years, and excluding Indians not taxed, three-fifths of all other persons. The actual enumeration shall be made within three years after the first meeting of the Congress of the United States, and within every subsequent term of ten years, in such manner as they shall by law direct. The number of Representatives shall not exceed one for every thirty thousand, but each State shall have at least one Representative; and until such enumeration shall be made, the State of New Hampshire shall be entitled to choose 3; Massachusetts, 8; Rhode Island and Providence Plantations, 1; Connecticut, 5; New York, 6; New Jersey, 4; Pennsylvania, 8; Delaware, 1; Maryland, 6; Virginia, 10; North Carolina, 5; South Carolina, 5, and Georgia, 3.*

4. When vacancies happen in the representation from any State, the Executive Authority thereof shall issue writs of election to fill such vacancies.

* See Article XIV., Amendments.

5. The House of Representatives shall choose their Speaker and other officers, and shall have the sole power of impeachment.

SECTION III. 1. The Senate of the United States shall be composed of two Senators from each State, chosen by the Legislature thereof, for six years ; and each Senator shall have one vote.

2. Immediately after they shall be assembled in consequence of the first election, they shall be divided as equally as may be into three classes. The seats of the Senators of the first class shall be vacated at the expiration of the second year, of the second class at the expiration of the fourth year, and of the third class at the expiration of the sixth year, so that one-third may be chosen every second year ; and if vacancies happen by resignation, or otherwise, during the recess of the Legislature of any State, the Executive thereof may make temporary appointment until the next meeting of the Legislature, which shall then fill such vacancies.

3. No person shall be a Senator who shall not have attained to the age of thirty years, and been nine years a citizen of the United States, and who shall not, when elected, be an inhabitant of that State for which he shall be chosen.

4. The Vice-President of the United States shall be President of the Senate, but shall have no vote unless they be equally divided.

5. The Senate shall choose their other officers, and also a President *pro tempore*, in the absence of the Vice-President, or when he shall exercise the office of President of the United States.

6. The Senate shall have the sole power to try all impeachments. When sitting for that purpose, they shall be on oath or affirmation. When the President of the United States is tried, the Chief Justice shall preside ; and no person shall be convicted without the concurrence of two thirds of the members present.

7. Judgment in cases of impeachment shall not extend further than to removal from office, and disqualification to hold and enjoy any office of honor, trust, or profit under the United States ; but the party convicted shall nevertheless be liable and subject to indictment, trial, judgment, and punishment, according to law.

SECTION IV. 1. The times, places, and manner of holding elections for Senators and Representatives shall be prescribed in each State by the Legislature thereof ; but the Congress may at any time by law make or alter such regulations, except as to the places of choosing Senators.

2. The Congress shall assemble at least once in every year, and such meeting shall be on the first Monday in December, unless they shall by law appoint a different day.

SECTION V. 1. Each House shall be the judge of the elections, returns, and qualifications of its own members, and a majority of each shall constitute a quorum to do business; but a smaller number may adjourn from day to day, and may be authorized to compel the attendance of absent members in such manner and under such penalties as each House may provide.

2. Each House may determine the rules of its proceedings, punish its members for disorderly behavior, and with the concurrence of two-thirds expel a member.

3. Each House shall keep a journal of its proceedings, and from time to time publish the same, excepting such parts as may in their judgment require secrecy ; and the yeas and nays of the members of either House on any question shall, at the desire of one-fifth of those present, be entered on the journal.

4. Neither House during the session of Congress, shall, without the consent of the other, adjourn for more than three days, nor to any other place than that in which the two Houses shall be sitting.

SECTION VI. 1. The Senators and Representatives shall receive a compensation for their services, to be ascertained by law, and paid out of the Treasury of the United States. They shall in all cases, except treason, felony, and breach of the peace, be privileged from arrest during their attendance at the session of their respective Houses, and in going to and returning from the same ; and for any speech or debate in either House they shall not be questioned in any other place.

2. No Senator or Representative shall, during the time for which he was elected, be appointed to any civil office under the authority of the United States which shall have been created, or the emoluments whereof shall have been increased during such time ; and no person holding any office under the United States shall be a member of either House during his continuance in office.

SECTION VII. 1. All bills for raising revenue shall originate in the House of Representatives, but the Senate may propose or concur with amendments, as on other bills.

2. Every bill which shall have passed the House of Representatives and the Senate shall, before it become a law, be presented to the President of the United States ; if he approve, he shall sign it, but if not, he shall return it, with his objections, to that House in which it shall have originated, who shall enter the objections at large on their journal, and proceed to reconsider it. If after such reconsideration two-thirds of that House shall agree to pass the bill, it shall be sent, together with the objections, to the other House, by which it shall likewise be reconsidered ; and if approved by two-thirds of that House, it shall become a law. But in all such cases the votes of both Houses shall be determined by yeas and nays, and the names of the persons voting for and against the bill shall be entered on the journal of each House respectively. If any bill shall not be returned by the President within ten days (Sundays excepted) after it shall have been presented to him, the same shall be a law in like manner as if he had signed it, unless the Congress by their adjournment prevent its return ; in which case it shall not be a law.

3. Every order, resolution, or vote to which the concurrence of the Senate and House of Representatives may be necessary

(except on a question of adjournment) shall be presented to the President of the United States ; and before the same shall take effect shall be approved by him, or being disapproved by him, shall be repassed by two-thirds of the Senate and the House of Representatives, according to the rules and limitations prescribed in the case of a bill.

SECTION VIII.   1.   The Congress shall have power :

To lay and collect taxes, duties, imposts, and excises, to pay the debts and provide for the common defence and general welfare of the United States ; but all duties, imposts, and excises shall be uniform throughout the United States.

2.   To borrow money on the credit of the United States.

3.   To regulate commerce with foreign nations, and among the several States, and with the Indian tribes.

4.   To establish an uniform rule of naturalization and uniform laws on the subject of bankruptcies throughout the United States.

5.   To coin money, regulate the value thereof, and of foreign coin, and fix the standard of weights and measures.

6.   To provide for the punishment of counterfeiting the securities and current coin of the United States.

7.   To establish post-offices and post-roads.

8.   To promote the progress of science and useful arts by securing for limited times to authors and inventors the exclusive rights to their respective writings and discoveries.

9.   To constitute tribunals inferior to the Supreme Court.

10.   To define and punish piracies and felonies committed on the high seas, and offences against the law of nations.

11.   To declare war, grant letters of marque and reprisal and make rules concerning captures on land and water.

12.   To raise and support armies, but no appropriation of money to that use shall be for a longer term than two years.

13.   To provide and maintain a navy.

14.   To make rules for the government and regulation of the land naval forces.

15.   To provide for calling for the militia to execute the laws of the Union, suppress insurrections, and repel invasions.

16.   To provide for organizing, arming, and disciplining the militia, and for governing such part of them as may be employed in the service of the United States, reserving to the States respectively the appointment of the officers, and the authority of training the militia according to the discipline prescribed by Congress.

17.   To exercise exclusive legislation in all cases whatsoever over such district (not exceeding ten miles square) as may, by cession of particular States and the acceptance of Congress, become the seat of Government of the United States, and to exercise like authority over all places purchased by the consent of the Legislature of the State in which the same shall be, for the erection of forts, magazines, arsenals, dry-docks, and other needful buildings.   And

18. To make all laws which shall be necessary and proper for carrying into execution the foregoing powers, and all other powers vested by this Constitution in the Government of the United States, or in any department or office thereof.

SECTION IX. 1. The migration or importation of such persons as any of the States now existing shall think proper to admit shall not be prohibited by the Congress prior to the year one thousand eight hundred and eight, but a tax or duty may be imposed on such importation, not exceeding ten dollars for each person.

2. The privilege of the writ of habeas corpus shall not be suspended, unless when in cases of rebellion or invasion the public safety may require it.

3. No bill of attainder or *ex post facto* law shall be passed.

4. No capitation or other direct tax shall be laid, unless in proportion to the census or enumeration hereinbefore directed to be taken.

5. No tax or duty shall be laid on articles exported from any State.

6. No preference shall be given by any regulation of commerce or revenue to the ports of one State over those of another, nor shall vessels bound to or from one State be obliged to enter, clear, or pay duties in another.

7. No money shall be drawn from the Treasury but in consequence of appropriations made by law ; and a regular statement and account of the receipts and expenditures of all public money shall be published from time to time.

8. No title of nobility shall be granted by the United States. And no person holding any office of profit or trust under them shall, without the consent of the Congress, accept of any present, emolument, office, or title of any kind whatever from any king, prince, or foreign state.

SECTION X. 1. No State shall enter into any treaty, alliance, or confederation, grant letters of marque and reprisal, coin money, emit bills of credit, make anything but gold and silver coin a tender in payment of debts, pass any bill of attainder, *ex post facto* law, or law impairing the obligation of contracts, or grant any title of nobility.

2. No State shall, without the consent of the Congress, lay any impost or duties on imports or exports, except what may be absolutely necessary for executing its inspection laws ; and the net produce of all duties and imposts, laid by any State on imports or exports, shall be for the use of the Treasury of the United States ; and all such laws shall be subject to the revision and control of the Congress.

3. No State shall, without the consent of Congress, lay any duty of tonnage, keep troops or ships of war in time of peace, enter into any agreement or compact with another State, or with a foreign power, or engage in war, unless actually invaded, or in such imminent danger as will not admit of delay.

ARTICLE II.

SECTION I. 1. The executive power shall be vested in a President of the United States of America. He shall hold his office during the term of four years, and, together with the Vice-President, chosen for the same term, be elected as follows:

2. Each State shall appoint, in such manner as the Legislature thereof may direct, a number of electors, equal to the whole number of Senators and Representatives to which the State may be entitled in the Congress; but no Senator or Representative or person holding an office of trust or profit under the United States shall be appointed an elector.

3. [The electors shall meet in their respective States and vote by ballot for two persons, of whom one at least shall not be an inhabitant of the same State with themselves. And they shall make a list of all the persons voted for, and of the number of votes for each, which list they shall sign and certify and transmit, sealed, to the seat of the government of the United States, directed to the President of the Senate. The President of the Senate shall, in the presence of the Senate and House of Representatives, open all the certificates, and the votes shall then be counted. The person having the greatest number of votes shall be the President, if such number be a majority of the whole number of electors appointed, and if there be more than one who have such majority, and have an equal number of votes, then the House of Representatives shall immediately choose by ballot one of them for President; and if no person have a majority, then from the five highest on the list the said House shall in like manner choose the President. But in choosing the President, the votes shall be taken by States, the representation from each State having one vote. A quorum, for this purpose, shall consist of a member or members from two-thirds of the States, and a majority of all the States shall be necessary to a choice. In every case, after the choice of the President, the person having the greatest number of votes of the electors shall be the Vice-President. But if there should remain two or more who have equal votes, the Senate shall choose from them by ballot the Vice-President.]*

4. The Congress may determine the time of choosing the electors and the day on which they shall give their votes, which day shall be the same throughout the United States.

5. No person except a natural born citizen, or a citizen of the United States at the time of the adoption of this Constitution, shall be eligible to the office of President; neither shall any person be eligible to that office who shall not have attained to the age of thirty-five years and been fourteen years a resident within the United States.

6. In case of the removal of the President from office, or of his death, resignation, or inability to discharge the powers and duties of the said office, the same shall devolve on the Vice-President,

---

* This clause is superseded by Article XII., Amendments.

and the Congress may by law provide for the case of removal, death, resignation, or inability, both of the President and Vice-President, declaring what officer shall then act as President, and such officer shall act accordingly until the disability be removed or a President shall be elected.

7. The President shall, at stated times, receive for his services a compensation, which shall neither be increased nor diminished during the period for which he shall have been elected, and he shall not receive within that period any other emolument from the United States, or any of them.

8. Before he enter on the execution of his office he shall take the following oath or affirmation :

" I do solemnly swear (or affirm) that I will faithfully execute the office of President of the United States, and will, to the best of my ability, preserve, protect, and defend the Constitution of the United States."

SECTION II. 1. The President shall be Commander-in-Chief of the Army and Navy of the United States, and of the militia of the several States, when called into the actual service of the United States ; he may require the opinion, in writing, of the principal officer in each of the executive departments upon any subject relating to the duties of their respective offices, and he shall have power to grant reprieves and pardons for offences against the United States except in cases of impeachment.

2. He shall have power, by and with the advice and consent of the Senate, to make treaties, provided two-thirds of the Senators present concur ; and he shall nominate, and by and with the advice and consent of the Senate, shall appoint ambassadors, other public ministers and consuls, judges of the Supreme Court, and all other officers of the United States whose appointments are not herein otherwise provided for, and which shall be established by law ; but the Congress may by law vest the appointment of such inferior officers as they think proper in the President alone, in the courts of law, or in the heads of departments.

3. The President shall have power to fill up all vacancies that may happen during the recess of the Senate by granting commissions, which shall expire at the end of their next session.

SECTION III. He shall from time to time give to the Congress information of the State of the Union, and recommend to their consideration such measures as he shall judge necessary and expedient ; he may, on extraordinary occasions, convene both Houses, or either of them, and in case of disagreement between them with respect to the time of adjournment, he may adjourn them to such time as he shall think proper ; he shall receive ambassadors and other public ministers ; he shall take care that the laws be faithfully executed, and shall commission all the officers of the United States.

SECTION IV. The President, Vice-President, and all civil officers of the United States shall be removed from office on impeachment for and conviction of treason, bribery, or other high crimes and misdemeanors.

ARTICLE III.

SECTION I. The judicial power of the United States shall be vested in one Supreme Court, and in such inferior courts as the Congress may from time to time ordain and establish. The judges, both of the Supreme and inferior courts, shall hold their offices during good behavior, and shall at stated times receive for their services a compensation which shall not be diminished during their continuance in office.

SECTION II. 1. The judicial power shall extend to all cases in law and equity arising under this Constitution, the laws of the United States and treaties made, or which shall be made, under their authority ; to all cases affecting ambassadors, other public ministers, and consuls ; to all cases of admiralty and maritime jurisdiction ; to controversies to which the United States shall be a party ; to controversies between two or more States, between a State and citizens of another State, between citizens of different States, between citizens of the same State claiming lands under grants of different States, and between a State, or the citizens thereof, and foreign States, citizens, or subjects.

2. In all cases affecting ambassadors, other public ministers, and consuls, and those in which a State shall be party, the Supreme Court shall have original jurisdiction. In all the other cases before-mentioned the Supreme Court shall have appellate jurisdiction both as to law and fact, with such exceptions and under such regulations as the Congress shall make.

3. The trial of all crimes, except in cases of impeachment, shall be by jury, and such trial shall be held in the State where the said crimes shall have been committed ; but when not committed within any State the trial shall be at such place or places as the Congress may by law have directed.

SECTION III. 1. Treason against the United States shall consist only in levying war against them, or in adhering to their enemies, giving them aid and comfort. No person shall be convicted of treason unless on the testimony of two witnesses to the same overt act, or on confession in open court.

2. The Congress shall have power to declare the punishment of treason, but no attainder of treason shall work corruption of blood or forfeiture except during the life of the person attained.

ARTICLE IV.

SECTION I. Full faith and credit shall be given in each State to the public acts, records, and judicial proceedings of every other State. And the Congress may by general laws prescribe the manner in which such acts, records, and proceedings shall be proved, and the effect thereof.

SECTION II. 1. The citizens of each State shall be entitled to all privileges and immunities of citizens in the several States.

2. A person charged in any State with treason, felony, or other

crime, who shall flee from justice, and be found in another State, shall, on demand of the executive authority of the State from which he fled, be delivered up, to be removed to the State having jurisdiction of the crime.

3. No person held to service or labor in one State, under the laws thereof, escaping into another shall, in consequence of any law or regulation therein, be discharged from such service or labor, but shall be delivered up on claim of the party to whom such service or labor may be due.

SECTION III. 1. New States may be admitted by the Congress into this Union; but no new State shall be formed or erected within the jurisdiction of any other State, nor any State be formed by the junction of two or more States, or parts of States, without the consent of the Legislatures of the States concerned, as well as of the Congress.

2. The Congress shall have power to dispose of and make all needful rules and regulations respecting the territory or other property belonging to the United States; and nothing in this Constitution shall be so construed as to prejudice any claims of the United States, or of any particular State.

SECTION IV. The United States shall guarantee to every State in this Union a republican form of government, and shall protect each of them against invasion, and, on application of the Legislature, or of the Executive (when the Legislature cannot be convened), against domestic violence.

ARTICLE V.

The Congress, whenever two-thirds of both Houses shall deem it necessary, shall propose amendments to this Constitution, or, on the application of the Legislatures of two-thirds of the several States, shall call a convention for proposing amendments, which, in either case, shall be valid to all intents and purposes, as part of this Constitution, when ratified by the Legislatures of three-fourths of the several States, or by conventions in three-fourths thereof, as the one or the other mode of ratification may be proposed by the Congress; provided that no amendment which may be made prior to the year one thousand eight hundred and eight shall in any manner affect the first and fourth clauses in the Ninth Section of the First Article; and that no State, without its consent, shall be deprived of its equal suffrage in the Senate.

ARTICLE VI.

1. All debts contracted and engagements entered into before the adoption of this Constitution shall be as valid against the United States as under the Confederation.

2. This Constitution and the laws of the United States which shall be made in pursuance thereof and all treaties made, or which shall be made, under the authority of the United States, shall be

the supreme law of the land ; and the judges in every State shall be bound thereby, anything in the Constitution or laws of any State to the contrary notwithstanding.

3. The Senators and Representatives before mentioned, and the members of the several State Legislatures, and all executive and judicial officers, both of the United States and of the several States, shall be bound by oath or affirmation to support this Constitution ; but no religious test shall ever be required as a qualification to any office or public trust under the United States.

ARTICLE VII.

The ratification of the Conventions of nine States shall be sufficient for the establishment of this Constitution between the States so ratifying the same.

AMENDMENTS TO THE CONSTITUTION

ARTICLE I.

Congress shall make no law respecting an establishment of religion, or prohibiting the free exercise thereof ; or abridging the freedom of speech or of the press ; or the right of the people peaceably to assemble, and to petition the Government for a redress of grievances.

ARTICLE II.

A well-regulated militia being necessary to the security of a free State, the right of the people to keep and bear arms shall not be infringed.

ARTICLE III.

No soldier shall, in time of peace, be quartered in any house without the consent of the owner, nor in time of war but in a manner to be prescribed by law.

ARTICLE IV.

The right of the people to be secure in their persons, houses, papers, and effects, against unreasonable searches and seizures, shall not be violated, and no warrants shall issue but upon probable cause, supported by oath or affirmation, and particularly describing the place to be searched, and the persons or things to be seized.

ARTICLE V.

No person shall be held to answer for a capital or other infamous crime unless on a presentment or indictment of a grand jury, except in cases arising in the land or naval forces, or in the militia, when in actual service, in time of war or public danger ; nor shall any person be subject for the same offence to be twice put in jeopardy of life or limb ; nor shall be compelled in any criminal case to be a witness against himself, nor be deprived of life, liberty, or property, without due process of law ; nor shall private property be taken for public use without just compensation.

ARTICLE VI.

In all criminal prosecutions, the accused shall enjoy the right to a speedy and public trial, by an impartial jury of the State and district wherein the crime shall have been committed, which district shall have been previously ascertained by law, and to be informed of the nature and cause of the accusation ; to be confronted with the witnesses against him ; to have compulsory process for obtaining witnesses in his favor, and to have the assistance of counsel for his defence.

ARTICLE VII.

In suits at common law, where the value in controversy shall exceed twenty dollars, the right of trial by jury shall be preserved, and no fact tried by a jury shall be otherwise re-examined in any court of the United States than according to the rules of the common law.

ARTICLE VIII.

Expensive bail shall not be required, nor excessive fines imposed, nor cruel and unusual punishments inflicted.

ARTICLE IX.

The enumeration in the Constitution of certain rights shall not be construed to deny or disparage others retained by the people.

ARTICLE X.

The powers not delegated to the United States by the Constitution, nor prohibited by it to the States, are reserved to the States respectively or to the people.

ARTICLE XI.

The judicial power of the United States shall not be construed to extend to any suit in law or equity, commenced or prosecuted against one of the United States, by citizens of another State, or by citizens or subjects of any foreign State.

ARTICLE XII.

The electors shall meet in their respective States, and vote by ballot for President and Vice-President, one of whom at least shall not be an inhabitant of the same State with themselves ; they shall name in their ballots the person voted for as President, and in distinct ballots the person voted for as Vice-President ; and they shall make distinct lists of all persons voted for as President, and of all persons voted for as Vice-President, and of the number of votes for each, which list they shall sign and certify, and transmit, sealed, to the seat of the government of the United States, directed to the President of the Senate ; the President of the Senate shall, in the presence of the Senate and House of Representatives, open all the certificates, and the votes shall then be counted ; the person having the greatest number of votes for President shall be the President, if such number be a majority of the whole number of electors appointed ; and if no person have such majority, then from the person having the highest numbers not exceeding three, on the list of those voted for as President, the House of Representatives shall choose immediately, by ballot, the President. But in choosing the President, the votes shall be taken by States, the representation from each State having one vote ; a quorum for this purpose shall consist of a member or members from two-thirds of the States, and a majority of all the States shall be necessary to a choice. And if the House of Representatives shall not choose a President, whenever the right of choice shall devolve upon them, before the fourth day of March next following, then the Vice-President shall act as President, as in the case of the death or other constitutional disability of the President. The person having the greatest number of votes as Vice-President shall be the Vice-President, if such number be a majority of the whole number of electors appointed, and if no person have a majority, then from the two highest numbers on the list the Senate shall choose the Vice-President ; a quorum for the purpose shall consist of two-thirds of the whole number of Senators, and a majority of the whole number shall be necessary to a choice. But no person constitutionally eligible to the office of President shall be eligible to that of Vice-President of the United States.

ARTICLE XIII.

1. Neither slavery nor involuntary servitude, except as a punishment for crime whereof the party shall have been duly convicted, shall exist within the United States, or any place subject to their jurisdiction.

2. Congress shall have power to enforce this article by appropriate legislation.

ARTICLE XIV.

1. All persons born or naturalized in the United States, and subject to the jurisdiction thereof, are citizens of the United States and the State wherein they reside. No State shall make or enforce any law which shall abridge the privileges or immunities of citizens of the United States ; nor shall any State deprive any per-

son of life, liberty, or property without due process of law, nor deny to any person within its jurisdiction the equal protection of the laws.

2. Representatives shall be apportioned among the several States according to their respective numbers, counting the whole number of persons in each State, excluding Indians not taxed. But when the right to vote at any election for the choice of electors for President and Vice-President of the United States, Representatives in Congress, the executive and judicial officers of a State, or the members of the Legislature thereof, is denied to any of the male members of such State being of twenty-one years of age, and citizens of the United States, or in any way abridged, except for participation in rebellion or other crime, the basis of representation therein shall be reduced in the proportion which the number of such male citizens shall bear to the whole number of male citizens twenty-one years of age in such State.

3. No person shall be a Senator or Representative in Congress, or elector of President and Vice-President, or holding any office, civil or military, under the United States, or under any State, who, having previously taken an oath, as a member of Congress, or as an officer of the United States, or as a member of any State Legislature, or as an executive or judicial officer of any State, to support the Constitution of the United States, shall have engaged in insurrection or rebellion against the same, or given aid and comfort to the enemies thereof. But Congress may, by a vote of two-thirds of each House, remove such disability.

4. The validity of the public debt of the United States, authorized by law, including debts incurred for payment of pensions and bounties for services in suppressing insurrection or rebellion, shall not be questioned. But neither the United States nor any State shall assume or pay any debt or obligation incurred in aid of insurrection or rebellion against the United States, or any claim for the loss or emancipation of any slave ; but all such debts, obligations, and claims shall be held illegal and void.

5. The Congress shall have power to enforce by appropriate legislation the provisions of this article.

ARTICLE XV.

1. The right of the citizens of the United States to vote shall not be denied or abridged by the United States or by any State, on account of race, color, or previous condition of servitude.

2. The Congress shall have power to enforce the provisions of this article by appropriate legislation.

RATIFICATION OF THE CONSTITUTION.

The Constitution was ratified by the thirteen original States in the following order :

Delaware, December 7, 1787, unanimously.
Pennsylvania, December 12, 1787, vote 46 to 23.
New Jersey, December 18, 1787, unanimously.
Georgia, January 2, 1788, unanimously.
Connecticut, January 9, 1788, vote 128 to 40.
Massachusetts, February 6, 1788, vote 187 to 168.
Maryland, April 28, 1788, vote 63 to 12.
South Carolina, May 23, 1788, vote 149 to 73.
New Hampshire, June 21, 1788, vote 57 to 46.
Virginia, June 25, 1788, vote 89 to 79.
New York, July 26, 1788, vote 30 to 28.
North Carolina, November 21, 1789, vote 193 to 75.
Rhode Island, May 29, 1790, vote 34 to 32.

RATIFICATION OF THE AMENDMENTS.

I. to X. inclusive were declared in force December 15, 1791.

XI. was declared in force January 8, 1798.

XII., regulating elections, was ratified by all States except Connecticut, Delaware, Massachusetts, and New Hampshire, which rejected it. It was declared in force September 28, 1804.

XIII., the emancipation amendment, was ratified by 31 of the 36 States ; rejected by Delaware and Kentucky, not acted on by Texas ; conditionally ratified by Alabama and Mississippi. Proclaimed December 18, 1865.

XIV., reconstruction amendment, was ratified by 23 Northern States ; rejected by Delaware, Kentucky, Maryland, and 10 Southern States, and not acted on by California. The 10 Southern States subsequently ratified under pressure. Proclaimed July 28, 1868.

XV., negro citizenship amendment, was not acted upon by Tennessee ; rejected by California, Delaware, Kentucky, Maryland, New Jersey, and Oregon ; ratified by the remaining 30 States. New York rescinded its ratification January 5, 1870. Proclaimed March 30, 1870.

BIBLIOGRAPHY

For an exhaustive bibliography of the period covered by this volume, see Vol. VII. of Justin Winsor's Narrative and Critical History of America.

GENERAL HISTORICAL ACCOUNTS, 1783-1817.

George Bancroft : History of the United States. (Vol. VI. of the author's last revision, 1783-89.)

George T. Curtis : Constitutional History of the United States, Vol. I. (1783-89). (Originally published in 2 vols., and entitled A History of the Constitution.)

John Fiske : Critical Period of American History (1783-89).

James Schouler : History of the United States, Vols. I. and II. (1783-1817).

John B. McMaster : History of the People of the United States, Vols. I.-III. (1784-1812).

Richard Hildreth ; History of the United States, Vols. III.-VI. (1773-1821).

George Tucker : History of the United States, Vols. I.-III.

Timothy Pitkin : Political and Civil History of the United States (1763-1797), 2 volumes.

George Gibbs : Administrations of Washington and John Adams, 2 volumes.

Tench Coxe : A View of the United States of America (1787-1794).

Adam Seybert : Statistical Annals (1789-1818).

A. Bradford : History of the Federal Government (1789-1839).

H. von Holst : History of the United States, Vol. I. (1750-1832).

Henry Adams : History of the United States (1801-1817), 9 volumes.

Histories of the War of 1812 by C. J. Ingersoll, 4 volumes ; B. J. Lossing ; Theodore Roosevelt (naval).

Edward Stanwood : History of Presidential Elections.

The articles on American History in Lalor's Cyclopædia of Political Science, etc. (3 volumes), especially those by Alexander
Johnston ; most of them are accompanied by bibliographical
references.

WORKS OF A LEGAL AND CONSTITUTIONAL CHAR-
ACTER.

John Fiske : Civil Government in the United States (elementary).

T. M. Cooley: Principles of Constitutional Law.

Joseph Story : Commentaries on the Constitution of the United
States, 2 volumes.

J. I. C. Hare : American Constitutional Law, 2 volumes.

H. von Holst : Constitutional Law of the United States.

J. C. Hurd : Theory of our National Existence.

B. J. Sage : The Republic of Republics.

J. A. Jameson : Treatise on Constitutional Conventions.

J. F. Jameson (editor) : Essays on the Constitutional History of
the United States (1775–1789).

C. E. Stevens : Sources of the Constitution of the United States.

P. L. Ford (editor) : Pamphlets on the Constitution of the United
States (1787–1788).

P. L. Ford (editor) : Essays on the Constitution of the United
States (1787–1788).

And particularly The Federalist (Editions by Dawson, Lodge,
and others).

S. F. Miller : Lectures on the Constitution of the United States.

H. L. Carson : History of the Celebration of the 100th Anniver-
sary of the Promulgation of the Constitution, 2 volumes.

H. L. Carson : The Supreme Court of the United States, 2 volumes.

Francis Wharton : State Trials of the United States during the
Administration of Washington and John Adams.

Constitutional History of the United States as Seen in the Development of American Law. Lectures by T. M. Cooley, H.
Hitchcock, and others.

WORKS.

George Washington, edited by Jared Sparks, 12 volumes ; by W.
C. Ford, 14 volumes.

Benjamin Franklin, edited by Jared Sparks, 10 volumes ; by John
Bigelow, 10 volumes.

Alexander Hamilton, edited by J. C. Hamilton, 7 volumes; by
H. C. Lodge, 9 volumes.

Thomas Jefferson, edited by H. A. Washington, 9 volumes; by
P. L. Ford, 10 volumes (now in course of publication).

John Adams, edited by C. F. Adams, 10 volumes.

John Jay, edited by H. P. Johnston, 4 volumes.

Albert Gallatin, edited by Henry Adams, 3 volumes.

Diary and Letters of Gouverneur Morris, edited by Anne C. Morris, 2 volumes.

Memoirs of J. Q. Adams, edited by C. F. Adams, Volumes I.-III.
(12 volumes in all).

Papers of James Madison, 3 volumes.

Letters and other Writings of James Madison, 4 volumes.

Writings of John Marshall (some of his most important opinions
as Chief Justice).

Fisher Ames, edited by Seth Ames, 2 volumes.

BIOGRAPHIES.

George Washington, by John Marshall, 5 volumes; Washington
Irving, 5 volumes; Jared Sparks; H. C. Lodge, 2 volumes.

Alexander Hamilton, by J. C. Hamilton, 2 volumes; J. T. Morse,
2 volumes; H. C. Lodge; W. G. Sumner.

John Adams, by J. Q. and C. F. Adams, 2 volumes; John T.
Morse.

Thomas Jefferson, by H. S. Randall, 3 volumes; George Tucker,
2 volumes; James Parton; John T. Morse; James Schouler;
Sarah N. Randolph.

James Madison, by W. C. Rives, 3 volumes; S. H. Gay.

Samuel Adams, by W. V. Wells, 3 volumes; J. K. Hosmer.

Patrick Henry, by W. W. Henry, 3 volumes (including correspondence and speeches); M. C. Tyler.

Gouverneur Morris, by Jared Sparks, 3 volumes (with selections
from his writings); Theodore Roosevelt.

Benjamin Franklin, by Jared Sparks; James Parton, 2 volumes;
J. T. Morse; J. B. McMaster.

John Jay, by William Jay, 2 volumes; George Pellew; W.
Whitelock.

Robert Morris, by W. G. Sumner, 2 volumes (Financier and
Finances of the American Revolution).

Timothy Pickering, by O. Pickering and C. W. Upham, 4
volumes.

William Pinkney, by William Pinkney.

John Marshall, by A. B. Magruder.

Aaron Burr, by M. L. Davis, 2 volumes ; James Parton ; Trial of Aaron Burr, by D. Robertson, 2 volumes.

Elbridge Gerry, by J. T. Austin, 2 volumes.

Albert Gallatin, by Henry Adams ; J. A. Stevens.

James Monroe, by D. C. Gilman.

John Randolph, by H. A. Garland, 2 volumes ; Henry Adams.

George Cabot, by H. C. Lodge.

Josiah Quincy, by Edmund Quincy.

Lives of the Chief-Justices of the United States, by George Van Santvoord ; Henry Flanders, 2 series.

FOREIGN RELATIONS.

Treaties and Conventions concluded between the United States and other Powers since July 4, 1776.

Freeman Snow : Treaties and Topics in American Diplomacy.

W. H. Trescot : Diplomatic History of the Administrations of Washington and Adams.

Theodore Lyman : The Diplomacy of the United States (1778–1828), 2 volumes.

Francis Wharton : Digest of the International Law of the United States, 3 volumes.

WORKS IN ECONOMIC HISTORY.

F. W. Taussig : Tariff History of the United States.

W. G. Sumner : American Currency.

J. L. Bishop : History of American Manufactures, 2 volumes.

A. S. Bolles : Financial History of the United States, 1774–1789 ; Financial History of the United States, 1789–1860.

H. C. Adams : Taxation in the United States, 1789–1816.

HISTORIES OF STATES.

New Hampshire, by Jeremy Belknap, Volumes II. and III. ; J. N. McClintock.

Vermont, by R. E. Robinson.

Massachusetts, by J. S. Barry, Volume III.

Rhode Island, by S. G. Arnold, Volume II.

Connecticut, by G. H. Hollister, Volume II. ; Alexander Johnston.

New York, by E. H. Roberts, 2 volumes.

Pennsylvania, by W. M. Cornell.

Maryland, by J. T. Scharf, Volumes II. and III. ; W. H. Browne.

Virginia, by R. R. Howison, Volume II. ; J. E. Cooke.

North Carolina, by J. W. Moore, Volume I.

South Carolina, by David Ramsay, Volume II. ; W. G. Simms.

Georgia, by C. C. Jones, 2 volumes.

Alabama, by W. Brewer.

Kentucky, by N. S. Shaler.

Ohio, by Rufus King.

Indiana, by J. P. Dunn, Jr.

Michigan, by T. M. Cooley.

The Old Northwest, by B. A. Hinsdale.

MISCELLANEOUS.

Martin Van Buren : Political Parties in the United States.

R. McK. Ormsby : History of the Whig Party.

J. D. Hammond : History of Political Parties in New York, 2 volumes.

E. D. Warfield : The Kentucky Resolutions of 1798.

Henry Adams : Documents Relating to New England Federalism (1800–1815).

Theodore Dwight : History of the Hartford Convention.

Journal of William Maclay (1789–1791), edited by E. S. Maclay.

William Maclay : Sketches of Debate (1789–1791), edited by G. W. Harris.

William Sullivan : Familiar Letters on Public Characters and Public Events (1783–1815).

R. W. Griswold : The Republican Court, or American Society in the Days of Washington.

S. G. Goodrich : Recollections, 2 volumes.

Timothy Dwight : Travels in New England and New York, 4 volumes.

E. S. Maclay : History of the United States Navy, 2 volumes.

Francis A. Walker : The Indian Question.

The American Register (1806–1809), 7 volumes.

Niles's Weekly Register, Volumes I.–XII. (1811–1817).

A large number of valuable historical monographs and papers may be found in the seventh volume of Justin Winsor's Narrative and Critical History of America, in the publications of the American Historical Association, the Massachusetts Historical Society, the New York Historical Society, the Johns Hopkins University, Columbia College, the Magazine of American History, the Magazine of Western History, and various other historical and economic publications.

The following will appeal to the teacher or special student of history, rather than to the general reader :

Jonathan Elliot (editor) : Debates, etc., 5 volumes.
Journals of Congress (1774–1788), 13 volumes.
Secret Journals of Congress (1775–1788), 4 volumes.
Annals of Congress, Volumes I.–XXX. (1789–1817).
T. H. Benton : Abridgment of Debates.   Volumes I.–V. (1789–1817).
Journal of the House of Representatives (1789–1815), 9 volumes.
Legislative Journal of the Senate (1789–1815), 5 volumes.
Executive Journal of the Senate (1789–1829), 3 volumes.
Statutes at Large.   Volumes I.–III.
T. B. Waite : State Papers and Public Documents of the United States (1789–1818), 12 volumes.
Edwin Williams (editor) : The Statesman's Manual.   Volume I.
United States Supreme Court Reports, by Dallas, Volumes II.–IV., and by Cranch, 9 volumes (to 1815) ; or, edition by Curtis, Volumes I.–III.

American State Papers :
 Foreign Relations (1789–1828), 6 volumes.
 Indian Affairs (1789–1827), 2 volumes.
 Finances (1789–1828), 5 volumes.
 Commerce and Navigation (1789–1823), 2 volumes.
 Military Affairs (1789–1838), 7 volumes.
 Naval Affairs (1789–1836), 4 volumes.
 Post Office (1789–1833), 1 volume.
 Public Lands (1789–1837), 8 volumes.
 Claims (1789–1823), 1 volume.
 Miscellaneous (1789–1823), 2 volumes.

INDEX

from, oppose constitution in Massachusetts convention, 56; population in 1790, 64.

Manufactures repressed in the Colonies, 68-9; protection of, 84-5; growth promoted by War of 1812, 258-61, 269-70; the real manufacture of the United States, during the first fifty years, was the manufacture of farms, 267.

Marshall, Chief Justice, 105; his views of the liability of a State to be sued by a citizen of another State, 127, n.; envoy to France, 138-9; enters Adams's cabinet, 161; appointed chief justice, 167, 252; presides at Burr's trial, 206; his chief contributions to the theory of the constitution, 253, 270.

Martin, Luther, in constitutional convention, 27; opposes constitution, 57.

Maryland, its colonial dispute with Virginia, 3, 19; votes against Bill of Rights, 53; Tories, 55; ratifies constitution, 57; cedes district for seat of government, 107-8; presidential election of 1800, 164, 170; representation in Congress after second census, 174; election of 1804, 188; Hanson riot, 2.7-9; election of 1812, 251; representation in Congress after third census, 251-2.

Mason, George, in constitutional convention, 25, 36, n.; opposes ratification, 58.

Massachusetts, its colonial dispute with Connecticut, 1647-50, 2; Tories, 55; convention to ratify constitution, 55-7; second State in population, 1790, 108; presidential election of 1800, 164; representation in Congress after second census, 174; election of 1804, 188; last stronghold of federalism, 217; opposition to the War of 1812, 242-4; represented in Hartford convention, 244; election of 1812, 251; representation in Congress after third census, 251.

Maumee River, operations on, 235.

Mechanical genius of American people, accounted for, 67-72; in-

fluence on naval power, 232-3; promoting the rapid settling up of the West, 266-7.

Meigs, Fort, 235.

Miami Confederation, war with, 104-6, 123.

Michigan, base of operations against Canada, 234-5.

Midnight appointments, so-called, of President Adams, 169-70.

Milan decree, 196, 217-21, 225.

Military Academy established at West Point, 174.

Militia of States, relation of general government to, 44; employment of militia, instead of "regulars," advocated by democratic-republican party, 106-7, 233; called out to enforce whiskey tax, 125; to enforce direct tax, 147; refusal of governors of Massachusetts and Connecticut to allow the militia to march, 233-4; Pennsylvania militia called out to resist execution of decree of United States court, 252-3.

Mint, established, 81; proposition to abolish it under Jefferson, 176.

Miranda, Francisco de, his Spanish-American projects, 141.

Mississippi, navigation of, importance of the question, 3-4, 58, 74, 111-12, 141, 178, 2(8, 270.

Mississippi Territory, 155; State of, 257.

Monocrats, epithet by Jefferson applied to federalists, 113.

Monroe, James, minister to Paris, recalled, 122; his treaty with England, 177-8; his claims to the succession in 1808, 212, 215; becomes secretary of state under Madison and "heir-apparent," 220; his correspondence with British minister following declaration of war, 224; assumes duties of secretary of war, 263; nominated for presidency, 263; elected, 264.

Montreal, expedition against, 236.

Morris, Gouverneur, in constitutional convention, 55.

Mosquito fleet, so-called, in Jefferson's term, 204.

Murray, William Vans, envoy to France, 142.

THE AMERICAN HISTORY SERIES

A series of 5 volumes containing Connected History of the United
States from the Discovery of America to the present day, divided
into five distinct epochs, each of which is treated by a writer of
eminence and of special authority in this field. The volumes are
sold separately, and each contains maps and plans.

The Colonial Era — 1492=1756.

*By GEORGE PARK FISHER, Professor of Ecclesiastical History
in Yale University. 12mo, 348 pages.*

The French War and the Revolution — 1756=1783.

*By WILLIAM M. SLOANE, Professor of History in Columbia
University. 12mo, 409 pages.*

The Making of the Nation — 1783=1817.

*By General FRANCIS A. WALKER, President of the Massachu-
setts Institute of Technology. 12mo, 314 pages.*

The Middle Period — 1817=1858.

*By JOHN W. BURGESS, Professor of History, Political Science,
and International Law in Columbia University. 12mo.*

The Civil War and Reconstruction — 1858=1877.

*By JOHN W. BURGESS, Professor of History, Political Science,
and International Law in Columbia University. 12mo.*

THE NEW YORK SUN.—" The 'American History Series,' now in the
course of publication by the Scribners, constitutes one of the most valuable
contributions as yet made to the connected history of the United States, and
is certain to find a place in every city and town library, and among the prescribed text book of our colleges and schools."

THE COLONIAL ERA.

*By GEORGE P. FISHER, D.D., LL.D., Professor of Ecclesiastical
History, Yale University. 12mo, $1.25.*

This initial volume of the American History Series carries
the narrative down to 1756, thus embracing the beginnings of
the decisive struggle for dominion in America. To this point

the Colonies are treated one by one. Though brief, the narrative is not a mere sketch ; not only do the political events have prominent place, but manners, customs, and phases of intellectual progress are noticed.

THE CRITIC.—" Professor Fisher's work shows the hand of a master still in its strength. He seems to have a positive genius for clear, compact, and readable condensation."

PRES. C. K. ADAMS, *University of Wisconsin.* — " The best of what we know concerning the age."

THE FRENCH WAR AND THE REVOLUTION.

By WILLIAM M. SLOANE, Ph.D., Professor of History in Princeton University. 12mo, $1.25.

The French and Indian War and the Revolution are so closely related logically, as well as chronologically, that their treatment as one epoch is eminently fitting, and Professor Sloane's volume has accordingly the unity of Professor Fisher's. In addition to being a popular narrative of the events of the era which succeeded the Colonial, it is a thoroughly philosophical account of political causes, and effects and a picture of the times as well, exhibiting the social and private life, as well as the public feeling of the Colonies during the agitated period which closed the birth of a new nation.

stitutional Revolution, 1770–1774. XIV. Resistance to Oppression, 1773–1774. XV. The Beginning of Hostilities, 1774–1775. XVI. The Battle of Bunker Hill, February–July, 1775. XVII. Overthrow of Royal Authority, 1775–1776. XVIII. The Movement for Independence, January–June, 1776. XIX. Independence and Confederation, July–August, 1776. XX. The Loss of New York City, April–December, 1776. XXI. Trenton and Princeton, December, 1776. XXII. Bennington and the Brandywine, 1777. XXIII. Saratoga and the French Alliance, September–December, 1777. XXIV. Recognition of American Independence, January–July, 1778. XXV. Evil Effect of the Foreign Alliance, 1778–1779. XXVI. Camden and King's Mountain, 1779–1780. XXVII. The Southern Invasion Repelled, 1780–1781. XXVIII. Yorktown, 1781. XXIX. The Peace of Versailles, 1782–1783. XXX. Weakness and Strength. Appendix—I. Chronological Table. II. Bibliography.

Prof. Moses Colt Tyler, *Cornell University.*—" I have read very carefully, and with great interest and pleasure, Prof. Sloane's book on 'The French War and Revolution.' Being a field in which I have done special work, I have been gratified to find my own conclusions confirmed by a scholar so discriminating and so thorough. The book seems to me to furnish new and important help to the study and understanding of the great period of which it treats."

THE MAKING OF THE NATION.

By General FRANCIS A. WALKER, President of the Massachusetts Institute of Technology. 12mo, $1.25.

General Walker's volume deals with the era of the adoption of the Constitution and the subsequent welding together of the different States which had hitherto been distinct and independent communities. It begins with the close of the Revolution and ends with the conclusion of Madison's second administration.

Contents: I. The Confederation, 1783–1787. II. The Constitutional Convention of 1787. III. The Constitution as Submitted to the People. IV. Ratification and the Inauguration of the Government. V. Washington's First Term. VI. Washington's First Term—Continued. VII. Washington's Second Term. VIII. The Administration of John Adams. IX. Jefferson's First Term. X. Jefferson's Second Term. XI. The Controversy with England. XII. The War of 1812–15. XIII. The Civil Events of Madison's Administration. Appendix—I. The Electoral Vote in Detail, 1789–1876. II.—1. Population at the First Four Censuses; 2. Net Ordinary Receipts and Expenditures and Disbursements on Account of the Public Debt, 1790–1817. III. The Cabinets of Washington, John Adams, Jefferson, and Madison, 1789 to March 3, 1817; Bibliography.

The Sunday School Times.—" Scholarship, patriotism chastened by a rich historic sense, clever character sketching, a style lively but always dignified, a bibliography sufficiently full, a good index, useful tables, and clear maps, which betray the author's long training as our national census taker, all unite in this volume.

THE MIDDLE PERIOD.

By JOHN W. BURGESS, Ph.D., LL.D., Professor of History, Political Science and Constitutional Law in Columbia University. 12mo, $1.75.

Professor Burgess has made an important contribution to American History in this thoroughly original work. It is not only written exclusively from the sources, but the view it takes of the great slavery controversy, of which it is at once the chronicle and commentary, distinguishes it among the histories of the period for absolute impartiality and a luminous appreciation of the motives and conduct of both sides. It is written from the judicial standpoint of the constitutional lawyer, rather than that of the politician or the philanthropist, and giving chapter and verse substantiation of its every position, will certainly revolutionize public opinion on several vital particulars, with the incidental result of dignifying the too often belittled figures of this important period of our national history, in a way that cannot fail to appeal to the reader's patriotism.

IN PREPARATION.

THE CIVIL WAR AND RECONSTRUCTION.

By JOHN W. BURGESS, Ph.D., LL.D.

The volumes of the series will be sent post-paid at the given price. Correspondence in regard to class use is cordially invited.

CHARLES SCRIBNER'S SONS,

Publishers,

153-157 Fifth Avenue,   -   -   New York.